Market Power and the Economy
Industrial, Corporate, Governmental,
and Political Aspects

Recent Economic Thought Series

Warren J. Samuels, Editor
Michigan State University
East Lansing, Michigan, U.S.A.

Previously published books in the series:

Feiwel, G., *Samuelson and Neoclassical Economics*
Wade, L., *Political Economy: Modern Views*
Zimbalist, A., *Comparative Economic Systems: Recent Views*
Darity, W., *Labor Economics: Modern Views*
Jarsulic, M., *Money and Macro Policy*
Samuelson, L., *Microeconomic Theory*
Bromley, D., *Natural Resource Economics: Policy Problems and Contemporary Analysis*
Mirowski, P., *The Reconstruction of Economic Theory*
Field, A., *The Future of Economic History*
Lowry, S., *Pre-Classical Economic Thought*
Officer, L., *International Economics*
Asimakopulos, A., *Theories of Income Distribution*
Earl, P., *Psychological Economics: Development, Tensions, Prospects*
Peterson, W., *Market Power and the Economy*

This series is devoted to works that present divergent views on the development, prospects, and tensions within some important research areas of international economic thought. Among the fields covered are macromonetary policy, public finance, labor, and political economy. The emphasis of the series is on providing a critical, constructive view of each of these fields, as well as a forum through which leading scholars of international reputation may voice their perspectives on important related issues. Each volume in the series will be self-contained; together these volumes will provide dramatic evidence of the variety of economic thought within the scholarly community.

Market Power and the Economy

Industrial, Corporate, Governmental,
and Political Aspects

edited by
Wallace C. Peterson
Department of Economics
University of Nebraska–Lincoln

Kluwer Academic Publishers
Boston / Dordrecht / London

Distributors for North America:
Kluwer Academic Publishers
101 Philip Drive
Assinippi Park
Norwell, Massachusetts 02061 USA

Distributors for the UK and Ireland:
Kluwer Academic Publishers
MTP Press Limited
Falcon House, Queen Square
Lancaster LA1 1RN, UNITED KINGDOM

Distributors for all other countries:
Kluwer Academic Publishers Group
Distribution Centre
Post Office Box 322
3300 AH Dordrecht, THE NETHERLANDS

Library of Congress Cataloging-in-Publication Data

Market power and the economy.
  (Recent economic thought)
  Includes index.
  1. Capitalism. 2. Power (Social sciences)
3. Economic policy. 4. Industrial concentration.
5. Industry and state. I. Peterson, Wallace C.
II. Series.
HB501.M3312 1988   338.9   88-576
ISBN 0-89838-267-X

Copyright © 1988 by Kluwer Academic Publishers

All rights reserved. No part of this publication may be reproduced, stored in a retrieval system, or transmitted in any form or by any means, mechanical, photocopying, recording, or otherwise, without the prior written permission of the publishers, Kluwer Academic Publishers, 101 Philip Drive, Assinippi Park, Norwell, Massachusetts 02061.

Printed in the United States of America

Contents

Contributing Authors — vii

Preface — ix

**1
Industrial Power: Meaning and Measurement** — 1
Rodney Peterson

**2
Economic Power: History and Institutions** — 27
John R. Munkirs

**3
The Concentration of Economic Power** — 53
Douglas F. Greer

**4
Corporate Power and Economic Performance** — 83
William Dugger

**5
National Economic Management and the Supranational Economy** — 109
John Willoughby

**6
Economic Power and the Political Process** — 127
Jerry L. Petr

**7
Concluding Observations** — 157
Wallace C. Peterson

Index — 171

Contributing Authors

William Dugger
Department of Economics
DePaul University
Chicago, Illinois 60604

Douglas Greer
Department of Economics
San Jose State University
San Jose, California 95192

John Munkirs
Department of Economics
Sangamon State University
Springfield, Illinois 62702

Rodney Peterson
Department of Economics
Colorado State University
Fort Collins, Colorado 80523

Wallace C. Peterson
Department of Economics
University of Nebraska–Lincoln
Lincoln, Nebraska 68588

Jerry L. Petr
Department of Economics
University of Nebraska–Lincoln
Lincoln, Nebraska 68588

John Willoughby
Department of Economics
American University
Washington, D.C. 20016

Preface

A situation in economics that is little short of scandalous is the almost total neglect by mainstream economics of the importance of power in economic affairs. Power in this context means the ability to bend market forces in one's favor, influencing and shaping key economic variables such as prices, wages, and other income determinants. As John Kenneth Galbraith astutely observes: a dominant fact in economic life is the desire of people everywhere and in all circumstances to get control over their personal lives and their incomes—to escape from the "tyranny of the market." Power is the means to this end. Ever since Adam Smith, economists have been fascinated by and lavish in their praise for the workings of the market. All modern textbooks are built around Smithian ideas about markets and the way the "invisible hand" works through competition for society's betterment. Yet one can search nearly in vain through leading texts, undergraduate and graduate alike, for any reference to market or economic power. This is the situation in spite of the fact that the drive for power, the urge to get control over one's income, permeates the economy as much as does competition. This is a scandal! For a discipline that claims for itself the mantle of a science—one which wants to be accorded the same respect given the natural sciences—it is almost incomprehensible that it should ignore a major force at work in the real economic world. This, sad to say, is the case.

Fortunately, there are those within the profession who are unwilling to allow this condition to continue unchallenged. The authors of the chapters in this book belong in that category. Collectively and individually, they are concerned with understanding and analyzing power and the many ways in which it has an impact upon the economy. No claim is made by either the editor nor any of the individual authors that the present book represents a definitive statement on the subject. That is far from being the case. But the claim can be made that an attempt is put forth here to remedy to some degree the long-standing neglect of this important subject by mainstream economics. This is, at least, a beginning.

In the opening chapter ("Industrial Power: Meaning and Measurement"), Professor Rodney Peterson of Colorado State University takes a broad look at power and its many dimensions, including discussion of its historic origins, how it can be measured, and some of the differing concepts of power that have meaning in relation to the economy and its performance. His essay sets the stage for those that follow. In the second chapter ("Economic Power: History and Institutions"), Professor John R. Munkirs of Sangamon State University examines from a historic perspective the forces that have permitted the business corporation to emerge as the dominant institution through which market power is exercised in the modern economy. He does this by developing an innovative "power mosaic," a five-fold classification scheme that shows how the modern global corporation emerged over the last century and the way in which through government the corporation's exercise of power is all too frequently given public sanction.

Professor Douglas F. Greer of San Jose State University in the third chapter on "The Concentration of Economic Power" examines in depth concentration in America's industrial economy. Because he finds that the standard measures of industrial concentration fail to identify fully the impact that power has on economic life, he develops a new, 12-way classification system that probes into the roots of power. The specific question of how power affects the economy's performance is addressed by Professor William M. Dugger of DePaul University ("Corporate Power and Economic Performance"). Technological innovations have enhanced corporate power, giving rise to the "imperial conglomerate," an entity which knows no national boundaries and which enriches itself more through financial manipulation than production. As far as the American economy is concerned, the rise of the imperial conglomerate has led to domestic deindustrialization, import penetration, and a worsening in the distribution of income.

International dimensions of economic power are the subject of the fifth chapter ("National Economic Management and the Supranational Economy"). Here Professor John Willoughby of the American University demonstrates how the growth of the multinational corporation in conjunction with the explosive expansion of the Eurodollar market under flexible exchange rates created a supranational economy that is largely beyond the economic control of any national state, even the largest. To cope with these new developments, Professor Willoughby suggests a series of banking and trade reforms that are workable precisely because they do not require an unrealistic amount of international cooperation for their implementation. His vision is practical, not Utopian. In the sixth chapter ("Economic Power and the Political Process"), Professor Jerry Petr of the University of Nebraska–Lincoln probes in depth the linkages between the raw political power in the United States that money and wealth command, and the formulation and implementation of economic policy. As Mark Green has said, the "Golden Rule" of politics is "he who has the gold, rules." Professor Petr explores how the rule actually works, how the political exercise of economic power in our society is carried out. In the final chapter ("Concluding Observations"), I attempt, first, to summarize the diverse strands of thought in the prior chapters; second, to examine power in a macroeconomic context; and, finally, to offer some comments from a theoretical perspective, the objective being to suggest what a workable theory of economic power might entail.

Market Power and the Economy
Industrial, Corporate, Governmental,
and Political Aspects

1 INDUSTRIAL POWER: MEANING AND MEASUREMENT
Rodney Peterson

Power in General

Power has been the subject of comment and analysis for centuries. Recently several excellent inquiries have appeared that consider the nature of power and problems generated by its presence.[1] Not only have economists identified sources and expressions of power but other social scientists have investigated the uses and results of power. This chapter introduces the topic of power and questions its prevalence within modern American capitalism. What is power? How can it be measured? Where does it reside in our system? What impact has it had on the citizens of this society?

Etymology

Power has been defined in many ways, for it means different things to different people. The Latin word for power is *potis*. In Old French it is *poeir*, and in Middle English, *pouer*. Singularly, all refer to being *able* to do something. Consistent with an agreement on capability, a contemporary dictionary offers nearly a dozen synonyms for power: ability, capacity, strength, force, might, influence, effectiveness, aptitude, faculty, authority, and forcefulness.[2] When one considers the ordinary usage of these words, a continuum from strong to weak emerges and suggests the extent to which power-oriented terms permeate our vocabulary and reflect our existence. Indeed, some power is benign and some is blatant, as will be noted when discussions of contemporary business power unfold in this book.

Concerns About Power

Why do social scientists, sometimes economists, continuously inquire into the nature of power? Is it because a feeling of powerlessness arises whenever dealing with business, government, and other societal organizations? Is it because our democratic heritage stresses freedom over authority? Is it because of fears that power is increasing in society? Is it because conventional analyses of power do not go far enough? Is it because measures of power fail to describe adequately recent developments in the world?

Surely, "all of the above" can be marked as the correct answer to the question. Indeed, power is all around us! There is power in the domestic economy, on the international scene, in the political arena, in the financial sector, in city hall, in the neighborhood, the church, the family, and on and on. Concerns about power are not limited to control and influence wielded by and in various American institutions. Combatting power and creating power for the individual to use against the system have become important, too.

A profound change has occurred recently in American values. In the arts, for example, killers had not escaped punishment no matter how their actions might be rationalized. Lately, however, violence is being glorified in the cinema whenever revenge is involved. Consider the roles played in these movies: Charles Bronson (*Death Wish*), Sondra Locke (*Sudden Impact*), Sylvester Stallone (*First Blood*), and Denise Coward (*Sudden Death*). On each stage, murders were committed with impunity because the killers were "justifiably" fighting back. Why has Bernard Goetz become a minor folk-hero for shooting first and asking questions later? And why have some states passed "make my day" statutes to strengthen the taking of lives in self-defense? One answer continues to resound loudly to explain this phenomenon: a sense of powerlessness increasingly pervades America, not only for crimes against the person but in day-to-day living.

Powerlessness and the Market

Under mercantilism, franchises granted to special interests by parliament gave them some economic power. Jeffersonian democracy[3] and the competitive market supposedly negated those relations by dispersing power widely among many relatively small units. With the harsh guidance of a Smithian invisible hand, everyone struggled to pursue his/her own self-interest, but no one person was able to influence price and terms of trade. The outcome confirmed that economics was a dismal science, for price was competed down to the cost of production causing profit rates to be low. In this way, the competitive market became an economic existentialism which made everyone feel powerless.

In a nation populated by yeoman farmers, artisans, and small shopkeepers, Jefferson's dream would be a reality. It turned into a nightmare when the corporate form of business organization and other forms of bigness began to dominate the economy. Experience under American capitalism attests that it was not long before mercantilist-like perquisites crept back into the system. Occupational licensure, subsidies, import quotas, tariffs, and industrial protectionism were created and extended. Power positions reappeared. As a result of actions by voluntary organizations which exercise their first amendment rights—trade associations, unions, and other pressure groups—power became vested into the hands of various bodies. Persons belonging to, or represented by, a particular body felt a sense of power because special privileges allowed them some control over their environment, and over their social, political, and economic destinies.

Recently, however, as quotas, tariffs, and regulations have been reduced, some remnants of competition have been re-established in the domestic economy. In addition, new technology in communications and transportation, as well as advances in production, distribution, and finance, have created a system of global competition. Members in both domestic and international groups felt that they rightfully possessed power when they had it, but feel powerless upon being deprived of it. Perhaps an invisible hand of Smithian competition is to blame rather than some larger conspiratorial body.

Objectives

The broad purpose of this book is to discuss industrial power and to explore how it affects the performance of our economy. Neoclassical theory has generally downplayed the possession of power, although attempts to measure its exercise can be found. In a competitive market, compared to production and exchange in mercantilism and fascism, price and output are jointly determined in a powerless realm. Whenever power is introduced into neoclassical economics, it has been treated as an aberration. Indeed, models of imperfect competition presented in the 1930s were considered to be exceptions to the theory of the competitive firm. Even today, rigid-thinking neoclassical economists reject Chamberlin's hypothesis regarding monopolistic competition,[4] and some oligopoly explanations are dismissed as being inaccurate.[5]

Economics is alleged to be an empirical science. If it is, economists are obligated to investigate, analyze, and identify cause-and-effect relationships about power in the real-world economy (rather than in some imaginary context based on century-old theory and institutions). As a start, this chapter reviews traditional concepts of power in a private-enterprise system, and then considers several dimensions of power that appear germane to industrial capitalism. To do this, the way that power is treated in various disciplines must be confronted. Of particular interest are the standard ways of measuring industrial power, chiefly based on cost and revenue functions of neoclassical economics. But power is more than just numbers, indices, and ratios. There are qualitative aspects of power in an organizational context which must also be considered.

Alternative Concepts of Power

It is an understatement that little agreement exists on the definition of power. Just as an ordinary dictionary shows nearly a dozen synonyms for power, so do academic disciplines attach various meanings to the word. A difference is especially apparent between the way that power is treated in the natural and social sciences. In physics, for example, power is the rate at which work is done, and is expressed quantitatively as the first derivative of work with respect to time. In mathematics, a power takes the form of an exponent which alters the magnitude of a number; and in statistics, a power is the probability of rejecting the null hypothesis. In all three situations, a transformation of one thing into something else occurs in a positive, rather than a normative, way. Whenever power is contemplated in the social sciences, change is involved; however, normative aspects necessarily creep into the analysis.

In addition to economics, four disciplines in social science and humanities treat power seriously. These fields have, among other features, one attribute in common: they deal with the behavior of people toward one another. In the human arena, diverse views exist as to the extent of power in society. Among the citizenry, certain advocates for the present distribution of income and wealth have concocted an argument that minimizes the presence of power. By contending that power refers to the absolute ability to force someone to do something, the presence of power can be disavowed summarily: "What power? Where? No one is holding a gun to your head!" Moreover, some observers view control over anything negatively because they believe that power in society or over the economic system is not desirable. Yet, others readily admit that power allows certain groups to obtain otherwise unattainable collective goals.

Sociology

Power was not a topic of primary concern for sociologists prior to the 1960s. Since then, interest has increased in social organization, which treats the problem of social power. In sociology, power is the result of human interaction and refers to the ability to affect group activities. In a society of only one person, there could be no power.

Most introductory sociology texts[6] adopt Max Weber's definition of power: "the capacity of an individual or group to control or influence the behavior of others, even in the face of opposition."[7] It is recognized that "power is not a 'thing' possessed by social actors, but rather a dynamic process that occurs in all areas of life."[8] In economic language, power is a flow, not a stock, concept.

Social theorists have identified several attributes of power. Etzioni believes that power is relative, not absolute.[9] To Bierstedt, the sources of power are people who interact with resources.[10] For Dubin, power in a social context depends on the functions that a person performs, and the importance of those functions to members of the group.[11] The belief by sociologists that power is exercised by social institutions—behavioral arrangements established and sanctioned by people to accomplish some purpose—fits well with the assertion that societal organizations (such as unions, churches, corporations) make decisions that often limit the range of human choice for some people.

Political Science

Political scientists also understand that power is a human, behavioral process by stressing that it relates to who will govern, and how government will be conducted. Most introductory texts of American government follow the definition of power developed by Robert A. Dahl: "the capacity to get people to do something that they would not otherwise do."[12] Being interested in achieving representative government, political scientists view power broadly, from the application of pressure and persuasion to the use of threats and coercion. A benefit-cost framework can even be used to analyze power: "the strengths of A's influence is measured by the 'cost' to B of complying."[13] Yet, power is only a subset of influence; for it is the threat of sanction that differentiates the former from the latter.[14] An extensive literature in political science considers how power is expressed in a democracy, as will be noted when the subjects of elitism and pluralism are discussed.

Management Science

In an organization, a manager seeks to achieve the goals of the unit by motivating subordinates to accomplish tasks. A question naturally arises as to the locus and extent of power and authority in the exercise of assigned responsibilities.

Management scientists have classified several sources of power: (1) reward power (managers can praise, give raises, and promote); (2) coercive power (managers can reprimand, suspend, and fire); (3) legitimate power (managers have a superior position usually recognized by subordinates); (4) expert power (managers often have special skills, talent, and abilities); (5) referent power (managers may be admired because of age, charisma, and reputation).[15] These facets of power are not mutually exclusive, for any given manager may possess all simultaneously. But power by itself is not sufficient in a management context. To get things done, power needs to be buttressed by authority—the sanction given from the organization and the acceptance by those who are managed.

Jurisprudence

Jurispurdence, being the science of law, treats power in the context of control over property. The largest 200 industrial corporations in America, for example, have rights to the use of more than half of the manufacturing assets in the nation.[16] Interlocking directorates and other organizational practices indicate that effective control of these 200 companies rests in the hands of a few individuals. Whereas this control may have been derived legally within the framework of constitutional, statutory, and case law, whether it is *legitimate* has been questioned.[17] "Legitimacy" refers to the morality of acquiring, possessing, and using industrial power based on property ownership, and the rightfulness of how control came to be vested in the hands of those who possess it. Legal scholars have challenged the legitimacy of the corporation's power over property by asking some important questions: Whose property is it, anyway? Where did it originate? Why does the holder have it? How is the holder able to retain control over property and use it as a basis for power? Has the system been rigged so only a few persons have control over vast amounts of property? Has the rigging mechanism been the corporate form of ownership? Is the corporation a natural capitalist institution (or is it an alien form of organization which is not democratic, competitive, and capitalist at all)? The finger of blame is pointed at the modern corporation by those who question the legitimacy of its control over property and the derivative power it provides. The corporation originally was an agency of the state—a public body—but today, private interests have expropriated the corporate form of organization and perverted it to their own use.

Power and Political Economy

Two contrasting views on power in political economy are elitism and pluralism. The former holds that a handful of influential persons shape public policy. The latter, in its idealistic form, holds that American democracy allows anyone and everyone to participate equally in political affairs. The cluster hypothesis, a realistic variation of pluralism, holds that power becomes consolidated in the hands of special interest groups. In either situation, elitism or the pluralistic cluster, power exists and permeates the economic system.

Elitism

The elitist hypothesis confronts power directly by admitting that it exists, identifying where it resides, and describing how it affects public policy decisions. Elitism in political theory was summarized by G. Mosca in 1939,[18] and popularized by C. Wright Mills in 1956.[19] According to this view, society is divided into two classes: "the few who govern [elites] and the many who are governed [masses]."[20] Elites are organized and united; the masses are not.

The elitist hypothesis holds that American institutions are controlled by a small number of persons whose backgrounds, characteristics, and values are similar. Elites come from the upper classes of society—the wealthy and the educated—and are usually white, Anglo-Saxon, and Protestant. Elites form a relatively homogeneous body that caters to its members, and who are organized into special-interest groups that become platforms for power in the economic system. As elites wield power and govern, they do so by balancing their own economic interests with the general welfare.

Research results suggest that elites are more tolerant and committed to democratic values than the masses.[21] Some political scientists claim that democracy would not survive if the masses were in control rather than elites. As a result, from the standpoint of preserving American democracy and capitalism, power in the hands of elites is desirable.

Pluralism and Power Clusters[22]

A variation of pluralism holds that public policy decisions are made through a system of semi-autonomous power clusters. Policy specialization occurs within this framework. A power cluster deals with a given group of interrelated social, political, or economic issues, but may be fragmented into subclusters. There are clusters for each primary area of domestic and foreign policy: agriculture, banking, commerce, defense, education, environment, health, welfare, and so on. Each cluster operates apart from others to identify policy issues, design proposals, offer legislation, and execute policy. The political parties, per se, are rarely involved in this process. Each power cluster is comprised of administrative agencies, executive review personnel, legislative committees, interest groups, and certain influential citizens. Policy decisions are the product of intensive interaction among the basic components of one or more power clusters. This system provides an effective means to simplify the gigantic and difficult job of accommodating the nation's policy goals. The interest group is at the center of this process.

Interest Groups and Power[23]

In modern American capitalism, most people receive money income based on the amount and type of physical and human resources they control. As a result, there is an incentive to acquire productive resources and to join with persons of similar circumstances to influence legislation and its execution.

If a property-owning group is successful in having laws passed and interpreted which will enhance the value and productivity of its property resources, then members can increase their incomes relative to others. An elaborate network of voluntary associations—special-interest groups—provides representation in the political economy for many individuals. American capitalism is a vast array of these competing groups which are engaged in a continuous process of building alliances, appealing for popular support, bargaining, pressuring, negotiating, and compromising. The outcome is often economic advantage for the victorious group.

As political pressure groups from different segments of the citizenry assemble to negotiate, the result is often a compromise skewed in favor of those who were most successful at using their bargaining strengths. Success is often based on the number of persons a bargainer represents and the property and wealth backing the bargainers. Those with the most political influence are often groups with the most economic advantage. Once both have been acquired, they reciprocate and reinforce each other, especially if property holders are active in the political arena, pressuring to get laws passed for their benefit, or to gain privileges, subsidies, and favors for themselves from the system. All of this is a logical extension of freedom, self-interest, and profit seeking, being constitutional under the first amendment.

Neoclassical Indicators of Power

For several decades, neoclassical economists have attempted to define and measure industrial power. Several of these attempts have become a standard part of orthodox economics, so much so that textbooks on price theory and industrial organization are considered remiss if they neglect them. These measures are tied to the neoclassical model of the firm, and refer, either directly or indirectly, to its cost and revenue functions.

Lerner

For the firm in a perfectly competitive market, price eventually equals marginal cost ($P = MC$, or $P - MC = 0$); but with imperfect competition, the extreme form of which is monopoly, price is greater than marginal cost ($P > MC$). In 1934, Abba Lerner suggested that this divergence between price and marginal cost be expressed as a ratio to measure monopoly power:[24]

$$L = \frac{P - MC}{P}, \text{ where } \begin{array}{l} L = \text{index of monopoly power,} \\ P = \text{profit-maximizing price, and} \\ MC = \text{marginal cost.} \end{array}$$

Once computed, L varies between zero and one: the ratio would be zero in perfect competition, but the nearer L is to 1.0, the greater the monopoly power. It has been shown that L also equals the reciprocal of the absolute value of the coefficient of price elasticity of demand:[25]

$$L = \frac{1}{|E|}, \text{ where } \begin{array}{l} L = \text{index of monopoly power, and} \\ E = \text{the elasticity coefficient.} \end{array}$$

Indeed, the more price inelastic is the demand for a firm's product, the smaller the value of E, and the more monopoly power the firm possesses. In the case of pure competition, the firm's demand curve is flat, or perfectly elastic, and E approaches infinity (so that L approaches zero).

Rothchild

In 1942, based on work of Edward Chamberlin[26] and Morris Copeland,[27] Kurt Rothchild proposed measuring the extent of monopoly power for a specific product by dividing the slope value of the firm's demand curve by the slope value of the market demand curve.[28] In monopoly, the demand curve for a firm and the market are coexistent: their slopes are the same and the Rothchild index equals 1.0. In a competitive market, the firm's demand curve is horizontal and the Rothchild Index is equal to zero. As with the Lerner Index, the critical values of Rothchild's Index vary from zero to one: the closer to zero, the less the presence of monopoly power and the greater the competition; but the closer to 1.0, the greater the extent of monopoly power.

Papandreau

Andreas Papandreau, the current Premier of Greece, was Professor of Economics at the University of Minnesota during the 1950s. In 1949, he published a landmark paper in *The American Economic Review* proposing that cross-elasticity be used to approximate the extent of monopoly power.[29] Papandreau's analysis focused on whether one firm, by lowering its price, could penetrate the markets of other firms, and whether a firm was insulated from the price cutting of its rivals. Whereas cross-elasticities of supply and demand are appropos for measuring such penetration and insulation, they are difficult to apply in actual situations. For one thing, in a pure monopoly, there are no close substitutes for the sole seller's output; and in pure competition, every firm's output is alike. In both situations, it is not possible to assemble a meaningful measure of cross-elasticity. Nevertheless, Papandreau's index is revealing whenever the rigid extremes of the two polar market structures are relaxed.

Bain

Rather than measure monopoly power with elasticities, slopes, or revenue-cost divergence, Joe Bain used profit rates directly. In 1941, he proposed a direct connection between monopoly profit and monopoly power.[30] Nearly 20 years later,[31] he estimated economic profits from business accounting data via the following procedure:

$$EP = R - C - D\,(i\,V), \text{ where}$$

EP = economic profit,
R = sales revenue,
C = costs and expenses,
D = depreciation,
i = net interest, and
V = value of owner's investment.

When the dollar amount of economic profit is estimated, it can be expressed as a percent of sales or equity. Bain warned that not all economic profit is due to monopoly, and he identified four sources of above-competitive profit: windfalls, risk rewards, innovation rewards, and monopoly power.[32] To separate them, information about the firm, the market, and the economy must be obtained to understand the reasons for economic profits at various points over time. Profit due to monopoly power is separated subjectively from the other categories of economic profit.

Collins and Preston

To measure the extent of monopoly power, Lerner computed the divergence between price and *marginal* cost, and Bain calculated the difference between price and average *total* cost. Norman Collins and Lee Preston compute a "price-cost margin" to determine if monopoly power is present in a market.[33] A price-cost margin is the difference between price and average *variable* cost. Collins and Preston use U.S. Department of Commerce, Census of Manufacturers data on four-digit Standard Industrial Classification (SIC) industries to compute:

$$PCM = \frac{VA - PR - OC}{VS}, \text{ where}$$

PMC = price-cost margin,
VA = value-added,
PR = payroll
OC = other costs, and
VS = value of shipments.

Since *VS* is the same as total revenue, the data translate into:

$$PCM = \frac{\text{Total Revenue less Total Variable Cost}}{\text{Total Revenue.}}$$

However, total revenue is equal to price times quantity, so the right-hand side of the above expression reduces to:

$$PCM = \frac{P - AVC}{P}$$

Collins and Preston regressed price-cost margins on the four-firm concentration ratios for each of several dozen industries, and found a direct, positive relation. As a result, they concluded that the higher the *PMC*, the higher the concentration, and the greater the amount of industrial power in those markets.

Reflections on Neoclassical Measures

The maximization hypothesis undergirds neoclassical economics, and is embodied within its functional relations. Indeed, the cost curve is derived from tangencies of isoquants and isocosts, and the demand curve is derived from tangencies of the budget constraints and preference functions of the consumer. Both sets of tangencies indicate optimizing conditions. Orthodox analyses of power relations using elasticity of demand and the height of price above cost necessarily presume maximization. However, if maximization is being neither pursued not reached for various reasons, then the efficacy of the different measures of monopoly power may be incomplete.

Measuring Power with Concentration Ratios

The traditional industrial organization paradigm holds that market structure is directly related to market conduct, and that both interact to determine market performance. This set of interconnections abstracts from the basic biological framework that environment (structure) shapes behavior (conduct), and that both govern outcomes or results (performance).[34] In economics, these interconnections are expressed within the neoclassical models of perfect competition and pure monopoly. In the former, a large number of relatively small firms producing a homogeneous output are unable to distinguish and promote their respective products. As a result, they accept the going market price, which is competed down near production costs, and thereupon receive only normal profits. In the latter, a few relatively large firms are able to differentiate and promote their outputs. As a result, each firm has control over its own price (which is set somewhere above production costs), and it receives above-normal profits.

Among the elements of market structure, seller concentration holds a central position. *Industrial* concentration refers to the extent that some part of economic activity is centralized in the hands of a few companies. The concentration ratio for a monopolist would be equal to 100 percent; but for any single perfect (pure) competitor, it would be near zero. Thus, the higher the one-firm seller concentration ratio, the closer is that market structure to the monopoly side of the economic ledger. Whenever seller concentration is used to infer monopoly power, the analyst implicitly applies a standard based on elasticity of demand, and divergence of marginal revenue from marginal cost.

Construction of Ratios

Industrial power ordinarily has been measured by a concentration ratio.[35] Generally, the higher the ratio, the greater is said to be the presence of industrial power. A concentration ratio can refer to the entire economy (*overall* or *aggregate* concentration), or it can refer to a specific line of commerce (*market* or *industry* concentration). Moreover, a ratio of concentration can be constructed to account for all entities being measured (a *summary* index), or it can account for only some of the entities contained in the total group being measured (a *partial* index). Finally, a concentration ratio can be computed with different indicators of economic activity— such as assets, sales, value-added, profits, or employment. There are other measures as well.

In 1981, the largest 100 manufacturing corporations held approximately 47 percent of all assets in domestic manufacturing in the nation.[36] This is a measure of *aggregate* concentration using a *partial* index with an *indicator* of economic activity called assets. Note that the ratio considers the entire economy (rather than just a single line of commerce), that it focuses on only 100 companies (rather than on all firms), and that it uses a specific piece of statistical accounting data (assets rather than sales, value-added, or some other quantitative information). This *aggregate* index could have been computed for any other number of firms—50, 100, 500, and so on —but unless the measure reports a breakdown which encompasses a distribution containing all firms in the entire group, it remains a *partial* index.

To compensate for the shortcomings of a partial index, concentration can be measured by a *summary* index which includes all firms (either in the economy, if an aggregate approach is used, or in a specific product line, if a market approach is used). Consider the following measure of aggregate concentration using a summary index: in 1983, 80 percent of all firms in the United States were unincorporated and received only 10 percent of all business receipts in the nation; whereas all corporations comprised only 20 percent of the country's firms and received 90 percent of all business sales.[37] Next, consider how a measure of aggregate concentration can also be combined with a partial index. To illustrate, based on the above analysis, the 400 largest corporations in the United States received nearly 30 percent of all business receipts in 1983.[38] Note that this measure is a partial index because concentration was cited with respect to only 400 firms rather than some comparative distribution containing *all* firms.

Probably the most meaningful and often-used concentration ratio is one that measures *market* or *industry* concentration. Many economists believe that competition, or the lack of it, occurs among a group of firms that produce substitutable products with similar production processes that are sold to a common group of buyers. In this way, competition in a relevant product and geographic market occurs on the basis of both price and nonprice rivalry among firms that challenge each other for customers. By confining a concentration ratio to an industry or a market, the analyst can identify competitiveness narrowly in a sector of the economy rather than broadly for the entire economy itself.

As with aggregate concentration ratios, an industry concentration ratio can be constructed as a partial or a summary index, and can use a variety of indicators of economic activity. Several methods or procedures have been proposed during the past several decades for measuring industrial concentration,[39] but two have gained widespread use: the four-firm (FF) ratio and the Hirschman-Herfindahl (HH) index.

Four-firm Ratio

The four-firm (FF) concentration ratio is a partial index at a market or industry level. It measures the percent of total economic activity in a market or industry held by the four leading firms in that same industry. For example, the FF ratio in cigarette manufacturing was .84 in 1982, and signifies that the largest four cigarette manufacturers produced 84 percent of all the value-added in domestic cigarette manufacturing in the United States during that year.

A concentration ratio of this general form can be computed for any number of firms—four, five, six, and so on. In this country, the four-firm ratio is used because the U.S. Department of Commerce publishes data for various lines according to the leading four firms in each of approximately 450 separate four-digit Standard Industrial Classification[40] groups. Concentration ratios are also published for the leading 8, 20, and 50 largest firms. Frequently, concentration at those levels is reported in research studies. The smallest aggregation is at the four-firm level because public policy officials, having responded to lobbying efforts of business, will not allow government to release information that identifies companies. In England, because reporting is according to the leading three firms, the British use a three-firm concentration ratio. And whenever an alleged Sherman Act, Section I violation is analyzed in court, defendant's share is ordinarily expressed as a one-firm concentration ratio. No matter the basis—whether one-firm, three-firm, or four-firm—these ratios are partial indices at the market or industry level.

Hirschman-Herfindahl Index

The other measure is the Hirschman-Herfindahl (HH)[41] index which is a *summary* rather than a partial indicator of market or industry concentration. As an index, HH has certain desirable statistical properties which makes it preferable to the FF ratio.[42] HH is computed by squaring the market share of each market participant (i.e., each firm in the industry), and then summing the results. In this way, the relation of each firm to the other is embodied within the ratio.

In 1982, the Merger Guidelines published by the U.S. Department of Justice[43] installed the HH index as an official measure of concentration in specific types of antitrust cases. Rather than using the traditional FF ratio to determine if a merger might violate the Clayton Act, Section 7, the Department of Justice began using HH, which ranges from zero to 10,000:

the higher the number, the more concentration there is in the industry being analyzed. Because HH is computed from data for each firm in the industry, it summarizes into a single measure the entire range of economic activity within a given line of commerce. Increasingly, HH is being used by industrial organization economists and antitrust officials to measure market concentration.

Concentration Ratios and Power

Industry concentration ratios, whether computed by the FF or HH procedure, have been used to compare different industries cross-sectionally at a given point in time, or as a time series over some duration within a given industry. Whenever concentration is high or increasing, the conclusion is usually drawn that power (or control, or influence, or domination) exists in the extant market. The same conclusion is drawn whenever aggregate concentration indicates that a relatively small portion of the nation's corporations contributes to a relatively large share of the nation's economic activity. Indeed, concentration and power tend to be connected as a cause-and-effect relation, or even equated in the sense that high concentration *is* power, control, and dominance. But such an assertion, even if true, fails to identify the effects of power on the individual, or to uncover the pervasiveness of power in society.

Institutional Analysis of Power

Power can be analyzed directly and indirectly as well as quantitatively and qualitatively. Whenever appraising monopoly power, market power, or economic power, contemporary economists ordinarily use concentration ratios to measure directly how much power resides in various parts of the business system. Unfortunately, quantitative measures fail to capture the essence of industrial power. Many observers believe that power—social, political, economic—is thoroughly embedded in the woof and warp of the national fabric. This interweaving involves business, government, labor, education, and the military from the supranational level down through regional and local levels. Such interconnections form a complex maze of relationships which are difficult to disentangle. Some creative scholars have tried,[44] but the result is often a counting of something either in absolute or relative terms, the magnitude of which suggests the extent of power. To confront this shortcoming, an institutional framework is developed to assess the ubiquity of power in modern American capitalism.

Economic activity involves the level, composition, and distribution of national output. This output is created from scarce resources which, by themselves, are not very productive. Economic activity occurs when technology is applied to the resource base. But economic institutions—coordinating mechanisms of planning, organizing, and directing according to some agenda—are needed to bring technology and resources together productively. A nation tries to satisfy as many unlimited human wants as possible from its scarce resources by striving to be efficient. Unfortunately, a nation often fails to achieve its potential and operates chronically in a state of unemployment and underemployment: it could produce additional output; it could allocate a different mix of resources to investment and consumption goods; and it could alter the division of output to reduce misery. These objectives are rarely reached because economic institutions do not allow technology to be applied to resources as fully as possible. Economic institutions are shackled by the rigidities of ceremonial behavior[45] which impede economic progress.

The economic process is plagued by institutional drag and cultural lag. As Alfred Marshall stated on the title page of his well-known principles text: *Natura non facit saltum*[46] (nature does not make great leaps). Technology continuously advances, albeit sometimes at a faster pace than at others. However, institutional adjustment to technological change takes time and imposes hardships during the adjustment period. *Why* do institutions take so long to adjust? Any society obtains its institutions from its values and its culture. Both are past-binding and resistant to change. New technology is slow to become accepted by society, embodied within its culture, and adjusted to its values. By the time that technological feedback absorbs that technology in the culture, and subsequently within values, which then begets the institutional adjustment to apply technology fully to the resource base for the improvement of level, composition, and distribution of economic activity, technology advances once again. The basic framework within which this process occurs is shown in figure 1-1. These conditions are pervasive and contribute to a perpetual feedback-and-adjustment process. As it occurs, some resources are wasted, some unmet wants are forestalled, and some members of society continue to be disadvantaged. Moreover, as the process is repeated from period to period, there is the possibility—indeed, a probability—that various persons or groups will influence the feedback mechanism and the institutional adjustment to technological change for their own benefit to the detriment of others.

The key to understanding power in our economic system is to recognize its role within this institutional framework. Power permeates the

Figure 1-1. An Institutional Model of the Economic Process

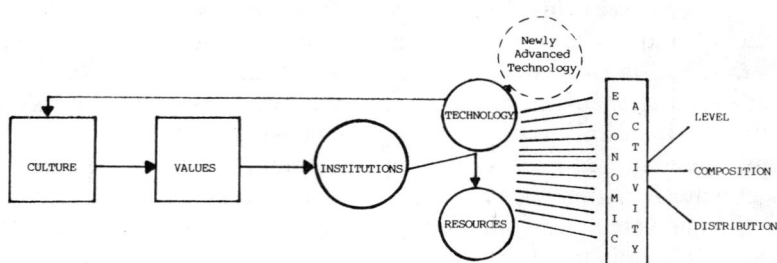

* The level, composition, and distribution of economic activity is a result of technology being applied to the resource base, with institutions acting as a coordinating mechanism to connect them. Institutions reflect the values of a society, and those values are derived from the cultural heritage. Because culture and values are past-binding, our institutions do not allow the latest technology to be applied full-force to existing resources. As a result, economic activity is less than it could be. By the time that existing technology is absorbed into the culture, and our values cause institutions to apply technology full-force to resources, technology advances and the same scenario of "cultural drag and institutional lag" occurs again.

entire system, from control over resources, to influence on the direction of technology, to decisions over what and how much will be produced and distributed (including the allocation mechanism), to the adjustment process wherein values affect institutions and their ability to connect technology to the resource base. Even the feedback mechanism itself—the way that advancing technology is absorbed into culture—must be analyzed carefully to detect power tampering.

Previously, neoclassical analyses of power have focused on only a part of the right-hand side of figure 1-1 in terms of the number of firms that produce some share of the level of output. Whereas the Lorenz curve and a Gini coefficient may be used to depict the pattern of income distribution among different groups in society, most components of figure 1-1 have been neglected. Whereas these incomplete evaluations may shed light on some of the *effects* of power, they do not identify where power is imbedded in the economic process, and how the *exercise* of power affects the members of society.

The Hierarchy of Industrial Power

It is not uncommon for economists to treat monopoly power, market power, and economic power as being synonymous. A careful reading of the literature of industrial organization, and of the case law in antitrust litigation, suggests three distinct facets of industrial power.[47] Just as Joe Bain[48] insists on differentiating among the sources of economic profit, to make the point that *monopoly* profit is really only a subset of *economic* profit, so must the hierarchy of industrial power be delineated. This separation sheds additional light on the meaning and measurement of power in economics.

Importance of Distinctions

Among these power terms—monopoly, market, economic—the latter is the most basic. Against this backdrop, monopoly power has become a red herring which helps create a myth about the nonexistence of power. Monopoly power is an extreme concept, and few situations meet its criteria. By denying the presence of monopoly power, other destructive forms of power silently continue to infiltrate society as long as the citizenry is fooled into believing that power is absent.

The first step in creating the myth is to casually mention "monopoly" and then to define it in terms of the textbook model of *pure* monopoly: only a solitary firm in an industry with no other existing or potential firms producing close substitutes. At this point in the discussion, it is important to mention that the definition of pure monopoly is touted by economists as being proper and accurate. The consequence of this step is to eliminate most of the economic system; for there are few markets with only one firm, and there are few products for which no substitutes exist.

The second step is to shorten "pure monopoly" to just "monopoly," and to pass the latter off as the former. As a result, whenever monopoly is mentioned, the image is conjured of a large firm facing no business rivals which could possibly challenge its price and production policies. This maneuver solidifies the nexus established in the first step.

The third step is to equate both monopoly and pure monopoly with monopoly power. This quantum leap allows the subterfuge of claiming that a firm with a substantial share of industry sales is *the only* firm, obviously a logical inconsistency. If the intent of the myth is to make claims of power seem vacuous, this step is successful.

The fourth step is to equate monopoly power with both market power and economic power. By contending that all three terms are interchangeable—that each refers to essentially the same condition—the stage has been set to draw the ultimate conclusion: that economic power does not exist (and the same goes for market power)!

A complaint about the evils of monopoly power can be defeated directly on the grounds that the extant situation does not involve a single firm or a nonsubstitutable product (or, in technical language, that no *pure* monopolist is present). The myth is solidified when the argument is extended. Whenever someone complains of the presence or exercise of economic (or market power), its existence can be disavowed with the same reasoning. But these three forms of power are distinguishable, and a delineation of them is crucial to how industrial power is evaluated.

Monopoly Power

As noted above, pure monopoly refers to the sole seller of a product (or service) for which there are no close substitutes. *Monopoly power* refers to a dominant firm in an industry which is able to exercise substantial control over the seller side of the market. Sepecifically, monopoly power exists if the dominant firm has the ability to influence significantly price, output, and entry for all firms in the industry. This condition refers to whether or not a single decision-making unit dominates the market in terms of productive capacity, employment, sales, profits, and business practices. Some observers suggest that monopoly power necessarily embodies the ability to exclude competitors and to discipline rivals. The key factor giving rise to monopoly power is the obvious dominance of one relatively large firm in an industry containing other firms.

Market Power

The typical industry is not dominated by a single, large seller. As a result, monopoly power does not characterize the bulk of the American economy. In most industries, whether at the national, regional, or local levels, a number of large- and small-sized firms compete with one another. In some markets, however, a few large firms—oligopolists—may be in a position of influencing market price, output, entry, and terms of trade. These situations are characterized by *market power*. Monopoly power and market power are similar—namely, the ability to influence market price and output, and even to exclude competitors and to discipline rivals. In the former, ability and influence are possessed and exercised by a single dominant firm, but in the latter, they are in the hands of a few firms that share market dominance. In both situations, several relatively small companies divide part of total industry sales with the large firm(s). Market power may reside with one of the oligopolists or among them. The distinguishing feature is whether interdependence among a few large firms allows one of the oligopolists to make decisions that others will follow for fear of starting a destructive price war. Such mutual forbearance by the major firms in the industry thwarts rivalry over the terms of trade. The result is a relatively stable price and above-normal profits.

Economic Power

Monopoly power is narrow in its applicability to our present-day economic system because there are few industries in which one dominant firm influences price, output, and other matters. Likewise, not all industries are oligopolistic so that interdependent market power renders similar results. But a firm does not have to be a monopolist, or even a dominant firm, to possess and exercise *economic power*. If a seller or a buyer is able to extract concessions from the party on the other side of the transaction, it probably has economic power. Conditions giving rise to economic power may be continuous, transitory, major, or minor. A seller may be one of many small firms in a line of commerce, but if it has an element of uniqueness, for which a buyer has a strong preference, it may have economic power. Economic power is superior bargaining ability based on some attribute of the product, conditions of sale, or buyer preference. Edward Chamberlin had economic power in mind when he assembled the market structure of monopolistic competition.[49] Differences between monopoly power and market power, on the one hand, and economic power, on the other, are demonstrated in the following situation.

A tire manufacturer (TM) owned a large lot on a busy thoroughfare in a metropolitan area. There had been built an ultra-modern, fully equipped retail tire store (RS). This outlet had been operated by TM as a company-owned retail tire store, but the regional manager leased the premises to a small, local independent businessman (LF) who wanted his own retail tire outlet. No similar units were available at the time within a three-mile radius of RS. Other nearby properties were for sale and lease, but required extensive renovation before serving as a tire outlet. After the lease was signed, TM asked if LF wanted to sell its tires, and the parties made a separate franchise agreement for that purpose. The term of the lease of RS was only for one year, whereas the customary period was five years. After several months of operating his own store, LF decided to stock two other brands of tires to provide customers with the additional choice they were requesting. TM informed LF that the lease would not be renewed if competing brands were sold in RS. LF reluctantly agreed, and another one-year lease was executed. A comprehensive but restrictive franchise agreement was also signed. Toward the end of the term of the second lease, TM demanded that LF sell only its tires on the premises of RS, and also sell its batteries and accessories as well, or else a third one-year lease would not be granted. LF acquiesced in order to continue in business.

TM was not the leading manufacturer of tires, and had a minor share of all tire sales in the metropolitan area. Thus, TM was not a monopolist, and had neither monopoly power nor market power. Moreover, TM owned only three other of its own retail tire outlets within a five-mile radius of the leased property. TM had no monopoly power or market power in the real estate market, either generally or specifically, with respect to retail tire store outlets. Nevertheless, TM was able to extract concessions from LF. The RS was unique and a scarce item; LF strongly desired that particular RS; LF was tied down to its own business with sunken investments in start-up costs, inventories, and promotional expenditures for establishing a clientele base. LF's choice was to accept TM's demands or suffer a greater loss than was incurred by selling only TM's products.

It is hollow rhetoric to claim that LF created the problem because of a preference for RS, or that physical force was not used to require LF to sign the lease and franchise agreements. Economic coercion, based on the power held and exercised by TM, is difficult to deny. The first lease was unconditional, but thereafter, a condition of the lease was the set of covenants in the franchise, against the backdrop of RS which was no longer a company-owned outlet or even a company-franchised store. TM leased RS to independent LF, and then used its economic power on LF to achieve its objectives.

Concluding Remarks

This digression into the meaning and measurement of industrial power barely scratches the surface of a vast area of concern. Much more could be said, and is in the chapters that follow. A number of topics are considered there, and each focuses on a unique aspect of business power, not necessarily confined to the meanings and measures shown in this chapter, but according to contemporary developments in the world which have had a serious impact on modern American capitalism.

A central theme runs through the essays that follow: deeply imbedded *coalitions of power* permeate our economic system. As industrial capitalism is practiced around the globe, the main undercurrent is control of financial arrangements for purposes of influencing international trade relations. The main players are giant corporate enterprises that are both subsidized and protected by various agencies of government. On this stage, business often outmaneuvers the actions of government for the benefit of selected private interests to the detriment of the public. In order to trace the interconnections of control and influence, several analyses are performed to identify the loci of power among business and government and to explain how such power is expressed in the real world. The result is an expose of the internal dynamics of modern American economy. Join now a journey into the fascinating world of industrial power and contemporary capitalism.

Notes

1. Some excellent examples are: (1) Adolf A. Berle, *Power* (New York: Harcourt, Brace, and World, 1967); (2) Andrew Cox, Paul Furlong, and Edward Page, *Power in Capitalist Societies: Theory, Explanations, and Cases* (New York: St. Martins Press, 1985); (3) John Kenneth Galbraith, *The Anatomy of Power* (Boston: Houghton Mifflin, 1983); (4) Norman Cousins, *The Pathology of Power* (New York: W.W. Norton, 1987); and (5) Walter Adams and James W. Brock, *The Bigness Complex* (New York: Pantheon Books, 1986).

2. *The American Heritage Dictionary* 2nd college ed. (Boston: Houghton Mifflin, 1983), pp. 971–972.

3. A historical account is presented in: Kenneth G. Dolbeare, *American Political Thought* (Monterey: Duxbury Press, 1981), pp. 171–203.

4. G.C. Archibald, "Chamberlin V. Chicago," *Review of Economic Studies*, Vol. XXIX, 1962-4, pp. 2–28.

5. See: George J. Stigler, "The Economist Plays with Blocs," *The American Economic Review*, May, 1954, pp. 7–14; and George J. Stigler, "The Kinky Oligopoly Demand Curve and Rigid Prices," *Journal of Political Economy*, October, 1947, pp. 432–49.

6. As examples: Caroline Hodges Persell, *Understanding Society* (New York: Harper and Row, 1987), p. 354; and Ian Robertson, *Sociology* (New York: Worth, 1987), p. 596.

7. Max Weber, *The Theory of Social and Economic Organization* (New York: Free Press, 1957), as quoted in Alex Thio, *Sociology: An Introduction* (New York: Harper and Row, 1986), p. 357.

8. Marvin E. Olsen, *Power In Societies* (New York: Macmillan, 1970), p. 3.

9. Amatai Etzioni, *The Active Society* (New York: The Free Press, 1968), pp. 314–23 and 357–61.

10. Robert Bierstedt, "An Analysis of Social Power," *American Sociological Review*, December, 1950, pp. 730–38.

11. Robert Dubin, "Power, Function, and Organization," *Pacific Sociological Review*, Spring, 1963, pp. 16–22.

12. Robert A. Dahl, "The Concept of Power," *Behavioral Science*, July, 1957, p. 202.

13. Dahl, *op. cit.*, p. 204.

14. Harold D. Lasswell and Abraham Kaplan, *Power and Society* (New Haven: Yale University Press), 1950.

15. Don Hellriegel, John W. Slocum, and Richard W. Woodman, *Organizational Behavior* (St. Paul: West, 1986), pp. 462–64.

16. *Statistical Abstract of the United States, 1984* (Washington, D.C., U.S. Bureau of the Census), p. 780.

17. This analysis is based on: Adolf A. Berle, *The American Economic Republic* (New York: Harcourt, Brace and World, 1963), pp. 24–54; and David A. Bazelon, *The Paper Economy* (New York: Random House, 1963), pp. 175–90.

18. Geatano Mosca, *The Ruling Class* (New York: McGraw-Hill, 1939).

19. C. Wright Mills, *The Power Elite* (New York: Oxford University Press, 1956).

20. Thomas R. Dye and L. Harmon Zeigler, *The Irony of Democracy* (North Scituate: Duxbury Press, 1982), pp. 3–18.

21. Peter Bachrach, *The Theory of Democratic Elitism* (Boston: Little, Brown, 1967).

22. This section is based on: Daniel M. Ogden, Jr., "How National Policy Is Made," *Increasing Understanding of Public Problems and Policies* (Chicago: Farm Foundation, 1971), pp. 5–9.

23. This section is derived from: R.D. Peterson, "Pluralist Democracy, Political Economy, and Modern American Capitalism," *Akron Business and Economic Review*, Summer, 1978, pp. 14–19.

24. Abba P. Lerner, "The Concept of Monopoly and the Measurement of Monopoly Power," *Review of Economic Studies*, June, 1934, pp. 157–75.

25. This relation is shown in James V. Koch, *Industrial Organization and Prices*, 2nd ed. (Englewood Cliffs: Prentice-Hall, 1980), pp. 62–3.

26. Edward H. Chamberlin, *The Theory of Monopolistic Competition* (Cambridge: Harvard University Press, 1933).

27. Morris A. Copeland, "Competing Products and Monopolistic Competition, *Quarterly Journal of Economics*, Vol. 55, No. 1, 1940.

28. Kurt W. Rothchild, "The Degree of Monopoly," *Economica*, February, 1942, pp. 24–40.

29. Andreas G. Papandreau, "Market Structure and Monopoly Power," *American Economic Review*, September, 1949, pp. 883–97.

30. Joe S. Bain, "The Profit Rate As A Measure of Monopoly Power," *Quarterly Journal of Economics*, February, 1941, pp. 271–93.

31. Joe S. Bain, *Industrial Organization* (New York: Wiley, 1959), pp. 365–69.

32. Joe S. Bain, *Industrial Organization* (New York: Wiley, 1968), pp. 398–401.

33. Norman R. Collins and Lee E. Preston, *Concentration and Price Cost Margins in Manufacturing Industries* (Berkeley: University of California Press, 1968), pp. 119–21.

34. See R.D. Peterson, "Product Differentiation, Implicit Theorizing, and the Methodology of Industrial Organization," *Nebraska Journal of Business and Economics*, Spring, 1980, pp. 22–36.

35. For an excellent discussion of the nature of industrial concentration ratios, see: William L. Baldwin, *Market Power, Competition and Antitrust Policy* (Homewood: R.D. Irwin, 1987), pp. 149–78.

36. *Statistical Abstract of the United States, 1982–83*, p. 535.

37. *Statistical Abstract of the United States, 1987*, p. 503.

38. *Ibid*.

39. For example, see: E. Singer, "The Structure of Concentration Indexes," *Antitrust Bulletin*, April, 1965, pp. 75–103; and C. Marfels, "A Bird's Eye View to Measures of Concentration," *Antitrust Bulletin*, Fall, 1975, pp. 485–501.

40. Executive Office of the President (OMB), *Standard Industrial Industrial Classification Manual* (Washington: U.S. Government Printing Office, 1972).

41. D. Baker and W. Blumenthal, "De-Mystifying the HH Index," *Merger and Acquisition*, Summer, 1984, pp. 42–46.

42. G. Rosenbluth, "Measures of Concentration," *Business Concentration and Price Policy* (Princeton: Princeton Unviersity Press, 1955), p. 62.

43. See: "The 1982 Merger Guidelines and Pre-existing Law," *Columbia Law Review*, Vol. 311, 1983, pp. 333–35.

44. One illuminating attempt is: John Munkirs, *The Transformation of American Capitalism* (Armonk, New York: M.E. Sharpe, 1985).

45. This point is discussed in C.E. Ayres, *The Theory of Economic Progress* (New York: Schrocken Books, 1962), pp. 155–76.

46. Alfred Marshall, *Principles of Economics*, 8th ed. (New York: Macmillan, 1948).

47. See: W.G. Shepherd, *The Economics of Industrial Organization* (Englewood Cliffs: Prentice-Hall, 1985), pp. 27–37, 41–43, and 125–40. Northern Pacific Railway Company v. U.S., 356 U.S. 1, 1958.

48. Bain, (1968), *op. cit.*, p. 401.

49. Chamberlin, *op. cit.*, pp. 56–7.

2 ECONOMIC POWER: HISTORY AND INSTITUTIONS

John Munkirs

Introduction

The primary purpose of this chapter is to examine the source and exercise of corporate power from a historical perspective. Subsidiary, yet integral, to this disputation is an analysis of the concomitant existence and exercise of power by labor organizations and government (power that emerged in direct response to the rise of corporate power).

The key characteristics forming the power mosaic as it is delineated herein consist of the following: first, definitionally, power is the capacity (implicit or explicit) of an organization to impose its views on the general public, to impose its will, or to win submission to its purposes; second, economic power pertains to an organization's ability to affect a community's standard of living, employment opportunities, income distribution, growth, environmental quality, etc.; third, the locus of economic power in the United States resides primarily in corporate enterprise.

And finally, the wellspring of corporate power flows from the community's beliefs and opinions, i.e., its ideology. Economics, like other social sciences, consists of a body of knowledge, a set of analytical techniques, and an ideological perspective. But economics in particular (especially since the mercantilist and physiocratic regimes) has always "...been partly a vehicle for the ruling ideology of each period as well as partly a method of scientific investigation."[1] The central role that ideology plays in everyday economic and political affairs is of crucial importance. For example, if a Senator from Louisiana, Oklahoma, or Texas strongly denounces government regulation of natural gas prices, what reasons are normally given? Are we told that these three states account for approximately 80 percent of the United States' natural gas production and that powerful vested interests back home expect forceful representation? Are we told that their position is a practical consideration since to do otherwise might cause campaign contributions to dry up? Are we told that they themselves have stock in, or relatives working for, the natural gas industry and that it's just a matter of representing their own interests? In fact, such considerations as these are never mentioned—at least not in the public forum. Instead, we hear that prices should be freely determined by the laws of supply and demand, and that free private enterprise is a more efficient and equitable mechanism for assuring both adequate supplies and just prices than government regulation or government enterprise.

In reality, there is nothing more important for men of action (political or business) than to have a firm command of the canonical rhetoric that forms the corpus of the ruling ideology. In the words of John Maynard Keynes: "...the ideas of economists and political philosophers, both when they are right and when they are wrong, are more powerful than is commonly understood. Indeed, the world is ruled by little else."[2]

Now, this chapter is about corporate power, not ideology. Nonetheless, while corporate power may be effected through either coercion or compensatory rewards, it is more often and more easily effected through the community's willing acquiescence due to its adherence to prevailing ideological tenets, tenets such as laissez-faire and self-interest.[3] Indeed, it is arguable that the laissez-faire and self-interest doctrines are the two greatest contributors to the emergence, cultivation, and effective exercise of corporate power. And just as economics divorced from power lacks meaning and relevance, economics divorced from ideology also lacks meaning and relevance. Throughout this chapter, then, ideology is treated as an essential ingredient in the power mosaic.

The American Corporation, 1860–1915

The importance of the corporate form of enterprise lies in the fact that the material well-being of the American people has become ever more closely tied to corporate performance. Such was not always the case. Prior to the Civil War the vast majority of the country's economic enterprise was conducted in partnerships or proprietorships. Corporations, while not a novelty, were "...relatively unimportant within the economic organization."[4]

But after the Civil War there was a gradual increase in the importance of corporations. Many important markets became national in scope which in turn required large aggregates of capital; financial structures evolved from one of simple common stock to increasingly complex pyramids of stocks and bonds of differentiated types; and a national public market for corporate stocks and bonds emerged. In the 1880s gradualism gave way to an avalanche. By 1905 corporate enterprise was the dominant form of enterprise, while trust and holding companies were the dominant corporate forms.[5]

The holding company actually superseded the trust, but from the standpoint of both management and economic concentration there was little difference between the two. To form a trust the stockholders of several individual companies assigned their stock, without revocation, to a single board of trustees. The trustees then, controlling all or the majority of the voting stock of each individual company, could elect the directors of the various companies participating in the trust. Holding companies operated in much the same manner, except that a holding company owned outright all the stock of its various operating companies instead of merely functioning as a trustee. Holding companies did not actually operate production facilities but, through stock ownership, elected the directors of the various producing companies in the same manner as did the trustees.

The trust/holding company movement set trends and forces in motion that still today dominate the country's production and distribution processes in terms of both reality and ideas. From an organizational perspective these trends and forces inaugurated the separation of ownership and control in economic enterprise (discussed in the next section), and the structural origins of the concentration and exercise of different forms of corporate power. Initially these consisted of *corporate coercive power* and *corporate micro-market power*.

Corporate coercive power was an important element in the creation of trust/holding companies; i.e., dominance was not achieved through utilizing more efficient production techniques than one's competitors. Rather, success came through utilizing fiercely aggressive tactics and strategies. For example, the American Tobacco Company came to dominate its industry by what Clair Wilcox described as waging "...relentless war on its competitors."[6] American Tobacco subsidized independent companies, undercut competitors' prices, signed exclusive contracts with the major distributors, and even bought and then dismantled competing plants. Such tactics enabled American Tobacco, by 1910, to control 76 percent, 80 percent, 85 percent, and 96 percent, respectively, of the industry's smoking tobacco, fine-cut tobacco, plug tobacco, and snuff.

In like manner, National Cash Register Company retained a group of agents referred to as the "knock-out men," whose assignment was, of course, to knock out National's competitors. Their methods included efforts both nefarious and illicit: luring away the competition's best employees, bribing employees of the competition to spy on other manufacturers, spreading false rumors and/or misrepresenting the quality of its competitors' goods, interfering with its competitors' sales efforts, and even physically damaging its competitors' merchandise. In fact, National put its competitors' cash registers on public display with huge signs labelling them as "junk" and also created a "graveyard" for obsolete machines made by former competitors. It brought frivolous suits against competitors for alleged patent violations, and threatened suits against others unless they repudiated contracts held with its competitors. Twenty years of such activities gave National control over 95 percent of the cash register industry;[7] the knock-out squad alone managed to eliminate 158 rivals.[8]

The Standard Oil Trust (the original alliance from which the word "trust" was derived) was itself not to be outdone in what its founder John D. Rockefeller termed a "survival of the fittest" struggle. Standard gained control over the industry not on the basis of efficiency but, rather, by virtue of discriminatory rate arrangements negogiated with the railroads. Standard was allowed to claim rebates amounting to almost 50 percent of its own transport costs. In addition, the railroads would rebate to Standard 50 percent of the transportation costs that they (the railroads) charged Standard's competitors, which for all practical purposes eliminated Standard's transportation expenses. With the deck thus stacked, Standard was able to freely manipulate prices, destroy its competitors, and acquire their properties. By 1899 Standard had acquired the property of 400 of its competitors and controlled approximately 84 percent of the market. Between 1896 and 1906, Standard's net income "...ranged between 48.8 percent and 84.5 percent of the cost of its properties."[9]

In short, it is but a truism to describe the trust-holding company movement as one where deception, fraud, illegality, and outright aggression were the norm and not the exception: the movement's very essence was simply how clever and imaginative corporate coercive power could be brought to bear against one's competition.

But effective control in a particular market also brought with it the power to manipulate output, prices, wages, and product quality as well as to control entry by potential competitors. This type of power is best described as corporate micro-market power; that such power was freely exercised in the market place is well documented in the literature. Also well documented is the public outcry which, in turn, led to the growth and exercise of *government micro-market power* (as evidenced at the turn of the century by enactment of the antitrust laws and the institutionalization of regulatory commissions).

For example, the Act to Regulate Commerce of 1887 created the Interstate Commerce Commission (ICC). The Commission's primary function was to regulate railroads and water carriers. The creation of the ICC was in direct response to agitation from Midwestern farmers and small business owners who contended that freight rates charged by the railroads were unjustly high. In fact, it was widely believed that in order to give Standard Oil rebates (in essence, shipping Standard's products below cost), the railroads set prices for shipping other commodities considerably above cost. Possessing little if any market power themselves, farmers and small business owners turned to government for help. In response, the Act to Regulate Commerce of 1887 directed the ICC to prohibit all discriminatory practices by railroads and water carriers, and to require that all rates be "just" and "reasonable."

In like manner the Food and Drug Act of 1906 created a standing commission known as the Food and Drug Administration (FDA). By the 1880s mass production and distribution within the food industry had become widespread. Toxic food additives in the form of mineral substances and coloring agents were frequently used to make mass distribution possible. In addition, large-scale production of many dangerous and habit-forming drugs and medicines commenced. To dramatize and help solidify public opinion concerning these problems, Dr. Harvey W. Wiley (the U.S. Department of Agriculture's Chief Chemist) went so far as to organize a "poison squad." This squad would eat and/or take food and medicines produced by firms most noted for distributing toxic products: prominent papers and magazines ran daily serials on the deteriorating health of squad members.[10] And the nation's press popularized a jingle which immediately entered into the folklore of the meat-packing industry: "Mary had a little lamb, and when she saw it sicken, she shipped it off to Packingtown, and now it's labeled chicken."[11]

More and more people became disgusted and shocked upon realizing that many processed foods were rotten, diseased, and/or toxic; finally, Upton Sinclair's book, *The Jungle*, published in 1906, crystallized public outrage and, within six months of the book's publication, Congress responded by passing the Food and Drug Act. This act prohibited the "adulteration and misbranding"[12] of all food and drugs that were considered to be part of interstate commerce, and also established the Food and Drug Administration (FDA) to administer the act's provisions.

In 1913, and again in response to grassroots public pressure, the federal government passed the Federal Reserve Act. In 1893 there were a phenomenal 496 bank failures; while between 1904 and 1913, nearly 100 banks per year closed their doors. Bank suspensions and failures had become so prevalent and disruptive of general economic activity that Congress was besieged by both bankers and the general public to intervene, i.e., to exercise government micro-market power. The main provisions of the Federal Reserve Act included the establishment of a national clearinghouse for bank checks, the creation of a flexible currency system, and the establishment of a more flexible credit system to meet the needs of the business community. The act also called for the creation of a regulatory commission, the Federal Reserve Board (FRB), to oversee and enforce the established regulations. In principle, creation of the FRB was a move toward central control of the monetary system; and again, it was a move instigated by both the business community and the general public.[13]

Other examples of the growth of government micro-market power during this period could be given, but the point would remain essentially unchanged: the growth in government micro-market power was a direct result of the growth and exercise of corporate micro-market power, with corporate micro-market power, in turn, being a direct result of corporate concentration.

In attempting to deal with the broader issue of the evolution of corporation concentration itself the government also enacted legislation that became known collectively as the antitrust laws: the Sherman Act of 1890, and the Clayton and Federal Trade Commission Acts of 1914. The acts in part prohibited "...every contract, or combination in the form of trust or otherwise, or conspiracy, in restraint of trade or commerce among the several states or with foreign nations"; price discrimination that would "...substantially lessen competition or tend to create a monopoly in any line of commerce"; mergers where their effect may be "...to substantially lessen competition or tend to create a monopoly in any line of commerce"; and "...unfair methods of competition in commerce...."

While the number of trust and holding companies actually broken up under the antitrust laws was small, so small as to leave the industrial panorama essentially unchanged, the frenzied merger movement did slow down, and was not renewed until the mid 1920s. However, ideology notwithstanding, both corporate and government micro-market power had become forceful structural entities within the economy. Self-adjusting markets and the nightwatchman state were quickly passing into limbo.

The American Corporation, 1915–1960

Growing slowly at times, and at times rapidly lurching forward, corporate concentration had by the early 1930s fundamentally transformed the economic landscape. To appreciate the significance of this change, and to also understand the impending and equally dramatic shift in economic ideas, it will be useful to refer to Adam Smith's vision of competitive captialism. For over 100 years Smith's economic system had held center stage. In much of the Western world, and particularly in America, his ideas evoked the type of reverential treatment and respect usually associated with religious canons. Smith's system rested on two pillars, one economic and one political.

From an economic perspective Smith posited a stark contrast between economic organizations typified by competitive impersonal market forces, as opposed to those typified by monopoly market power. On the one hand, although individuals were assumed to be motivated by self-love or self-interest, they would be guided by an invisible hand in such a manner that their economic actions would be beneficial to society as a whole. The invisible hand of competitive impersonal market forces would produce the following real world results: (1) prices equal to value; (2) allocative and X-efficiency;[14] (3) economic progress or dynamic efficiency; (4) economic rewards equal to one's marginal productivity; and, finally, (5) production of the type and quantity of goods and services for which consumers had effective demand. In short, economic organizations would have zero market power—the consumer would be sovereign.

On the other hand, where monopoly market power obtained, Smith contended that individuals motivated by self-love or self-interest would tend to make economic decisions that resulted in (1) market prices higher than natural prices; (2) allocative and X-inefficiency;[14] (3) retarded economic progress/growth or dynamic inefficiency; (4) economic rewards less than one's marginal productivity; and (5) diminished opportunities for individual freedom of choice.

In terms of government's role in the economy, Smith's prescript, while much more subtle and complex than usually stated in the literature, was straightforward: *Laissez nous faire*.[15] This laissez-faire prescript followed logically from Smith's view that equity, efficiency, and material progress were best secured within a competitive impersonal market force environment. The twin ideas of competition and laissez-faire were enshrined as the doctrine of economic liberalism. And, while economic liberalism was never fully adhered to, it had a profound influence on public opinion, legislative policy, and business practice. It was also, up until the 1890s, a reasonably accurate description of economic reality. To be sure, the existence of great wealth was tempered by the concurrent existence of great poverty; economic expansions were often quickly followed by severe contractions or panics. Nonetheless the system did produce both qualitative and quantitative advances in society's material welfare: from decade to decade economic progress was considered self-evident.

However, as corporate concentration grew, the social costs associated with downturns in the business cycle also grew. In extent, depth, and duration, the depression of the 1930s was so severe that many economists undertook studies with the specific end-in-view of describing and explaining the underlying reasons for the economy's dismal performance. Five of these stuides (arguably of seminal or near seminal stature) set forth arguments that severely challenged the conventional wisdom. These were: Edward Hastings Chamberlin's *The Theory of Monopolistic Competition* (1933), Joan Robinson's *The Economics of Imperfect Competition* (1934), the National Resources Committee's study *The Structure of the American Economy* (1939) directed by Gardiner C. Means, Adolf A. Berle's and Gardiner C. Means' *The Modern Corporation and Private Property* (1932), and John Maynard Keynes' *The Theory of Employment, Interest and Money* (1936). Each will be discussed in turn.

Robinson and Chamberlin coined the terms *imperfect competition* and *monopolistic competition*, respectively. Both were in substantial agreement as to the negative effects of monopolistic or imperfect competition, but each stressed different aspects of the problem. Professor Chamberlin put greater emphasis on the negative impact of monopoly prices and excess capacity, while Professor Robinson underscored the problems of worker exploitation and inequitable income distribution. The main points of their *argument* may be summarized as follows:

- that the models of pure competition (many sellers) and pure monopoly (one seller) neither accurately describe nor explain the functioning of most real world markets;
- that while pure monopoly did not exist, monopoly market power did exist in monopolistically or imperfectly competitive markets (markets dominated by a few sellers);
- that the existence of *widespread* market power led to both micro and macro economic problems: idle capacity, allocative and X-inefficiency, high unemployment, monopoly prices, deadweight welfare loss, inflation, wage exploitation, increases in wealth and income maldistribution, etc.;
- that the negative effects of market power came about not through collusion but simply because businesses were being run in an "econ-

omically rational" manner, given existing *structural* market conditions; and therefore
- that while competition among competitors in Adam Smith's world of many sellers produced positive economic results, competition among competitors in monopolistically/imperfectly competitive market structures produced serious negative economic results.

As illustration, consider an industry dominated by four or five large firms: if one firm reduces its prices, each of the other firms, once aware of their competitor's price reduction, will be forced to reduce their own prices if they wish to maintain their market share. If, the additional quantity of items sold, on a percentage basis, is less than the price reduction, the net outcome will be less total revenue for the entire industry. In effect, once the number of firms in a particular market becomes so small that each expects that its actions will be countered by its competitors, price competition becomes irrational if the goal is to maximize profits. Simple logic allows each firm to understand (without any consultation with its competitors) that price competition will decrease each firm's profits. Thus, price competition is eliminated, not via overt collusion, but simply by producers (with corporate micro-market power) realizing their economic interdependence and, in turn, acting in their own economic self-interest.

In addition, both excess capacity and unemployment may result from a decrease in demand. Again, consider an industry dominated by a few firms: if demand declines, the industry will reduce either price or output. If each individual firm believes that a reduction in price will not significantly increase sales, each firm may choose to stabilize total revenue (maintain profits and/or minimize losses) by reducing supply as opposed to reducing price. Again no collusion need occur. Each firm is confronted with the same problem—falling demand. Given the existence of corporate micro-market power, the rational business decision may be to curtail production, but this will cause both idle machines and unemployment, i.e., excess capacity.

The potency of Chamberlin's and Robinson's arguments was twofold. First, the world was presented with an elaborate and technically sophisticated explanation for the existence of idle capacity and high unemployment. And the depression's foremost characteristics were high levels of unemployment and idle plants. Second, their explanation was "people neutral" since no ill motives were attributed to any group or economic class.

This last point is very important. Economic orthodoxy assumed that rational economic man was a maximizer—be it wages, interest, rent, or profits. Therefore, the businessman's decision to not price compete, or to reduce supply as opposed to price in the face of falling demand, was simply a function of rational profit-maximizing behavior. Yet the *power* to choose (to price compete or not, to reduce either price or output given falling demand) in conjunction with the community's self-interest and profit-maximizing cultural norms, was no more than an economic disaster waiting to happen. Of course it already had! And, with the Great Depression, the phrase *ruinous competition* entered the economic dictionary.

In 1935 Gardiner Means presented testimony before the U.S. Senate, sustained by persuasive statistical documentation, that supported Chamberlin's excess capacity/high unemployment thesis. In addition his conceptualization of the unemployment problem introduced into the micro-market power lexicon a new term—administered prices. Means' administered price hypothesis contained four fundamental propositions. First, the prices of goods and services produced in industries where output was concentrated in a few firms would not be set by competitive impersonal market forces, but, rather, would be administered by businessmen.

Second, Means contended that there was a direct and close relationship between the number of times a firm changed its prices and the magnitude of its price increases or decreases. As illustration, during the depression firms possessing significant market power administered price reductions infrequently and by small amounts, while firms subject to impersonal market forces reduced their prices frequently and by large amounts. On the one hand, as shown in figure 2-1, industries dominated by a few large firms (Group A) administered price changes from 0 to 7 times between 1926 and 1938: total absolute price decreases averaged 15 percent. On the other hand, during the same time period, industries for the most part typified by competitive market structures (Group E) changed prices from 78 to 95 times: total absolute price decreases average 60 percent.

Third, Means argued that in the country's concentrated industries declining consumer demand had been countered by decreasing production and employment while maintaining stable prices. On the other hand, where relatively competitive markets existed, declining consumer demand resulted in price reductions while production and employment remained stable. As illustrated in table 2-1, firms operating in administered price industries (Group A) had price and production decreases between 1929 and 1932 of 9.4 and 52.6 percent, respectively. During the same time period firms operating in relatively competitive market structures had price and production decreases of 53.4 and −0.4 percent, respectively.

In fact, in the highly concentrated agricultural implements industry (hay loaders, mowers, corn planters, combination harvester-threshers, etc.), as well as in the automobile industry, prices declined only 6 and 16 percent, respectively, from 1929 to early spring 1933, while production was cut back

Figure 2-1. Monthly Wholesale Prices for 5 Frequency Groups 1926–1938*

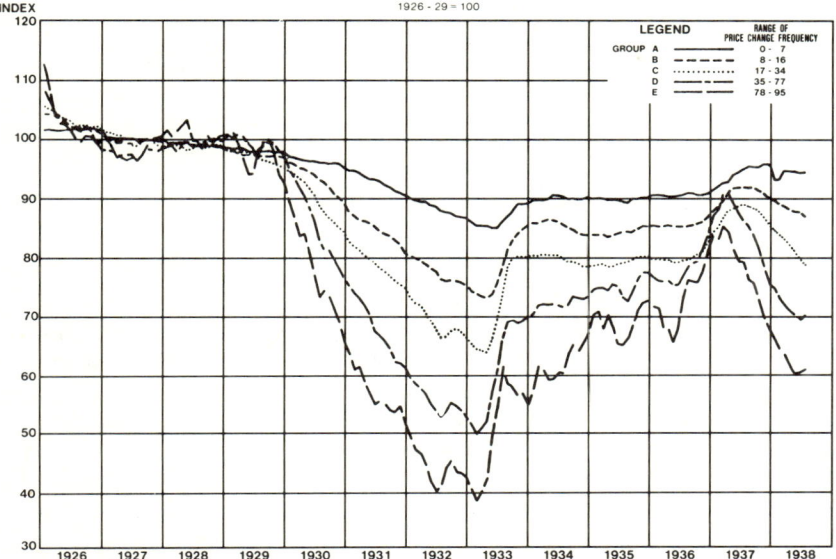

* Each of the 5 groups contains pricing and production information on approximately 120 products. As a general rule, the products in Group A represent more concentrated industries where market power exists, while products in Group E represent the least concentrated industries where competitive impersonal market forces still obtain.

Source: National Resources Committee, "The Structure of the American Economy," 1939, Part 1, (Washington, D.C.: U.S. Government Printing Office) Chart XXVI, p. 147.

by approximately 80 percent in both industries. During this same time period, the prices of agricultural commodities (dairy, livestock, grains, poultry, etc.) dropped by 63 percent with only a 6 percent drop in production. In short, where competitive impersonal market forces obtained, both prices and production responded as Smith had envisioned; however, where corporate micro-market power obtained, such was not the case.

Finally, Means, as did Chamberlin and Robinson, adopted the people neutrality concept. Administered prices were to be viewed simply as rational economic behavior on the part of individual businessmen, given the existence of corporate micro-market power.

In summarizing his disputation Means said that,

> Here we have evidence, not only of the power to choose between lowering production and lowering price but also evidence that the power tends to get

Table 2-1. Percentage Changes in Production and Prices for Five Frequency Groups from 1929 to 1932

	Percent Drop 1929–1932	
Group*	Price	Production
A	9.4	52.6
B	18.7	32.8
C	28.2	45.7
D	37.9	38.7
E	53.4	−0.4

Source: National Resource Committee, "The Structure of the American Economy," 1939, Part 1 (Washington, D.C.: U.S. Government Printing Office), Table VI, p. 148.

* Each of the five groups contains pricing and production information on approximately 120 products. As a general rule, the products in Group A represent more concentrated industries where market power exists, while products in Group E represent the least concentrated industries where competitive impersonal market forces still obtain.

exercised in the direction of lowered production and not lowered price.... A reduction of production throws workers out of employment, reduces their money income, and further reduces the demand for goods.... If all industry operated in this way, the result of an initial drop in demand would be an overpowering depression, unless some other factor, monetary or otherwise, intervened to prevent the initial drop in demand from destroying demand entirely.[16]

In essence, Means was arguing that the long duration and intensity of the Great Depression was directly related to the exercise of corporate micro-market power which, in turn, was a function of corporate concentration. But note: while micro in origin—once corporate concentration becomes widespread—the implications are of a macro nature. And therefore, we introduce the term *corporate macro-market power*.

Economic maladies directly attributable to the existence and exercise of corporate micro-macro-market power are primarily a derivative of structural changes (the replacement of competitive impersonal market forces by corporate concentration); however, an even more fundamental change took place that called into question the very essence of the concept of private property itself. From Locke to Smith private property was a central tenet in economic liberalism's philosophical construction: as Smith opined, "...the sacred right of private property..." is central.[17] But what role does private property play in the modern corporation?

On the one hand, in Smith's world (1776) companies were small; and a company's owners and managers were few in number and synonymous. Those who risked their capital (the owners) were also the managers of the company. In addition, the owners/managers often worked directly on the factory floor to produce and develop their products. Therefore, the owners/managers risked ruin if their decisions were unwise, and reaped economic gain if they provided a product or service that proved to be useful for the community.

On the other hand, in Berle's and Means' world (1930s) corporations were brobdingnagian, and the corporation's owners vastly more numerous in number. In addition, the ownership and management functions, for all practical purposes, were totally decoupled. Those who risked their capital (the owners) were essentially passive participants in the production process, while the corporate management team risked little, if any, of their own capital. What role, therefore, did private property play in the thinking and behavior of either owner or manager? Surely it was vastly different than in Smith's day!

In terms of the owners, Berle and Means note that they "...toil not, neither do they spin, to earn that reward. They are the beneficiaries by position only. Justification for their inheritance must be sought outside classic economic reasoning."[18] And what of managers—they control vast aggregates of capital that they do not own. Will they maximize profits, wealth, or income—if so, theirs, that of their friends and relatives, or the owners? Will they maximize sales, diversification, or survival? Will they minimize cost or will X-inefficiency (cost in excess of the competitive impersonal market force norm) become the norm? Do they have a right to maximize sales as opposed to profits—if so, is this right derived from the logic of private property? In the face of falling demand, do they have the right to reduce supply as opposed to price—if so, where does this right come from? Again, as noted by Gardiner Means:

> ...under the conditions created by the corporate revolution, most prices (are) not determined by trading in the market, but by administrative action...thus... converting a general fall in demand into a recession and unemployment.[19]

When management restricts supply as opposed to reducing price in the face of falling demand, in whose self-interest are they acting—their own, the stockholders, the general public?

Questions such as these are endless, and we have not yet as a society provided sufficient answers. But we do know that one cannot appeal to the logic of private property to find philosophical relief: the owners of private property exercise little if any control over society's provisioning processes, while those who control do so without the necessary encumbrances of ownership. In short, the separation of ownership and control severely limits, irreparably in the minds of many, the use of the idea of private property to sustain a laissez-faire brief on behalf of the modern forms of corporate enterprise.

The conceptual linkages between and among the undeniably stark reality of the depression, the emergence and exercise of corporate micro-macro-market power on a comprehensive scale due to structural changes in the economy's industries (a la competition among the few or industries dominated by a few firms), the creation of the administered price and monopolistic/imperfect competitive theories, and the nullification of the role of private property in the production process created a sharp cleavage between economic reality and Smith's competitive impersonal market forces ideal. And as is often the case in human affairs, the negative implications (supported by both reality and new ideas) of corporate micro-macro-market power summoned forth, as it were, a countervailing power as well as a supporting theoretical construct. This countervailing power may appropriately be referred to as *government micro-macro-market power*—with micro primarily denoting government regulation of specific industries, and macro primarily denoting the uses of monetary and fiscal policy to promote full employment, stable prices, and economic growth.

First, and from a micro perspective, during the depression years the government created additional tools in the areas of both antitrust and regulation. The original antitrust laws (Sherman, Clayton, and Federal Trade Commission) were amended by the Miller-Tydings Act (1937), the Robinson-Patman Act (1936), and the Wheeler-Lea Act (1938), respectively. Each represented an attempt to close legal loopholes that corporate lawyers had skillfully exploited. As illustration: Section 2 of the Clayton Act prohibited price discrimination that would "...substantially lessen competition or tend to create a monopoly in any form of business." The purpose behind this act was to prohibit a corporation from charging prices above actual cost in areas where it had a monopoly advantage while, at the same time, charging prices below actual cost in areas where it had competitors (thereby destroying its competitors).

But by the 1930s, more subtle methods of price discrimination prevailed than simply charging various customers different *initial* prices for the same products. For example, producers would often sell their products to small independent wholesalers and retailers for the same initial prices they charged larger chains. Subsequently though, the large chain dealers would be given what amounted to a reduction in their final bill by: (1) receiving discounts for purchasing in large volumes; (2) obtaining brokerage fees from the seller without actually employing an independent broker, or (3) obtaining advertising allowances. Such discounts and allowances allowed the large chain stores to sell products at lower prices than the smaller independent retailers could afford to match.

The independents argued that the discounts received by the chains were substantially higher than those justified by actual cost differences. Nevertheless, neither the Federal Trade Commission nor the Justice Department was successful in its attempts to forestall such practices. The courts simply did not agree that such practices violated Section 2 of the Clayton Act. Meanwhile, more and more small wholesale and retail enterprises were going out of business.

Pressures from the FTC and small independent businessmen persuaded Congress to pass the Robinson-Patman Act. Section 2(a) of the act permitted producers to vary prices among their customers based on actual cost differences, but the act also permitted the Federal Trade Commission to limit all price differences substantially above those justified by cost, where such price differentials were "promotive of monopoly." In effect, the act was designed to preserve the existence of small independent businesses and cooperatives: once again, corporate micro-market power engendered a countervailing government micro-market power.

During the 1930s grassroots organizations lobbied for, and the government responded by creating, four additional regulatory agencies—the Security and Exchange Commission (SEC), the Federal Communication Commission (FCC), the National Labor Relations Board (NLRB), and the Civil Aeronautics Board (CAB). The SEC (1934), FCC (1934), and the CAB (1938) were created primarily for the purpose of regulating, respectively, the securities, communications, and air transportation industries.

The National Labor Relations Act of 1935 (often called the Wagner Act) guaranteed workers the legal right to collective bargaining and specifically prohibited corporations from attempting to restrain or coerce workers in their unionization efforts. The Wagner Act was christened American labor's Magna Carta.

Not often mentioned but nonetheless one of the essential ingredients to successful union organizing was corporate concentration itself. The hundreds of thousands of workers employed in industries dominated by three or four firms brought to consciousness the economic power inherent in collective action. Likewise, such concentration also made organizational work much easier. Recognition of the ability to shut down an entire industry is simply power waiting to be actualized. And while deplorable working conditions and wages less than their marginal productivity became rallying points, it was the existence of highly concentrated industries that prefigured the success of the country's great labor leaders in their organizational efforts.

With the passage of the Wagner Act the government acknowledged the fact that worker power existed, attempted to encourage collective bargaining, and also provided for itself the role of referee. The idea was to mitigate the negative effects of the exercise of corporate (both union and management) micro-macro-market power on society as a whole.

The coexistence of worker and management market power in the concentrated industries resulted in a wage-price battle that, while benefitting both workers and management in those industries, impacted negatively on those employed in the less concentrated industries. On the one hand, in the concentrated industries management would raise prices, citing wage cost increases in excess of productivity gains. On the other hand, workers would demand higher wages, citing administered price increases in excess of actual cost increases. It was, of course, a chicken-and-egg type of argument with each side attempting to garner public support by blaming its adversary. In fact, both sides benefitted, the wage-price spiral theory of inflation was created, and for several decades at least, only those without market power had legitimate cause to complain.

Finally, by the end of the depression decade, the list of major regulatory agencies had expanded to nine (ICC—1886, FDA—1906, FRB—1913, FTC—1914, FPC—1920, SEC—1934, FCC—1934, NLRB—1935, and CAB—1938). Each represented an increase in the exercise of government micro-market power in the eocnomy; yet each had been created in direct response to the exercise of corporate micro-market power, e.g., the FDA to guarantee a safe food supply, the FRB to stem the tide of massive bank failures, or the SEC to reduce the risk of massive hemorrhages in the country's stock exchanges.

Also, from a macro-market power perspective the federal government was evolving toward a more activist role in the economy: such was legislatively codified just after the Second World War with the passage of the Employment Act of 1946. This act established a Council of Economic Advisors to assist the President and a Joint Economic Committee to act as a legislative liaison between the executive and legislative branches of government. It said in part that "...Congress hereby declares that it is the continuing policy and responsibility of the federal government to use all practical means...to promote maximum employment, production and purchasing power...."[20]

John Maynard Keynes set forth the economic analysis that provided the positive rationale for increasing government macro-market power. Keynes argued that it was not necessary for modern industrial economies to suffer the ill effects of inadequate aggregate demand. A sample of the Keynesian

ECONOMIC POWER: HISTORY AND INSTITUTIONS 43

macroeconomics approach is as follows: the level of aggregate demand is partially determined by consumer expenditures; consumer expenditures are partially determined by consumer disposable income, consumer disposable income is partially determined by the tax rate; the therefore, government can increase or decrease aggregate demand by increasing or decreasing taxes. In terms of unemployment the logic is equally straightforward and simple: reducing taxes increases consumer disposable income, which increases consumption expenditures, which increases the overall level of aggregate demand for goods and services, which increases the production of goods and services, which increases the demand for workers.

Though increased activism in monetary and fiscal policy arenas would greatly increase government's macro-market power, Keynes viewed his approach as being more conservative than radical—and, of course, it was. He concluded his book, *The General Theory of Interest, Employment, and Money*, by saying that:

> The foregoing theory is moderately conservative.... For whilst it indicates the vital importance of establishing certain central controls there are wide fields of activity which are unaffected.... If our central controls succeed in establishing

Figure 2-2. Interrelationships between Corporate and Government Micro-Macro-Market Power

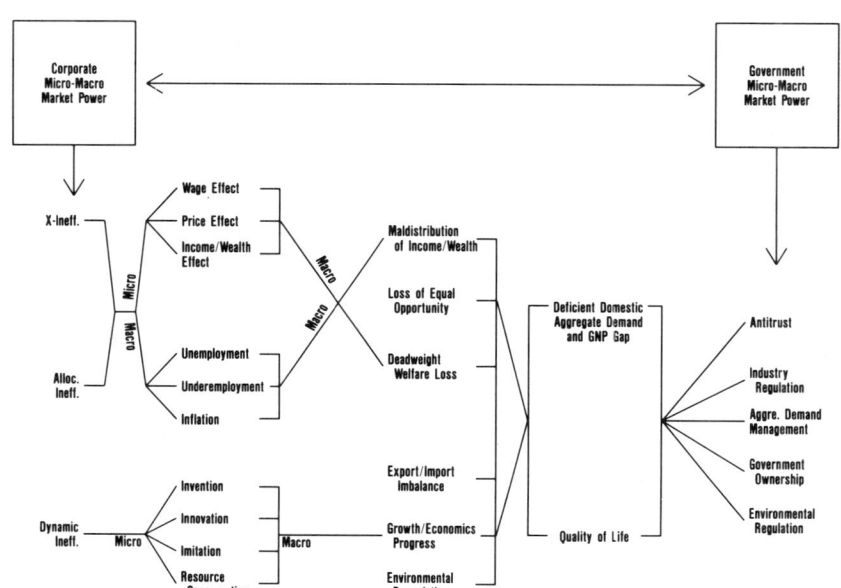

an aggregate volume of output corresponding to full employment as nearly as is practicable, then there is no objection to be raised against the classical analysis of the manner in which private self-interest will determine what in particular is produced, in what proportions the factors of production will be combined to produce it, and how the value of the final production will be distributed between them....[21]

Due primarily to the influence of Keynes and his followers, after the Second World War the teaching of economics was divided into two primary branches—micro and macro. And it is certainly arguable that the research and writing agendas of mainstream economists were, by and large, extensions, elaborations, refutations, and/or refinements of either the key concepts within the Chamberlin-Robinson-Means' micro approach or Keynes' macro approach. And in particular, whether working within a microeconomics or macroeconomics framework, great emphasis was placed on specification and measurement. The schematic structure shown in figure 2-2 is an anatomical characterization for presenting and interrelating these corporate and government micro-macro-market power concepts. Most are discussed, analyzed, and quantified in succeeding chapters.

The American Corporation, 1960–1980s

The analysis thus far has centered primarily on corporate enterprise's relationship to: (1) the decoupling of ownership and management; (2) the demise of private property's role in the production process; (3) the norms of self-interest and profit-seeking wreaking havoc in the economy; and (4) the concommitant emergence of corporate and government micro-macro-market power. If not revolutionary, certainly these changes were all momentous; but by the early 1960s an even more profound change was beginning to be perceived which had two core dimensions, planning and international interdependence.

Accompanying the evolving centralization of corporate power (1960s) was the emergence of the authority of economic planners and a further demise in the authority of markets. In the economy's key industries (finance, computers, telecommunications, iron and steel, automobiles, industrial chemicals, etc.) the corporation, for all practical purposes, had evolved into nothing less than a planning agency (Reagan, 1963; Bazelon, 1963; Schonfeld, 1965; Myrdal, 1967; Galbraith, 1967; Averitt, 1968; and Munkirs, 1985). As illustration, and, notwithstanding substantive differences among those cited above, Professor Galbraith's characterization of the corporate planning imperative is quite typical:[22]

- The process of modern industrial decision making entails drawing upon and appraising the specialized knowledge and information of numerous individuals due to:
  a. the massive technological and investment requirements necessitated by large-scale modern industry.
  b. the detailed and long-range planning necessitated by massive technological and investment requirements, and
  c. the need for *group decisions* necessitated by long-range planning;
- Decisions that require the specialized knowledge of a group (economic planners) are of necessity subject to review only by another group possessing similar knowledge and expertise; and that therefore
- The decisions of economic planners, unless acted upon by a similar technically competent group, tend to be peremptory.

But if the country's resources are allocated by corporate planners and not by markets, however flawed the markets might be, two issues of fundamental importance arise: first, to what *extent* is the economy characterized by private sector planning; and second, how does corporate planning affect, alter, enhance, or recast the exercise of micro-macro-market power? As to extent, there seems to be general agreement within the planning literature that the economy's planned and nonplanned sectors are roughly equal in size if measured by national income, business receipts, or employment.[23] Likewise, as to the economic power issue, there is also general consensus as to the important questions that planning raises; questions such as what criteria are used in selecting our economic planners; what criteria do they themselves use in their decision-making processes; or, for that matter, who are the key actors and in whose self-interest are they acting?

As illustration, when USX (one of the country's largest steel producers) spends billions to buy Marathon Oil and Texas Oil and Gas as opposed to modernizing the country's steel mills, in whose self-interest are they acting? Further, do the criteria used by the planning technocracy tend to forestall the kinds of entrepreneurial activities and dynamic efficiency essential to economic progress? Has X-inefficiency become a corporate norm because the decisions made by the country's economic planners are essentially free (at least in the short run) from critical review by either market forces, the government, or the general public? Does our inability to compete successfully with Japan's steel industry result from decisions where short-run considerations predominate over long-run considerations? Can economic planners motivated by short-run monetary considerations compete successfully with economic planners dedicated to technological excellence? Critical questions, all; but no doubt they take on even greater moment when viewed within the context of worldwide economic interdependence.

As first noted by Adam Smith, a country's ability to sell what it produces is limited by the extent of the market. And, as noted above, the American economy expanded dramatically after the Civil War due partially to regional markets becoming national in scope. After World War II, markets primarily national in scope expanded with such increasing and accelerated rapidity, that by the mid 1980s the world market had become a reality. Indeed, in order to properly classify or distinguish between corporations, a new taxonomy has evolved. And while both corporate and social science practitioners are not always precise in their usage, the following terms have gained general acceptance:

- *International Firm:* One in which international operations are consolidated in a home office on the division level and which, as a matter of policy, is willing to consider all potential strategies for entering foreign markets, up to direct investment.
- *Multinational Firm:* One in which, both structurally and policy-wise, foreign operations are co-equal with domestic.... Decisions remain nationally based for ownership, and headquarters' management remains uni-national.
- *Transnational Firm:* A multinational firm managed and owned by persons of different national origins.
- *Supranational Firm:* A transnational firm legally denationalized through allowing it the exclusive right to register with, be controlled by, and pay taxes to some international body.
- *Anational Corporation:* A supranational firm operating primarily within a laissez-faire environment.[24]

Proponents of the "world corporation" provide vivid amplification to the *truly* revolutionary changes emerging on the horizon. As illustration, George W. Ball, Undersecretary of State in both the Johnson and Kennedy Administrations, set forth his thoughts rather bluntly:

> The Nation State is no longer an adequate or even a very relevant economic unit. Conflict will increase between the World Corporation, which is a modern concept evolved to meet the requirements of the modern age, and the nation state, which is still rooted in armchair concepts unsympathetic to the needs of our complex world.[25]

In an equally direct manner, Jacques G. Maisonrouge, chairman of the IBM World Trade Corporation, stipulated that

...the world's political structures are completely obsolete. They have not changed in at least one hundred years and are woefully out of tune with technological progress. The critical issue of our time is the conceptual conflict between the search for global optimization of resources and the independence of nation states.[26]

In 1985, IBM's foreign operations accounted for 47.7 percent of its profits, 43.0 percent of its sales, and 40.7 percent of its assets. And finally Robert Stevens, Executive Vice-President, International Operations, Ford Motor Company, stated that it was Ford's

...goal to be in every single country there is, Iron Curtain countries, Russia, China. We at Ford Motor Company look at a world map without any boundaries. We don't consider ourselves basically an American company. We are a multinational company. And when we approach a government that doesn't like the U.S., we always say, 'Who do you like? Britain? Germany? We carry a lot of flags.' We export from every country.[27]

In 1985, Ford's foreign operations accounted for 20.9 percent of its profits and 44.7 percent of its assets.

The emergence of *world markets* and *economic interdependence* are but opposite sides of the same coin. Furthermore, both have the same antecedent—technological change. On the one hand, technological change allows corporate planners to produce and market their goods and services throughout the world. On the other hand, world markets create both economic interdependence and the emergence of anational attitudes and perspectives. As one example, consider financial markets: space satellites and computers have quite simply revolutionized communications and/or electronic data processing. In turn, financial markets have become, in point of fact, anational. Extraordinarily large sums of money (deutschmark, yen, dollar, lira, pound, rubel, etc.) can quickly, within hours, be transferred from one country or currency to another. The Eurocurrency market alone is approaching the $1.5 trillion dollar level. In short, the concept of a "domestic" money supply as traditionally conceived is quickly becoming irrelevant (the policy implications of which are discussed below). In addition, the large money-centered banks (e.g., Citicorp, Chase Manhattan, Chemical, and J.P. Morgan) now generate nearly half their net income as well as demand deposits from foreign operations. Summing up: technological change allows for the creation of world markets; corporate enterprise is, thus far, the primary vehicle being used to establish world markets; and concommitant with the emergence of world markets is the development of both worldwide economic interdependence and an anational mindset on the part of many corporate planners.

The raw power (social, political, and economic) of modern corporate enterprise is truly a tremendous force. The decisions made within today's "world corporations" can simultaneously endow great benefits on one community while totally devastating another. But one of the major themes in the argument thus far has been that when a new form of economic power comes into being, a countervailing power is usually called forth. Yet, can a democratically elected government, national in origin and setting, create an effective countervailing power to the worldwide micro-macro-economic power exercised by a planning technocracy housed within transnational or supranational corporations? The answer is necessarily complicated and involves both political and economic considerations.

Clearly from a political perspective, the asymmetry between increasing anational corporate power and the diminishing power of national governments will need to be addressed. Political organizations equally anational in perspective are essential and, however peripatetic, will undoubtedly in due time also arise.

As to the need for new economic concepts, this much is clear. From a micro perspective one must begin with the fact that the domestic economic system is composed of three distinct yet interrelated and *interdependent* sectors—the planned sector, the nonplanned sector, and government. Traditional micro theory is inadequate in terms of both description and explanation and therefore is also inadequate for purposes of domestic public policy. This is so because it does not take into account the important economic differences (production technologies, property relationships, logical, behavioral, motivational and power factors, etc.) that exist between the planned and nonplanned sectors. Additionally, traditional theory treats the government as an exogenous variable. Exogenous indeed! Where would we be without aggregate demand management? In 1984 government accounted for 20.4 percent, 14.8 percent, and 15.4 percent, respectively, of GNP, national income, and employment. Stated positively, we need a theory that explains where, when, and how government's micro-power can be effectively exercised in an economy where strong planned and nonplanned sectors coexist, wherein each sector performs a vital role, wherein corporate micro-macro-market power is all-pervasive, but nonetheless wherein government policy affects each sector differently.

On the other hand, from a macro economics perspective, we must also begin to understand that various policy options (monetary and fiscal) will affect the domestic economy's planned and nonplanned sectors quite differently. For example, interest rates driven high enough to affect the decisions of economic planners in the economy's planned sector may literally devastate large segments of the nonplanned sector.

ECONOMIC POWER: HISTORY AND INSTITUTIONS

And no doubt, of even greater importance, we must begin to develop a unified worldwide macro analytical model! The original setting of Keynesian macroeconomics was aggregate demand management primarily within the geographical confines of the nation state. But this is no longer appropriate. The modern form of corporate enterprise (supra-, trans-, or anational) simply transcends national markets. The level of output, employment, and capital flows in North American countries are significantly affected by the decisions of consumers, producers, and governments in Western Europe and Japan and vice versa. Indeed a decision by monetary authorities to expand or contract the money supply, so as to expand or contract domestic aggregate demand, will notably affect the economic decisions of both domestics and foreigners in ways not even contemplated just two decades ago. For example, the United States' recent and almost unbelievably high government deficits have not resulted in a crowding out of funds available to the private sector. Why? Simply because of capital flows from other industrial nations into United States' financial instruments—capital flows due primarily to the United States' relatively high interest rates. The Eurocurrency market alone has made measuring domestic money supplies, even if one can be defined, a tenuous exercise at best.

Stated somewhat differently, the exercise of corporate micro-macro-market power on a global scale has, to date, not yet summoned forth a countervailing government micro-macro-market power. Rather, and notwithstanding the many recently publicized attempts to coordinate macroeconomic policy between and among the industrial nations, the reality is closer to a "beggar thy neighbor" approach.

And a final observation: one must not assume that competition from "foreign" corporations is now effectively disciplining the marketplace. This is so for several reasons; two will be illustrated. First many of the imports coming into this country are, in fact, being produced by American anational corporations in foreign countries and then imported into American markets. Given the power to choose between investing in new technologies with long-run payoff potential, our corporate elite have opted instead, in far too many cases, to maximize short-run profits by simply moving their production facilities offshore, often moving to countries where labor is cheap, a middle-class nonexistent, and/or social and environmental standards minimal. Second, many manufacturing industries are quickly proceeding to become oligopolized on a worldwide scale: the prototypical example being the automotive industry. The power of worldwide oligopolized anational industries, especially where their own economic interests are concerned, simply transcends the power of legislatures within any given nation state.

Conclusion

First, the most obtrusive concrete reality in today's economy is the existence and exercise of corporate micro-macro-market power. On the other hand, the most obtrusive and enduring myth is that Smith's 200-year-old conceptualization of competitive impersonal market forces typifies the norm. The continued existence and widening of the economic dichotomy between myth and reality is monumental testimony to the fact that economic ideology is, and has been throughout the ages, as powerful a force, if not more so, than economic analysis based on *empirical scientific investigations*.

Second, the emergence and exercise of corporate micro-macro-market power, in the past, always summoned forth a countervailing exercise of power by other organizations. And to argue against the exercise of power by unions and government, while professing that corporate enterprise is adequately policed by market forces, is, quite simply, indefensibly disingenuous. Perhaps even fraud is not too strong an appellation.

And finally, the dichotomy between generally accepted orthodox economic theory and economic reality has almost reached the point where meaningful scientific discourse within the economics community is becoming impossible. Many in the economics profession, if not most, are occupied almost solely in the pursuit of creating ever more elaborate arguments to justify laissez-faire (a la rational expectations, contestable markets, public choice). However, global markets dominated by anational forms of enterprise have reduced the laissez-faire debate to such a level of absurdity as to make much of today's economics—and, therefore, today's economists—an actual impediment to social progress.

Notes

1. Joan Robinson, *Economic Philosophy* (New York: Doubleday & Company, Inc., 1964), p. 1.1
2. John Maynard Keynes, *The General Theory of Employment, Interest, and Money* (New York: Harcourt, Brace and Company, 1936), p. 383.
3. For an excellent analysis of the structural components of corporate power see John Kenneth Galbraith, *The Anatomy of Power* (Boston: Houghton Mifflin Company, 1983).
4. Arthur Stone Dewing, *The Financial Policy of Corporations*, 3rd rev. ed. (New York: The Ronald Press Company, 1934), p. 9.
5. In terms of Business Receipts in the year 1939, 1953, and 1975, corporations accounted for 77 percent, 71 percent, and 86 percent, respectively. As of 1983 corporations accounted for 90 percent of all business receipts.
6. Clair Wilcox, "Competition and Monopoly in American Industry," *Temporary National*

Economic Committee, Monograph 21 (Washington, D.C.: Government Printing Office, 1940), p. 66.

7. Charles R. VanHise, *Concentration and Control* (New York: The Macmillan Company, 1912), p. 190.

8. Wilcox, "Competition and Monopoly in American Industry," p. 68.

9. *Ibid.*, pp. 65–66.

10. Clair Wilcox, *Public Policies Toward Business*, pp. 588–89.

11. Upton Sinclair, *The Jungle* (New York: The New American Library, Inc., 1905), p. 348.

12. Adulteration was defined primarily as the use of diseased food, the use of coloring substances to disguise the age or quality of a food, or the use of toxic substances to prolong the shelf life of processed foods. Misbranding was defined primarily as the use of drugs or stimulants without so stating on the label, as well as the use of labels that claimed false healing remedies or labels that did not clearly state weights and/or measures properly.

13. H. H. Liebhafsky, *American Government and Business* (New York: John Wiley and Son, Inc., 1971), p. 148.

14. X-efficiency refers to the complete absence of any slack or waste within an individual firm's production processes; on the other hand, X-inefficiency refers to a situation where slack and waste exist within the firm's production processes. The degree of X-inefficiency in an individual firm is the ratio of excess cost (due to slack and waste) to minimum possible cost.

15. A careful reading of Smith's *Wealth of Nations* reveals his attitude toward government's role in the economy to be more complex than is usually thought. To facilitate domestic commerce Smith contended that government had a responsibility to establish and maintain public works "...such as good roads, bridges, navigable canals, harbours, etcetera;" and in order to facilitate international trade, to establish and maintain a foreign service apparatus including customs houses, boards of trade, ambassadors and embassies, etc. In addition, to establish tariffs and bounties (1) for "...the encouragement of domestic industry..." involved in the country's defense, and (2) in retaliation for tariffs and bounties being employed by its trading partners.

Smith also advocated regulation of specific industries as a means of protecting or promoting the public interest: he advocated (1) using taxes so as to promote increases in agricultural productivity, and (2) regulating interest rates so as to promote efficiency in investment projects. In addition, in banking, Smith supported replacing gold and silver with paper money, since in his view "...substituting paper in the room of a great part of this gold and silver, enables the country to...increase very considerably the annual produce of its land and labour"; and he also favored government regulating the supply of paper money.

Nor was Smith opposed to public enterprise; e.g., he opined that the post office was beneficial to commerce and should therefore be established by government; and finally, he believed in a progressive tax code with "...all the different members contributing, as nearly as possible, in proportion to their respective abilities."

16. U.S. Congress, Senate, Gardiner Means, "N.R.A., A.A. and the Making of Industrial Policy," Senate Documents, 74th Congress, 1st Session, Miscellaneous, 3 January 1935, pp. 2–22.

17. Adam Smith, *An Inquiry Into the Nature and Causes of the Wealth of Nation* (New York: The Modern Library, 1937), p. 365; also see pp. 121, 170.

18. Berle and Means, *The Modern Corporation and Private Property*, p. xxiii.

19. *Ibid.*, p. xxxii.

20. U.S. Joint Economic Committee, "Employment Act of 1946, as Amended, with Related Laws" (Washington, D.C.: Government Printing Offices, 1977).

21. John M. Keynes, *The General Theory of Employment, Interest and Money* (New York: Harcourt, Brace and Company, 1936), pp. 377–379.

22. John Kenneth Galbraith, *The New Industrial State* (Boston: Houghton Mifflin Company, 1967).

23. John R. Munkirs and Janet T. Knoedler, "The Dual Economy: An Empirical Analysis," *Journal of Economic Issues*, Vol. 21, No. 2, June, 1987, pp. 803–811.

24. John R. Munkirs, *The Transformation of American Capitalism* (Armonk, New York: M.E. Sharpe Inc., 1985) p. 197.

25. U.S. Congress, Senate Hearings before the Subcommittee on International Trade of the Committee on Finance, *Multinational Corporations*, p. 451.

26. Jacques G. Maisonrouge, "Address to the American Foreign Service Association," Washington, D.C., 29 May 1969.

27. U.S. Congress, Senate, *Multinational Corporations*, p. 451.

3 THE CONCENTRATION OF ECONOMIC POWER
Douglas F. Greer

Definition of Economic Power

Most economists define *market power* as the ability to control price and exclude rivals.[1] In turn, *economic power* is often assumed to be essentially the same as market power, but this equivalence raises serious problems. Real world economic power encompasses much more than market power, despite efforts by many economists to ignore the distinction. For example, a recent article in *Forbes* voluminously reports on the economic power of General Electric Corporation without ever even mentioning the company's market power in jet engines or television broadcasting. It states that during the first six years of the 1980s GE changed dramatically, reshuffling its "...corporate portfolio like a riverboat gambler, acquiring 338 business and product lines for $11.1 billion":

> Nothing like this has been seen in corporate America since the conglomerator days of LTV's Jimmy Ling and Gulf & Western's Charles Bluhdorn. With GE, it's a case of enormous financial might, coupled with the readiness to acquire—or to dump. Says one former GE official, "This company is prepared to buy or sell any business, depending on how it fits into its overall strategy."[2]

To encompass such behavior, economic power could be defined as "... the ability of some persons or firms to produce intended economic effects on others." This definition derives from Dennis Wrong's definition of *power* generally.[3] An alternative definition that conveys the same "capability of influence," yet stresses the limitations faced by even the most powerful firms, derives from Robert E. Smith. Each firm has, in Smith's words, a "constrained set of conduct options." Fewer and weaker constraints grant "greater discretion," more "economic power."[4] Clearly, the "conduct options" can include acquisitions, product innovations, public relations advertising, and many other things besides the price variables of conventional theory. Also, "greater discretion" would imply more substantial intended effects on others, like customers and rivals. Hence the two definitions overlap. This chapter is concerned with such broad economic power as well as the more traditional and narrow notion of market power. "Power holders" possess it. "Power targets" experience it.

How can such broad economic power be measured? In the abstract, it can be measured, at least qualitatively, according to three attributes—extensiveness, comprehensiveness, and intensiveness. *Extensiveness* refers to the number of people or the volume of business activity influenced, or potentially influenced, by power holders. *Comprehensiveness* indicates the range of issues or variables or conduct options that are affected by power holders. And *intensiveness* refers to the strength of influence or the degree of discretion exercised by power holders over power targets.[5]

Table 3-1 illustrates these three attributes for both market power and economic power so as to convey their meaning more concretely. Market power is a rather limited concept as measured by all three attributes. In

Table 3-1. Attributes of Market Power and Economic Power Selectively Illustrated

Attribute	Examples for Market Power	Examples for Economic Power
Extensiveness (spread of influence)	Number of buyers in the market	Number of people in the economy
Comprehensiveness (variables influenced)	Price of the product sold	Prices, asset size, and political beliefs
Intensiveness (strength of influence)	Price elasticity of demand (low being most intensive)	High intensity (e.g., jobs and plant locations) to low intensity (e.g., "United Way" endorsement)

extensiveness, market power concerns only market participants, or potential participants, so the number of buyers in the market would gauge this attribute. Price control is the essence of market power, so price level and price elasticity of demand best illustrate possible measures of the comprehensiveness and intensiveness of market power. The contrast with economic power should be clear. In this larger view, power targets, both actual and potential, can extend to economywide populations. The variables influenced by power holders can comprehensively include asset size and political beliefs plus many other things as well as product price level. And the intensities of influence can vary as widely as the variables involved.

It should be explicitly recognized that the "capacity to influence" that lies at the heart of our definition of economic power need not imply an "intensiveness" that always assures power holders of complete success in achieving their aims or of complete control over their power targets. The *Forbes* analysis of GE points out that GE is now doing more than acquiring companies. During the period it bought 338 businesses and product lines for $11.1 billion, the company also sold 232 others for $5.9 billion, and many of these divestitures were prompted by poor business performance. Defenders of giant corporate size would probably like to point to these divestitures as proof that GE lacks economic power, but failure in the economic world is not necessarily a sign of power's absence. Scientific man often fails in his attempts to tame nature—as dams crack open, as chlorofluorocarbon compounds destroy the earth's outer layer of protective ozone, and as nuclear power plants melt down. Yet these missteps would certainly not lead us to conclude that man is powerless against nature. Similarly, political man often fails in his attempts to solve disputes peacefully, resulting in violent conflicts. Yet such failures cannot justify sweeping conclusions of man's diplomatic impotence. As for corporate chieftains, they often stumble in their attempts to accumulate and manage assets (or in their attempts to manipulate consumers with advertising, etc.). Yet power, frequently immense power, is nevertheless commonly present, at least in the short run if not always in the long run. Indeed, the significance of that power may occasionally be gauged by the severity of the economic damage or disturbance that emerges in the wake of big mistakes.[6] Stated differently, our definition of economic power acknowledges constraints.

Likewise, power's presence does not require that the activities of corporate leaders always be guided by goals of profit maximization. Returning once again to the example of General Electric, *Forbes* reports that huge size is the source of GE's power and that still greater size is apparently one of its main objectives:

Clearly, GE has the stomach to swallow huge companies with barely a burp. The next takeover could be the size of Corning Glass, Honeywell, or Merrill Lynch. Outlandish? Not at all.... Only last December, in a rare and closed-door meeting with analysts in New York, GE Chairman Jack Welch, 51, noted that, in just six years since he took over as chief executive, the company had moved from tenth largest company in the U.S. as measured by stock market capitalization, to third largest. Then, astonishingly, he went on to suggest he would like GE to be the nation's largest company.[7]

In short, vast horizons appear once we move beyond the narrow confines of neoclassical theory's assumed motive and unit of analysis—profit maximization in a single market.

Sources and Targets of Economic Power

As just suggested, corporations and their managers are the principal power holders of interest to us here (as opposed to government agencies or others). Moreover, measures of size concentration will be the main yardsticks of their power. Our measures of concentration will refer to three different levels of aggregation—(1) single markets, such as "malt beverages" or "passenger cars," (2) sectors of related markets, such as "food industries" or "financial services," and (3) macro aggregates, which would encompass "all manufacturing" or "all services." In particular, corporate size concentration at any of these levels will disclose the *sources* of the "ability to influence" that comprises economic power (regardless of whether that size concentration derives from technical efficiencies, pecuniary efficiencies, or strategic conduct). Reference to these three levels, when coupled with explicit identification of those in the economy who are the *targets* of power's "influence," provides a convenient way to explain why measures of concentration are helpful in assessing economic power.

Table 3-2 presents the 12-part matrix that results from crossing the three possible *sources* of economic power with four classes of *targets* which are on the receiving end of the power holders' abilities. Brief discussion of each cell allows further defense of our broad definition of economic power and identifies some of the specific influences referred to in that definition. Let's take them in numerical order.

1. *Single market power with the customers and suppliers of the firm as targets.* This is the traditional case in neoclassical theory, where a pure monopolist raises selling price to customers and a pure monopsonist lowers purchase price to suppliers. Extensive empirical evidence verifies that

THE CONCENTRATION OF ECONOMIC POWER

Table 3-2. Sources of the "Capacity' and Targets of the "Influence" that Comprise Economic Power

Targets of the Influence	Source of Power is Size Concentration in...		
	Single Market	Related Markets	Macro Aggregates
Customers and suppliers	1	5	9
Market rivals (actual and potential)	2	6	10
Businesses at large	3	7	11
Society in general	4	8	12

market concentration is associated with these price effects—positively for selling prices received and negatively for buying prices paid.[8]

2. *Single market power with actual and potential rivals as targets.* Traditional theory and empirical analysis extend to this case also (at least among non-Chicagoans). Predatory and exclusionary conduct comprise the main topics of inquiry here. Two recent illustrative research projects of special interest to the present author concern (1) the effectiveness of American Tobacco Company's predatory activities around the turn of the century,[9] and (2) the importance and potency of raising rivals' costs in order to achieve exclusionary objectives.[10]

3. *Single market power vis-a-vis business enterprises in general.* How did General Electric obtain the resources to acquire RCA for $6.4 billion? GE's power in certain specific markets certainly helped considerably, illustrating that a firm's position in the traditional sense of item (1) above can have a very significant impact on that firm's relationships with other firms generally, especially as it concerns the acquisition of other firms (or defense against acquisition by others). Other acquisitions that illustrate this phenomenon include GM's purchase of Hughes Aircraft for $5.0 billion, Philip Morris' procurement of General Foods for $5.6 billion, and IBM's takeover of Rolm for $1.3 billion. These experiences, and countless others like them, undermine any notion that power in a single market—such as jet engines, automobiles, cigarettes, or computers—has no relevance whatever for enterprises operating in quite distant markets. Aside from this matter of acquisitions, which may be funded by single-market monopoly profits, there is one industry whose firms are strategically positioned vis-a-vis all other firms in the economy, so monopoly power in

that industry has substantial consequences for businesses generally. That key industry is, of course, commercial banking.[11]

4. *Single-market power influencing society in general.* Economists of the traditional, neoclassical stripe tend to deny or ignore the sociopolitical implications of single-market monopoly power. An extreme example of this narrow vision is provided by James Buchanan, who suggests that monopoly is good in organized crime as it concerns such activities as prostitution or illicit drug dealing, good because the typical economic effects of monopoly are raised price levels and restricted outputs. Although it may be true that monopolization of organized crime activities would indeed lessen society's allocation of scarce economic resources to their provision (below what they would otherwise be), this does not necessarily imply that, overall, such monopolization would be beneficial for society. As Steven Rhoads points out, Buchanan's position neglects a political factor of tremendous importance:

> Unlike disorganized crime, organized crime is a competing power center that corrupts our police and politicians. These corrupting crimes, committed in order to gain the power to offer illicit services, threaten political legitimacy. The gains made by having the syndicate organize and thus restrict the market for prostitution and drugs may be more than counterbalanced by the political legitimacy and legislative costs when public servants are on the take.[12]

More generally, there is evidence that corporate political activity is positively associated with single-market concentration.[13] And still more generally, single-market concentration can influence the "market" for ideas to the extent that increasing concentration in TV broadcasting, newspapers, and other media diminishes the diversity of views reaching the public. Finally, recent reports inform us that Pacific Bell, Ford Motor Company, and other prominent corporations with considerable labor market power have hired "New Age" consultants to train their workers to think "properly," the main objective being "homogeneity of thought" because "companies whose members agree on certain fundamental values and norms are more successful than those who do not."[14]

5. *Power in related markets: customers and suppliers.* Markets may be related in several possible ways. Because of high transportation costs, boundary legalisms, or other such factors, markets may be separated geographically while at the same time being related by product similarities or uniformities. For example, limited geographic markets for cement and ice cream in Boston and Baltimore are "related" in this sense, and firms are frequently structured into "multinationals" or "franchise" chains in order to exploit this relatedness. (Some, like McDonalds', become multinational

franchises.) Another form of market relatedness occurs in vertical, buyer-seller linkages, as when for instance, AT&T produces the equipment it uses in its long distance telecommunications service markets. Yet another form could be called "product-extension" conglomeracy, in which case firms occupy clusters of related but distinct markets. The airline companies that own hotel and car rental subsidiaries serve as examples. Even more prominent in this regard are companies like Procter & Gamble and Philip Morris-General Foods Inc., whose operations span a wide variety of products that are sold to the same ultimate buyers (household consumers), promoted on the same advertising media (television and magazines mainly), and distributed through the same retail outlets (grocery stores).

Prominent positioning in such related markets can easily bestow power to influence a firm's customers or suppliers in any single market. An instance of ancient heritage is price discrimination. This is especially true if the price discrimination is achieved by tying—as when IBM tied punch cards to its data processing equipment—or by vertical integration—as when GM gains especially high profits from the replacement parts it manufactures.[15] Firms well positioned in product-extention conglomeracy undoubtedly use their position to extract favorable terms and conditions from their input suppliers (such as the television broadcasters and grocery retailers who serve the Procter & Gambles of the corporate world).

6. *Power in related markets: actual and potential rivals.* Power in related markets often bestows exclusionary advantages, vis-a-vis actual or potential rivals. For example, IBM used its power in related markets to (1) establish itself in main-frame computers after Sperry-Rand's original innovaton, (2) establish itself in personal computers after ignoring the market for several years, (3) curb the growth of peripheral equipment suppliers who had the potential for competing with IBM in systems generally, (4) define technological interfaces in such a way as to disadvantage rivals, and (5) lend credence to its falsely inflated announcements of new products, announcements that hurt the sales of rivals.[16] Similarly, it can be argued that Kodak exploited its multimarket powers in photography to curb the competition of rivals who originally developed miniature cameras and cartridge-loading film formats.[17] It should be clear that raising rivals' costs in one way or another is often the essence of what is going on here.[18]

7. *Power in related markets: businesses at large.* The concepts of strategic groups and mobility barriers, developed by Richard Caves and Michhael Porter for intraindustry analysis, might well be applicable to the market for corporate control (and thereby to sectorwide levels of concentration).[19] At the intraindustry level of analysis undertaken by Caves and Porter, groups of firms can be distinguished by such criteria as degree of vertical integra-

tion, choice of distribution channel, and local or national scope. Applying this conception to a larger range of aggregation than the market or industry, it is possible to identify sectors or clusters of firms sharing similarities of product extension or some other major trait. In turn, we may deduce that firms within such clusters may have advantages over outsiders when it comes to the acquisition of fellow insiders. Thus the high frequency with which firms engage in product-extension acquisitions suggests that firms with strong related-market structures may have advantages over business enterprises in general when it comes to purchasing certain categories of companies. For example, food manufacturers in diverse food product categories share a common footing when it comes to (1) dealing with regulations of the Food and Drug Administration and the Department of Agriculture, (2) coping with grocery distributors, and (3) promoting low-priced convenience goods that are "pre-sold" to consumers. Firms in financial sectors have similar shared experiences. It seems, then, that related-market positioning may grant powers that go beyond those just identified in categories (5) and (6).

8. *Power in related markets: society in general.* Concentration across related markets may improve the political might of firms because concentration implies greater unification than otherwise. Food manufacturers with diverse food product lines might be better able to influence Food and Drug Administration (FDA) policy on artificial sweetners or Environmental Protection Agency (EPA) policy on pesticide residues. Examples from finance likewise come to mind. In the past commercial banks have favored and thrift institutions have opposed legislative proposals that would permit depository institutions to diversify much more freely into insurance, securities brokering, investment banking, and nonfinancial activities generally. This split in lobbying positions has helped block adoption of these proposals, but this split has apparently begun to dissolve as thrift institutions and commercial banks grow increasingly similar in service offerings and size, and as mergers bring about ever greater consolidations among their ranks.

9. *Aggregate power with customers and suppliers of the firm as targets.* A firm gains power in this respect most readily by pure conglomerate expansion. Pure conglomeracy pertains to the firm's customers and suppliers in at least two ways—reciprocity and mutual forbearance.[20] In the first case, some of the firm's customers and suppliers become *both* customers and suppliers, responding to the firm's admonition, "I buy from you, so you should buy from me." In the second case, collusive understandings reach multimarket dimensions. Here, a conglomerate firm gains greater power over its primary customers than otherwise because potential rivals of the

firm refrain from vying for those customers in accord with the mutual understanding that the conglomerate will likewise refrain from going after the customers of those potential rivals.

10. *Aggregate power with rivals as targets.* Empirical evidence indicates that, following their acquisition by conglomerates, formerly independent firms usually do not gain market share at the expense of their rivals.[21] Still, conglomerates often have the power to make such gains by their use of cross-subsidy, in which case monopoly profits obtained in some markets are used to finance losses in other markets, losses that, in effect, permit market share expansion or preservation vis-a-vis rivals or potential rivals. The consequences need not be anticompetitive. They may be procompetitive. The main point to recognize is that, either way, conglomeracy bestows power that otherwise would not exist. AT&T's recent plunge into the computer industry illustrates such power:

> So far the plunge has produced little more than a tremendous splash of red ink. AT&T refuses to discuss the matter, but insiders say that in 1985 the computer division lost $500 million, before taxes, on sales of $2.4 billion. Last year [1986] sales slumped to $2.2 billion and pretax losses more than doubled to a staggering $1.2 billion.[22]

Moreover, cross-subsidy need not be involved in order to elbow out rivals. In some cases, conglomerates may gain at the expense of rivals because of their clout with suppliers of promotion and distribution services, clout that gives the conglomerate access to bottlenecks and reduced costs.[23] For example, Procter and Gamble, whose total annual spending on advertising is now approaching $2 billion, undoubtedly has freer selection of network television sponsorships than a smaller more specialized rival. This probably gives Procter and Gamble especially favorable audience demographics per ad dollar spent on network television.

11. *Aggregate power vis-a-vis businesses in general.* As before in categories (3) and (7), the key issue here is the firm's power in acquiring other firms or in blocking its own acquisition by others. Immense absolute size, such as that easily obtained by conglomeracy, has proven to be helpful in making acquisitions and defending against them.[24] Aside from matters concerning mergers, the diversity and size fostered by pure conglomeracy may help to secure lines of credit when capital shortages arise. Moreover, they may help to bolster intercorporate ties grounded on interlocking directorates. It may be doubted that the interlocking directorships presently prevailing in the United States have any significant impact on specific market performance of the kind referred to in categories (1) and (2) of table 3-2. But they could plausibly affect the kinds of behavior covered

here, acquisitions especially. Where, for instance, do corporate "White Knights" come from if not at least occasionally from interlock relations?

12. *Aggregate power: society in general.* The political implications of pure conglomeracy are fairly easy to imagine. As Kenneth Elzinga observes, "...small enterprises, located in but one congressional district and without a potent trade association, cannot marshal the forces of a large, diversified firm with facilities in over a hundred districts."[25] Less apparent but no less real are the "image" campaigns that can be launched more readily with the kind of size afforded by conglomeracy. In 1974, for instance, International Telephone and Telegraph (ITT) successfully countered the bad publicity it was receiving for several embarrassing transgressions, including its involvement with the Central Intelligence Agency in Chile, by heavily advertising its sponsorship of a series of children's television programs. ITT's "social responsibility rating" among polled respondents jumped substantially when it spent more to *publicize* its good deeds than it spent to *produce* those good deeds.[26] More recently and more interestingly, Farley Industries, Inc., launched a 1987 campaign promoting the company's Chief Executive Officer (CEO), William Farley, for purposes of building Mr. Farley's public image "should he decide to run for political office" as well as for boosting the corporation's public image.[27]

The statistical measures of concentration that we consider shortly in section IV are not sufficiently refined, either in theoretical underpinnings or mathematical sophistication, to be assigned exclusively to any one of the 12 categories of table 3-2. Rather, they will refer broadly to the column clusters — namely, "single-market" measures (for categories 1 through 4), "related-market" measures (for 5 through 8), and "macro-aggregate" measures (for 9 through 12).

Statistical Measures of Power

Sidney Hook remarks that "the best hope of avoiding the abuse of power in our world is to share it."[28] It is fitting, then, that most statistical measures of economic power (or market power) focus on the "shares" of some economic variable, such as sales or value-added or assets, accounted for by a firm or group of firms. The more widely shared the shares, the greater confidence we tend to have that we will escape abuses. The less widely shared the shares, the more "concentrated" they become and the slimmer our chances of escape. This common sense generality has been formalized in economic theory, beginning with the work of August Cournot and continuing with the work of current contributors to periodicals like the *Journal* of *Industrial Economics*.[29] In this way, measures of share concentration are measures of *power*.

Once it is accepted that firm shares measure relative importance or power, and also that the collective shares of firms are important for explaining or predicting economic behavior, it can be argued that a good statistical measure of such concentration will possess certain desirable properties. L. Hannah and J. A. Kay, for instance, propose that meaningful concentration measures *have seven* properties, three of which might be deemed especially important:[30]

- Concentration should increase if the share of any firm is increased at the expense of a smaller firm.
- The entry of new firms below some arbitrary significant size should reduce concentration.
- Mergers should increase concentration.

These are substantive properties. Meeting them allows reality's statistics for power to represent accurately theory's concepts of power.

The concentration measure of greatest historical importance is the "concentration ratio," which is the cumulative share of some economic variable (such as sales or assets) accounted for by a certain absolute number of leading firms. The most common number of top firms for specific markets in the United States has been four or eight because of Census Bureau procedures. Aggregate concentration ratios typically refer to the top 50, 100, or 200 firms in, say, manufacturing.

Because the concentration ratio lacks certain desirable properties, a variety of alternatives have been proposed, the most popular of which is the "Hirschman-Herfindahl index," or "H-index." This is the sum of the squared values of the firms' shares. Unlike the concentration ratio, the H-index satisfies all the desirable properties proposed by Hannah and Kay. Accordingly, it has, among other things, been given a place of central importance in the Merger Guidelines of the Department of Justice and has been honored by Census Bureau calculation and publication in the *1982 Census of Manufactures*.[31]

The fact that the H-index satisfies numerous highly desirable properties does not necessarily mean that all other measures should be purged and the H-index deified. Many other measures likewise qualify under the same criteria. Indeed, Hannah and Kay identify an entire family of such measures, of which the H-index is but one member. Moreover, other measures, including especially the four-firm concentration ratio, are highly correlated with the H-index. In the end, then, the selection of any one particular measure can depend partly on value judgments, partly on statistical convenience, partly on the purposes at hand, and partly on its theoretical and empirical underpinnings.[32] For our purposes, the concentration ratio will be relied upon almost exclusively, with the number of leading firms in the ratio varying from 4 to 200, depending on the breadth of aggregation. A major reason for this selection is that we shall be keenly interested in broad historical trends, and the concentration ratio has the longest lineage of any measure of concentration.

Because the breadth of aggregation can vary widely, the issue of breadth has been as controversial as the issue of statistical formula. Should markets be defined by the four- or five-digit Standard Industrial Classification (SIC)? Are concentration data meaningful for manufacturing as a whole? These and other questions like them need not occupy us. Their answers are given by data availabilities or by our earlier discussion of table 3-2. In particular, we shall be interested in the full range of possible aggregations identified by the column headings of table 3-2—single markets, related markets, and macro aggregates. Within each of these divisions, we shall select from the best data available.

The Numbers: Levels and Trends

Single Markets

Current concentration levels in markets in U.S. *manufacturing*, as measured by the U.S. Census Bureau for 1982, are summarized in figure 3-1. Four-firm concentration ratios for four-digit industries (except those with sales "not elsewhere classified," or "nec") are shown there in two frequency distributions, one based on the percentage distribution of value of shipments (a weighted distribution) and one based simply on the percentage distribution of the 364 included industries. It may be seen that instances of very low concentration or very high concentration are relatively rare in manufacturing industries. Only about 6.6 percent of the total value of shipments, and about 4.9 percent of the number of industries, are associated with four-firm concentration ratios in the range between 0 and 10. At the opposite extreme, in the range where the top four firms have 90 to 100 percent of market sales, only 4.9 percent of the shipments and 1.9 percent of the industries are to be found. It is therefore in the middle ranges of concentration, where "tight" and "loose" oligopolies are depicted, that most manufacturing industries are located. The mean four-firm concentration ratio is 41.6 percent. On average, then, the top-four firms in manufacturing markets account for 41.6 percent of market sales.

Figure 3-1. Concentration Pattern in U.S. Manufacturing, 1982 (Excluding n.e.c. industries)

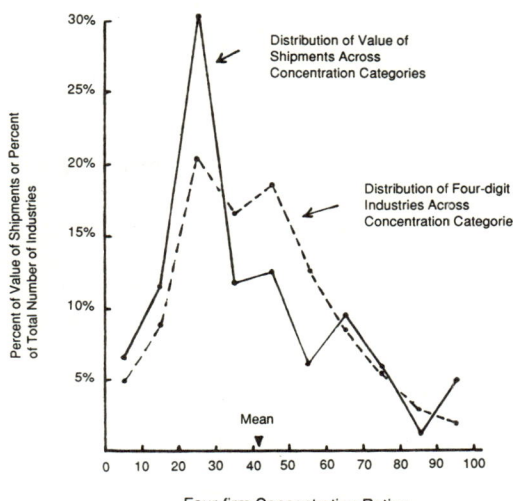

Source: U.S. Department of Commerce, Bureau of the Census, *1982 Census of Manufacturing: Concentration Ratios in Manufacturing*, MC82-5-7 (Washington, D.C., 1986), pp. 6–50.

The accuracy of the SIC market definitions used by the Census Bureau may be questioned. Here I have excluded all the "nec" industries so as to minimize the "catch-all" cases, which tend to be too broad to be meaningful. Some other adjustments, like narrowing the geographic scope of local and regional industries, would *raise* the mean concentration ratio above 41.6 if they were implemented. At the same time, however, some adjustments that would *lower* the mean concentration could also be justified. For example, adjusting for imports and exports, which are ignored in Census Bureau calculations, would lower the concentration ratio for "sewing machines" by about 50 percentage points and for "pulpmills" by about 35 points.[33]

If all possible adjustments could be made, the mean might be greater or lower than the 41.6 shown in figure 3-1. Adjustments to 1966 data tended to raise it.[34] Current adjustments might reverse that somewhat because of presently greater imports. Perhaps in the end the 41.6 of figure 3-1 would be pretty close to the true average.

Our reference to increased volumes of imports raises the issue of trend.

Has single-market concentration in manufacturing been rising, falling, or remaining unchanged? Looking at a few scraps of data over 100 years old, one might to argue that single-market concentration in 1850 and 1860 was not substantially less than it is today, assuming the relevant "markets" then were geographically restricted to single states because of restrictive state laws on corporate chartering and because of a lack of transportation compared to what we enjoy today.[35] Although *nationwide* the number of producers in most industries was apparently much larger in 1860 than it is today, an assumption of narrow, *statewide* relevant markets substantially lowers that old number of sellers as any individual buyer would see the situation, thereby raising concentration. However that may be, the accuracy of the data improves with time, and it appears that market concentration, at least by national geographic definitions, which with time tended to emerge for most manufacturing, experienced enormous increases between 1895 and 1902 as a result of a massive merger movement. Then between 1909 and the present, the trend is debated, but it appears that market concentration continued to rise (though less sharply than before) until 1947, after which it has remained, on average, fairly stable. According to Alfred Chandler, Jr., for instance:

> The percentage of total product value produced by the oligopolists rose from 16% in 1909 to 21% in 1929, and then jumped to 28% at the end of the depression in 1939. Since World War II the figure has remained stable, being 26% in 1947, 25% in 1958, and then up to 27% in 1963.[36]

Oligopoly in this case is defined as an industry in which 6 or fewer firms contributed 50 percent, or 12 or fewer contributed 75 percent of the total product value.

The post-World War II stability of single-market concentration in manufacturing is corroborated by Willard F. Mueller and Richard T. Rogers. For 165 consistently defined SIC industries over the period 1947–1977, they find that average concentration rose in consumer goods markets and fell in producer goods markets. On balance the overall average changed very little, rising slightly from 40.4 to 42.3.[37]

A more optimistic view of recent trends is propounded by W. G. Shepherd, but Shepherd's analysis is too qualitative to be strictly comparable to that of Mueller and Rogers. Whereas Mueller and Rogers stick to the census concentration ratios, Shepherd judges industries on such additional features as market share stability, price flexibility, profit levels, and entry barriers in order to assign them to one of his four categories of competitive condition. The "workably competitive" category accounted for 55.9 percent of all manufacturing industries in 1958 and 69.0 percent in

1980, a jump that Shepherd attributes mainly to import growth and official antitrust activity.[38] In Shepherd's view, then, the post-World War II trend has been favorable if factors other than census concentration ratios are included in the assessment.

Although single-market concentration in manufacturing has recently been steady or falling, it has been clearly rising in some other major sectors. *Grocery retailing* illustrates this. The upward trend is summarized by Bruce Marion:

> On average, local market concentration in grocery retailing increased between each of the six census years from 1954 to 1977. Moreover, the rate of increase accelerated since 1967. The market share held by the largest four grocery firms (CR 4) in each of 173 SMSAs that could be compared from 1958 to 1977 rose persistently from an average of 48.7 in 1958 to 56.4 in 1977....
>
> The proportion of highly concentrated markets (CR 4 greater than 60) expanded from 15.5 percent in 1958 to 42.0 percent in 1977.[39]

Energy mining industries, including coal and petroleum, are likewise on the rise.[40] Still, the overall picture is, as already suggested by the manufacturing data, rather mixed, with both ups and downs. Indeed, this mix even occurs within some sectors—*commercial banking*, for instance. At the national level, which is the relevant geographic market for large-company loans, bank concentration has been fairly low but is now rising.[41] On the other hand, at state and local levels, which are the relevant geographic markets for most other commercial banking services, concentration has been on average rather high but falling.[42] This recent downward trend in local markets is even greater than the statistics suggest to the extent that deregulation of thrift institutions has allowed them to compete with commercial banks in many local service markets.[43]

Deregulation has contributed to reduced concentration in single markets in other sectors as well, transportation especially. An important caveat must be added, however. The favorable effects from reduced regulation of the "public utility" type may be largely temporary because of reduced antitrust enforcement during Reagan's reign. In commercial banking, for instance, merger rates are running at historic highs as this is written, so the most recent trend in local concentration may well be skyward.[44] In airline services, new entry followed deregulation during the late 1970s, with the result that concentration apparently fell in many city-pair markets.[45] Most recently, however, a chain of mergers involving Continental, Eastern, Texas Air, TWA, Ozark, Northwest, Republic, and others has led to the result that in 1986 the leading six airlines accounted for about 71.4 percent of all U.S. passenger traffic nationally, up substantially from 64.4 percent in 1984.[46] Likewise, mergers among major railroads have contributed to the fact that, as of 1984, three railroads controlled roughly 80 percent of all rail traffic in the west (Burlington Northern, Santa Fe-SP, and Union Pacific), while three railroads garnered over 70 percent of all rail traffic in the east (CSX, Norfolk Southern, and Conrail).[47] Even where concentration is down, as it is in long-distance telecommunications (due chiefly to MCI and Sprint), it can be argued that competition is really no better now than it was before the substantial government policy changes of recent years.[48]

In sum, the concentration pattern for single markets is speckled. There are highs and lows plus trends in all possible directions. This allows for diverse assessments heavily flavored by value judgments:

- The extent of shared monopoly can modestly be called staggering. (Mark Green)[49]
- While there are some markets in which the number of competitors is limited, there is not an important national market today (with the possible exception of telephone service) which lacks active competition. (Lee Lovinger)[50]

The truth probably lies somewhere between.

Related Markets

In light of our discussion of categories (5) through (8) in table 3-2 it may well be instructive to look at concentration for certain broadly defined groups of related markets—that is, the top companies' share of the business across all related markets combined. Because we used food manufacturing industries, which range from breakfast cereals to soda pop, to explain the reasoning behind this approach, we can begin with that sector now that actual numbers are called for.

There are now roughly 17,00 firms that could be called "food manufacturers," suggesting that this segment of the economy is atomistic in structure. The asset and value-added concentration data of table 3-3 prove otherwise, though. Based on firms whose primary activity is food manufacturing of some kind, the 100 largest companies' share of assets rose from 46.3 percent in 1950 to 75.1 percent in 1981. The shares of the top 200 firms increased from 60.0 percent to 81.5 percent. Since these asset figures include foreign and nonfood assets of the included companies, they may overstate the levels of concentration (although they do reflect the overall size disparities of the top firms relative to the lesser firms). Value-added concentration data are therefore also reported in table 3-3, as they

THE CONCENTRATION OF ECONOMIC POWER 69

Table 3-3. Aggregate Concentration Among the Largest Food Manufacturing Companies, Selected Years, 1947–1981

	Percent of Assets		Percent of Value-Added*	
Year	100 Largest Companies	200 Largest Companies	100 Largest Companies	200 Largest Companies
1981	75.1	81.5	NA	NA
1977	74.4	81.1	53.0	64.4
1972	68.5	76.7	51.2	62.9
1967	67.4	73.4	49.0	58.2
1963	53.9	67.9	45.8	53.5
1958	NA**	NA	43.1	50.1
1954	NA	NA	41.9	48.7
1950	46.3	60.0	NA	NA

* Value-added data exclude alcoholic benerage manufacturers.
** Not available.

Source: John M. Connor, Richard T. Rogers, Bruce W. Marion, and Willard F. Mueller, *The Food Manufacturing Industries* (Lexington, MA: Lexington Books, 1985), p. 120.

reflect large company participation solely in domestic food manufacturing (although the numbers here exclude alcoholic beverages). The top 100 firms' share of value added jumped from 41.9 percent to 53.0 percent over the years 1954–1977, while the share of the top 200 went up from 48.7 percent to 64.4 percent.

Whether the absolute levels of concentration reported here could be considered especially high is a matter of debatable analytical judgment and value judgment. It is undisputably clear, however, that the trend is upward. After her analysis of this, Julie A. Caswell concludes that mergers have placed "heavy upward pressure on aggregate concentration in this sector." The list of acquired companies includes such notable entries as Nabisco Brands, General Foods, Carnation, Esmark, Norton Simon, Oscar Mayer, and Del Monte.[51]

Finance offers several other related-market sectors of interest. According to a recent Congressional report:

> The U.S. financial services industry is highly concentrated at the top, remarkably diversified at the bottom. In each sector, a very small number of institutions accounts for half of that sector's activity and resources.[52]

Table 3-4 presents the details. In each sector—commercial banks, secur-

Table 3-4. Aggregate Concentration in Major Financial Services Sectors, 1984

Sector	Percent of Total Sector Resources* Held by Top 10 Sector Firms	Number of Firms in Sector Accounting for 50 Percentage of Sector Resources*	Percent of Total Number of Firms in Accounting for 50 Percentage of Resources*
Commercial banks	25.6	64	0.55%
Thrift institutions	15.6	132	4.17
Securities firms	46.7	12	0.15
Life-health insurers	48.8	11	0.51
Property-casualty insurers	27.0	33	1.86

* "Resources" refers to assets except in the case of securities firms, where the relevent measure is total revenue.

Source: U.S. House of Representatives, Subcommittee on Telecommunications, Consumer Protection, and Finance of the Committee on Energy and Commerce, *Restructuring Financial Markets: The Major Policy Issues Report*, 99th Congress, 2nd session (1986), pp. 226–237.

ities firms, and so on—the geographic scope of reference is the entire United States. this is appropriate for present purposes. Although local markets would be more meaningful in a single-market context, the related markets of interest here would entail some geographic aggregation as well as some product aggregation. Except in the case of thrift institutions, the top 10 firms in each sector account for at least 25 percent of each sector's resources. Large securities firms (like Merrill Lynch and Salomon Bros.) and large life-health insurance companies (like Prudential and Metropolitan Life) are especially well positioned. Alternative statistics for concentration reveal that, with the exception of thrift institutions, relatively few firms in each sector account for 50 percent of each sector's resources.

The related-markets approach may be particularly relevant in this case of financial services. Apart from the regulatory and deregulatory considerations mentioned earlier, huge size concentration, regardless of specific markets, carries ominous implications for aggregate financial stability in the event failure visits the industry's leaders. In other words, size dispersion alleviates the problem of institutions getting "too big to fail." Moreover, dispersion increases the number of independent financial decision-makers, and this may yield nonprice benefits:

> ...the primary concern about the concentration of financial institutions is that it results in too few private lenders and investors choosing winners and losers— a result that could be as harmful as centralizing this function in government.[53]

Data for trends in financial services date back furthest for commercial banking, as shown in table 3-5. Overall, concentration rose from 1925, when the largest 100 commercial banks in the United States accounted for approximately 33 percent of all the banking business, until 1985, when the top 100 banks accounted nearly for 58 percent. The upward trend has not been steady, however. Massive bank failures during the Great Depression lifted concentration dramatically from 1928 through 1938. Concentration then fell during the World War II era. And since 1953 it has been on the rise.

Consistent data for life insurance concentration do not go back many decades (and old data for life *and* health combined, as specified in table

Table 3-5. Percentage of Commercial Bank Assets or Deposits Accounted for by the 100 Largest Banks, 1925–1985

Year	Percent Share*	Year	Percent Share**
1985	57.7	1978	51.4
1984	55.0	1973	49.6
1983	54.3	1968	48.2
1982	53.6	1963	47.4
1981	51.7	1958	46.3
1980	51.4	1953	45.1
1979	51.2	1948	44.5
1978	50.8	1943	51.4
1975	50.8	1938	53.3
1973	51.2	1933	52.4
1971	49.5	1928	39.3
		1925	33.7

Sources: * Donald T. Savage, "Interstate Banking Development, *Federal Reserve Bulletin*, February, 1987, p. 90. This series is based on domestic assets.
** Stephen A. Rhoades, "Size and Rank Stability of the 100 Largest Commercial Banks, 1925–1978," *Journal of Economics and Business*, Vol. 34, No. 2, 1982, pp. 123–128. This series is based on foreign and domestic deposits.

3-4, are unavailable). The very long-run trend for life insurance may, like banking, be upward, but recent data move to the contrary. By one series, the assets of the largest 50 life insurance companies as a percentage of the total fell from 87.7 percent in 1960 to 79.1 percent in 1977.[54]

A sector of related markets which has apparently witnessed a substantial decline in concentration since World War II is electronic data processing, or EDP. As defined by the economists who defended IBM in *U.S. versus IBM*, there is a "market" for all EDP products and services, including, besides mainframe computer systems suppliers such as IBM, NCR, and Burroughs, all firms that are plug compatable equipment maufacturers, all mini-computer and personal computer suppliers, all parts manufacturers, plus all nonmanufacturing leasing companies, systems integrators, brokers and dealers, service bureaus, and time-sharing suppliers. IBM's share of EDP product revenue in the United States apparently fell substantially from 90.1 percent in 1952 to 40.7 percent in 1972.[55] When coupled with the preceding data for food manufacturing and financial services, these data for electronic data processing illustrate an unsurprising conclusion. Concentration trends in sectors of related markets are mixed.

Macro Aggregation

The loftiest level of aggregation, that covering pure conglomeracy, has in recent years shown less tendency to rise than might be expected on the basis of the vigorous, even feverish merger activity of the past 20 years. Lawrence J. White, for instance, concludes his study of the recent numbers by commenting that "aggregate concentration in the United States has not increased in the 1960s and 1970s, despite the substantial merger wave of the late 1960s."[56]

Still, several interesting observations emerge from this level of analysis. First, the recent overall stability is partly due to the fact that sectors of traditionally low concentration—services in particular—are growing in economic importance relative to sectors of traditionally high concentration —such as manufacturing. Aggregation to the manufacturing level alone *does* reveal rising aggregate concentration over recent decades. Second, waves of mainly conglomerate mergers *have* contributed to aggregate concentration because, without them, that concentration would have fallen substantially. Third, looking backward beyond the last few decades discloses that the very long-term trend is *definitely upward*, and markedly so, even when nonmanufacturing lines of business are included.

Figure 3-2 verifies the last of these observations. Every aggregate con-

Figure 3-2. Long-term Trend in Aggregate Concentration.

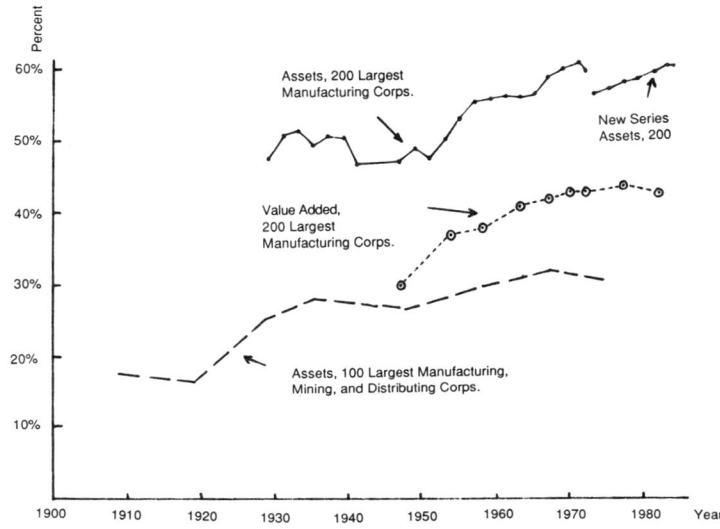

Sources: Federal Trade Commission Staff, *Economic Report on Corporate Mergers* (1969), p. 173; Lawrence J. White, "What has been Happening to Aggregate Concentration in the United States?" *Journal of Industrial Economics*, (March 1981), p. 225; Bureau of the Census, *1982 Census of Manufacturers: Concentration Ratios in Manufacturing*, MC82-5-7 (Washington D.C., 1986), p. 3; Robert J. Stonebraker, "Turnover and Mobility among the 100 Largest Firms: An Update," *American Economic Review* (December 1979), pp. 968–973; *1986 Statistical Abstract*, p. 534.

centration series dating back to the first half of this century, whether it is based on assets or some other measure of economic activity, indicates rising concentration in manufacturing over the long run.[57] Figure 3-2 shows the trend for assets and value added of the largest 200 manufacturing corporations. In addition, it shows the rising trend for assets of the largest 100 corporations in manufacturing, mining, and distributing from 1909 through 1974. (Note that the series on assets for the top 200 manufacturers changed in 1973 to exclude data on all foreign operations. The series therefore shifts down before continuing its long-term upward march.[58])

Greater detail for the value-added series on the leading 200 manufacturers is contained in table 3-6. There it may be seen that the share of the top 200 rose 13 percentage points; from 30 percent to 43 percent, and seven points of that can be credited to the largest 50 instead of those ranked 51 to 200. Moreover, most of this growth in concentration occurred before 1960,

Table 3-6. Share of Value-Added by Manufacturers Accounted for by the 50, 100, 150, and 200 Largest Manufacturing Companies, 1947–1982

Year	Company and Rank Group			
	50 Largest	100 Largest	150 Largest	200 Largest
1982	24%	33%	39%	43%
1977	24	33	39	44
1972	25	33	39	43
1970	24	33	38	43
1967	25	33	38	42
1963	25	33	37	41
1958	23	30	35	38
1954	23	30	34	37
1947	17	23	27	30

Source: U.S. Department of Commerce, Bureau of the Census, *1982 Census of Manufacturers: Concentration Ratios in Manufacturing*, MC82-5-7 (Washington, D.C., 1986), p. 3.

so the recent merger activity of the 1960s and 1970s has seemingly been less monumental than statistics on acquisitions alone might suggest.

This does not prove, however, that acquisition activity has been inconsequential. If the merging has been less intense, aggregate concentration would now be substantially less than it is. As Dennis Mueller explains:

> The fifties and sixties were a period of unprecedented economic growth and prosperity in the United States. Thousands of new firms were born and many grew to considerable size. That this period of prosperity was not accompanied by a relative decline in the importance of the largest firms is due to a considerable extent to the offsetting effects of mergers.[59]

Philip Silberg has estimated what concentration would be like in 1978 without the acquisitions of 1959–1978.[60] His sample included 14,676 companies in manufacturing, mining, transportation, wholesaling, and retailing. According to Spilberg the aggregate share of the largest 100 firms in these combined sectors would have been 14.1 percent less than it was in 1978 if these 100 firms had made no acquisitions (3.9 percentage points off their estimated share of 28.2). The aggregate share of the largest 200 firms would have been 16.3 percent lower without their acquisitions. Stated differently, acquisitions almost completely wiped out the concentration reducing effects of the economywide growth and new entry occurring over these two decades. Internal firm growth also helped the leaders maintain their position, but it made considerably less contribution than their acquisitions.

In sum, data through the 1970s, once analyzed, reveal rising aggregate concentration over the long run and hefty contributions from mergers. Although data are not yet available for 1984–1987, it seems safe to suppose that the merger movement of the mid-1980s has substantially fostered further aggregate concentration. The immensity of this current merger movement overshadows those of past decades.

As before (when assessing specific market and related market concentration), value judgments will determine whether, in an absolute sense, current levels of aggregate concentration are something to be deeply concerned about. My own judgment is that, given the importance of conglomerate mergers to the achievement of the present levels, and given the vast amount of evidence showing that conglomerate mergers do not further economic efficiency or technological progress or some other especially desirable social end,[61] presently observed levels of aggregate concentration generate very meager benefits. At the same time, the associated costs, such as those written of elsewhere in this book, are probably not trivial. On balance, then, I think there is a problem.

Other Measures of Power

Do the forgoing findings for rising concentration receive corroboration from any other measures of power? Does our neglect of other measures signal some embarrassing gaps in the data? The answers to these and related questions are sufficient to preserve the integrity of the preceding pages.

Completely apart from the very vast literature that reveals positive correlations between price levels or profit levels and concentration in cross-section analyses of market-by-market data, there are several additional methods of price behavior analysis that, broadly speaking, tend to confirm the findings of previous sections.

First, newly devised econometric studies of individual industries—including those for coffee roasting, tobacco, automobiles, and aluminum—reveal the presence of substantial market power. After surveying the literature of the "new empirical industrial organization" (NEIO), Timothy Bresnahan concludes that:

> By departing from the tradition of treating performance as observable in accounting cost data, the NEIO has provided a new form of evidence that there is substantial market power in the economy, a form of evidence that is not susceptible to the standard criticisms of earlier approaches. Further, the individual studies of particular industries are specific and detailed enough that alternative explanations of the findings can be rebutted.[62]

Second, the Lerner index, which places price in relation to marginal cost, or measures like the Lerner index, also provide interesting corroborations. While examining price and marginal cost behavior over the period 1949–1978, Robert E. Hall found that "most two-digit industries show signs of market power, and in a significant part of the economy, market power is substantial."[63] Addressing the question of whether market power has changed over the very long run, Myron J. Gordon updated Kalecki's aggregate Lerner indexes for manufacturing, with results shown here in table 3-7. Notice that the century-long trend of the index is up from 1.23 in 1879 to 1.46 in 1982, a trend that comes as no great surprise given the upward trend in concentration reviewed earlier. (Technically, the Lerner index as reported here is price divided by marginal cost. With perfect competition, price would equal marginal cost, yielding an index of one. In contrast, the data of table 3-7 indicate prices to be very high and rising relative to estimated marginal costs, thereby inviting a conclusion that monopoly power has been present and expanding.)

Although these several alternative approaches lend support to our earlier findings on power, these differ fundamentally from the earlier material. These approaches are, in particular, much narrower. Whereas concentration ratios measure the possession of economic power or potential power, as outlined throughout table 3-2, indices of price behavior measure the actual exercise of product market power in categories (1) and (2) of table 3-2, and perhaps (5) as well. Because our preferred definition of subject

Table 3-7. Degree of Monopoly (Lerner Indexes) in the Manufacturing Sector of the United States, 1979 to 1982

Year	Index*	Year	Index**
1982	1.46	1937	1.36
1977	1.46	1937	1.39
1972	1.49	1923	1.33
1967	1.48	1889	1.32
1958	1.39	1879	1.23
1950	1.33		
1947	1.31		
1939	1.38		

* Gorden's estimates.
** Kalecki's estimates.

Source: Myron J. Gordon, "The Postwar Growth in Monopoly Power," *Journal of Post Keynesian Economics*, Fall, 1985, pp. 3–13.

THE CONCENTRATION OF ECONOMIC POWER 77

matter broadly refers to "possessing *the ability*" to influence others, our own powers have been devoted most intently to a study of concentration in its various guises. Still, it is interesting to note in closing that possessing the ability usually means more than satisfying certain behavioral preconditions. Once power is possessed, temptation almost always assures its use.

Summary

Economic power, when broadly defined, includes a capacity to achieve intended effects, or stated differently, a large if constrained set of conduct options. In extreme cases this power will be extensive, comprehensive, and intensive—properties that range well beyond those contained in the narrow, single-market theorizing of traditional economic analysis.

The sources of a firm's power stem from its standing in single markets, related markets, and macro aggregates. At the same time, its influence can be felt by its customers, suppliers, rivals, businesses generally, or an entire society. Table 3-2 puts all the complex possibilities in a nutshell.

The collective power of firms is measured by concentration statistics over several levels of aggregation ranging from single markets to related markets and finally to pure conglomeracy. Among alternative statistical formulas for concentration, none can be declared universally superior to all others because value judgments affect the ratings of alternatives, and practicalities often dictate ultimate applications. Our analysis centered on concentration ratios, mainly 4-firm ratios for single markets and 100-firm and 200-firm ratios for related markets and aggregated data.

Single-market concentration varies widely, but its inclination centers in the middle ranges often described as "tight" or "loose" oligopoly. The very long-term trend, as disclosed in figures for manufacturing dating back to 1890, appears to have been for single-market concentration to increase, although very recently, since about 1950, the average level has remained unchanged or perhaps even fallen. Recent data in nonmanufacturing areas show both increases (as in grocery retailing) and decreases (as in local banking, at least until very recently). Concentration for related markets, or sectors, such as food manufacturing, has been high or rising in some cases, and has been better behaved in others. Merger activity has had adverse effects in food manufacturing and banking. Finally, concentration at the highest levels of aggregation has been rising over this century. In recent decades the skyward climb has stalled a bit, at least according to some measures at some levels of aggregation. Still, concentration in manufacturing drifts up and it would be much lower than it is at present if the leading firms had sat on the sidelines during the latest merger movements. Indeed, given the importance of mergers to current concentration, and given the fact that the largest mergers are more often predicated on managerial desires for growth or public notoriety than on seriously compelling economic efficiencies, it would seem that the social cost of the upper increments of this concentration could easily outweigh the social benefits. Corroboration for several of these results can be found in measures of power other than concentration ratios.

Notes

1. William L. Baldwin, *Market Power Competition, and Antitrust Policy* (Homewood, IL: Irwin, 1987), p. 3.
2. Edwin A. Finn, Jr., "General Eclectic," *Forbes*, March 23, 1987, p. 75.
3. Dennis H. Wrong, *Power: Its Forms, Bases, and Uses* (New York: Harper and Row Publishers, 1979), p. 2.
4. Robert E. Smith, "Economic and Political Characteristics of Cartel and Cartel-like Practices," in O. Schachter and R. Hellawell (Eds.), *Competition in International Business* (New York: Columbia University Press, 1981), p. 182.
5. These attributes are elaborately explored by Dennis Wrong, *op. cit.*, pp. 14–20.
6. Adams and Brock mention Mobil's error in acquiring Montgomery Ward and ITT's dismemberment following its sixties spurt, then they go on to say: "Whether or not the companies in question are eventually penalized for wrong decisions (by huge write-offs on their profit-and-loss statements) is of secondary importance. More significant is the fact that firms with command over vast social resources are free to make decisions of overarching social consequence with relative immunity from social accountability or social control...." Walter Adams and James W. Brock, *The Bigness Complex* (New York: Pantheon Books, 1986), p. 8.
7. Edwin A. Finn, Jr. "General Eclectic," *Forbes*, March 23, 1987, pp. 75–76.
8. For a review see D. F. Greer, *Industrial Organization and Public Policy*, 2nd ed. (New York: Macmillan, 1984), chapters 13 and 19. For recent further evidence, see, e.g., Lance Brannman, J. Douglas Klein, and Leonard W. Weiss, "The Price Effects of Increased Competition in Auction Markets," *Review of Economics and Statistics*, February, 1987, pp. 24–32; Gwen Quail, Bruce Marion, Frederick Geithman, and Jeffrey Marquardt, "The Impact of Packer Buyer Concentration on Live Cattle Prices," N.C. Project 117, Working Paper 89 (University of Wisconsin, 1986).
9. Malcolm R. Burns, "Predatory Princing and the Acquisition Cost of Competitors," *Journal of Political Economy*, April, 1986, pp. 266–296.
10. Steven C. Salop and David T. Scheffman, "Raising Rivals' Costs," *American Economic Review*, May, 1985, pp. 267–271; Thomas G. Krattenmaker and Steven Salop, "Anticompetitive Exclusion: Raising Rivals' Costs to Achieve Power over Price," *Yale Law Journal*, December, 1986, pp. 209–293.
11. For discussions see David M. Kotz, *Bank Control of Large Corporations in the United States* (Berkeley: University of California Press, 1978); Beth Mintz and Michael Schwartz, *The Power Structure of American Business* (Chicago: University of Chicago Press, 1985).
12. Steven E. Rhoads, *The Economist's View of the World* (Cambridge: Cambridge University Press, 1985), p. 196.

13. Russell Pittman "Market Structure and Campaign Contributions," *Public Choice*, Fall, 1977, pp. 37–52.

14. "Corporate Mind Control," *Newsweek*, May 4, 1987, pp. 38–39. To quote further: "Some workers say the programs constitute mind control or promote values inimical to their religious beliefs."

15. M.L. Burstein, "A Theory of Full-Line Forcing," *Northwestern University Law Review*, March–April, 1960, pp. 62–95. Robert Crandall, "Vertical Integration and the Market for Repair Parts in the United States Automobile Industry," *Journal of Industrial Economics*, July, 1968, pp. 212–234. For general theorizing on related-market power see David Encaoua, Alexis Jacquemin, and Michel Moreaux, "Global Market Power and Diversification," *Economic Journal*, June, 1986, pp. 525–533.

16. Richard Thomas DeLamarter, *Big Blue: IBM's Use and Abuse of Power* (New York: Dodd, Mead & Co., 1986); Russell W. Pittman, "Predatory Investment: U.S. *v.* IBM, "*International Journal of Industrial Organization*, Vol. 2, No. 4, 1984, pp. 341–365.

17. James W. Brock, "Structural Monopoly Technological Performance, and Predatory Innovation: Relevant Standards Under Section 2 of the Sherman Act," American Business Law Journal, Fall, 1983, pp. 291–306. On both IBM and Kodak see Walter Adams and James W. Brock, "Integrated Monopoly and Market Power: System Selling Compatability Standards, and Market Control," *Quarterly Review of Economics and Business*, Winter, 1982, pp. 29–42.

18. Krattenmaker and Salop, *op. cit.*

19. Richard E. Caves and Michael E. Porter, "From Entry Barriers to Mobility Barriers," *Quarterly Journal of Economics*, May, 1977, pp. 241–261.

20. Willard F. Mueller "Conglomerates: A 'Nonindustry'," in Walter Adams (Ed.), *The Structure of American Industry*, 7th ed. (New York: Macmillan Publishing Co., 1986), pp. 363–381; Arnold A. Heggestad and Stephen A. Rhoades, "Multi-Market Interdependence and Local Market Competition," *Review of Economics and Statistics*, November, 1978, pp. 523–532.

21. Dennis C. Mueller, "Mergers and Market Share," *Review of Economics and Statistics*, May, 1985, pp. 259–267; Lawrence G. Goldberg, "The Effect of Conglomerate Mergers on Competition," *Journal of Law and Economics*, April, 1973, pp. 137–158.

22. Peter Petre, "AT&T's Epic Push in Computers," *Fortune*, May 25, 1987, p. 42.

23. See, e.g., Jolie Solomon, "P&G Banks on becoming Dominant Drug Company," *Wall Street Journal*, November 25, 1986, p. 6. This might be a better example for category (6), however.

24. D.F. Greer "Acquiring in Order to Avoid Acquisition," *The Antitrust Bulletin*, Spring, 1986, pp. 155–186. Leasco provides a case study in the importance of size to an acquiring company. Beth Mintz and Michael Schwartz, *The Power Structure of American Business* (Chicago: University of Chicago Press, 1985), pp. 1–3.

25. Kenneth G. Elzinga, "The Goals of Antitrust: Other than Competition and Efficiency, What Else Counts?" *University of Pennsylvania Law Review* June, 1977, p. 1197.

26. Erik Barnouw, *The Sponsor* (New York: Oxford University Press, 1978), pp. 85–86.

27. *Wall Street Journal*, April 9, 1987, p. 31.

28. Sidney Hook, "The Conceptual Structure of Power—An Overview," in *Power: Its Nature, Its Use, and Its Limits*, D.W. Harward (Ed.), (Cambridge, MA: Schenkman, 1982), p. 16.

29. For reviews see F.M. Scherer, *Industrial Market Structure and Economic Performance*, 2nd ed. (Chicago: Rand NcNally, 1980), pp. 151–228; Michael Waterson, *Economic Theory of the Industry* (Cambridge: Cambridge University Press, 1984), pp. 17–55.

30. Leslie Hannah and J. A. Kay, *Concentration in Modern Industry* (London: Macmillan Press, 1977), pp. 48–55.

31. Actually their H-index covers only the 50 largest companies in each 4-digit and 5-digit SIC class, but this is close enough to an index covering all firms.

32. For elaborations of this point see Hannah and Kay, *op. cit.*: B. Curry and K. D. George, "Industrial Concentration: A Survey," *Journal of Industrial Economics*, March, 1983, pp. 203–255; Alexis Jacquemin, *The New Industrial Organization* (Cambridge, MA: The MIT Press, 1987), pp. 50–53.

33. John Lunn, "Trade-Adjusted Concentration Ratios," *Antitrust Bulletin*, Fall, 1984, pp. 523–534.

34. William G. Shepherd, *Market Power and Economic Welfare* (New York: Random House, 1970), pp. 106–107.

35. Fred Bateman and Thomas Weiss, *A Deplorable Scarcity* (Chapel Hill: University of North Carolina Press), pp. 143–156.

36. Alfred D. Chandler, Jr., "The Structure of American Industry in the Twentieth Century: A Historical Overview," *Business History Review*, Autumn, 1969, p. 257.

37. Willard F. Mueller and Richard T. Rogers, "Changes in Market Concentration of Manufacturing Industries: 1947–1977," *Review of Industrial Organization*, Vol. 1, No. 1, 1984, pp. 1–14.

38. William G. Shepherd, "Causes of Increased Competition in the U.S. Economy, 1939–1980," *Review of Economics and Statistics*, November, 1982, pp. 616–619. Shepherd argues for similar results in public utilities, but see Harry M. Trebing, "Apologetics of Deregulation in Energy and Telecommunications," *Journal of Economic Issues*, September, 1986, pp. 613–632.

39. Bruce W. Marion, *The Organization and Performance of the U.S. Food System* Lexington MA: Lexington Books, 1986, pp. 306–307.

40. Joseph Mulholland and Douglas Webbink, *Economic Report on Concentration Levels and Trends in the Energy Sector of the U.S. Economy* Washington, D.C.: Federal Trade Commission, 1974, p. 148.

41. Stephen A. Rhoades, "Size and Rank Stability of the 100 Largest Commercial Banks, 1925–1978," *Journal of Economics and Business*, Vol. 34, No. 2, 1982, pp. 123–128.

42. Between 1966 and 1978, average SMSA three-firm concentration ratios fell from 77.3 to 69.0 in statewide branching states, from 72.1 to 62.9 in limited branching states, and from 58.8 to 50.7 in unit banking states. Donald T. Savage and Elinor H. Soloman, "Branch Banking: The Competitive Issues," *Journal of Bank Research*, Summer 1980, p. 114.

43. Arnold A. Heggestad and William G. Shepherd, "The Banking Industry," in Walter Adams, editor, *The Structure of American Industry*, New York: Macmillan, 1986, 7th edition, pp. 309–311.

44. Jim Burke, "Antitrust Laws, Justice Department Guidelines, and the Limits of Concentration in Local Banking Markets," Staff Study 138, Washington, D.C.: Board of Governors of the Federal Reserve System, June 1984: Stephen A. Rhoades, "Mergers and Acquisitions by Commercial Banks, 1980–1983," Staff Study 142, Washington, D.C.: Board of Governors of the Federal Reserve System, January 1985.

45. Thomas Gale Moore, "U.S. Airline Deregulation: Its Effects on Passengers, Capital, and Labor," *Journal of Law and Economics*, April 1986, pp. 1–28.

46. Based on data from *Fortune*, March 31, 1986, p. 55 and Daniel Kaplan, "The Changing Airline Industry," in L. W. Weiss and M. W. Klass, editors, *Regulatory Reform*, Boston: Little Brown & Co., 1986, pp. 40–77.

47. *Forbes*, March 25, 1985, p. 154.

48. Harry Trebing, *op. cit.*
49. Mark Green, *The Closed Enterprise System*, New York: Grossman Publishers, 1972, pp. 7-8.
50. Lee Lovinger, "The Closed Mind Inquiry—Antitrust Report is Raiders' Nadir," *Antitrust Bulletin*, Fall 1972, p. 758.
51. Julie A. Caswell, "Aggregate Concentration: Significance, Trends, and Causes," in Robert L. Wills, et al., editors, *Issues After a Century of Federal Competition Policy*, Lexington, MA: Lexington Books, 1987, pp. 237-249.
52. U.S. Congress, House, Subcommittee on Telecommunications, Consumer Protection, and Finance of the Committee on Energy and Commerce, *Restructuring Financial Markets: The Major Policy Issues Report*, 99the Congress, 2nd session, 1986, p. 226.
53. *Ibid.*, p. 225.
54. Lawrence, J. White, "What has been Happening to Aggregate Concentration in the United States?" *Journal of Industrial Economics*, March, 1981, pp. 223-230.
55. Franklin M. Fisher, John J. McGowan, and Joan E. Greenwood, *Folded Spindled, and Mutilated* (Cambridge, MA: The MIT Press, 1983), pp. 116-117.
56. Lawrence J. White, *op. cit.*, p. 230.
57. For more series than shown in figure 3-2, see John M. Blair, *Economic Concentration* (New York: Harcourt Brace Jovanovich, Inc., 1972), pp. 63-64.
58. For details see David W. Penn, "Aggregate Concentration: A Statistical Note," *Antitrust Bulletin*, Spring, 1976, pp. 91-98.
59. Dennis C. Mueller, *The Corporation: Growth, Diversification and Mergers* (New York: Harwood Academic Publishers, 1987), p. 46.
60. Philip Spilberg, Mergers and Aggregate Concentration, unpublished Ph.D. dissertation, University of Maryland, 1985, as reported by D.C. Mueller, *ibid.*, pp. 46-47.
61. For reviews of the evidence see D.C. Muller, *The Corporation, op. cit.*, pp. 49-73; Alan A. Fisher and Robert H. Lande, "Efficiency Considerations in Merger Enforcement," *California Law Review*, December, 1983, pp. 1580-1696; F.M. Scherer, *Industrial Market...*, *op. cit.*, pp. 118-141; Richard Roll, "The Hubris Hypothesis of Corporate Takeovers," *Journal of Business*, April, 1986, pp. 197-216.
62. Timothy F. Bresnahan, "Empirical Studies of Industries with Market Power," in R. Schmalensee and R. Willig, Eds. *Handbook of Industrial Organization*, forthcoming.
63. Robert E. Hall, "Market Structure and Macroeconomic Fluctuations," *Brookings Papers on Economic Activity*, No. 2, 1986, pp. 285-322.

4 CORPORATE POWER AND ECONOMIC PERFORMANCE
William M. Dugger

Introduction

Power Defined: Conspicuous and Inconspicuous

Economic power is the ability to go beyond supply and demand to determine in one's own favor the parameters within which exchanges are made. Public power in the economy is exercised by the nation-state to determine and enforce the rules by which we must live. Public power in a democracy is responsible because it is directly accountable. So public power is hedged in; private power is not. Public power is conspicuous and works in the hot glare of publicity, but private power is inconspicuous and works in the shadows. The inconspicuous exercise of private power in modern capitalism weakens the substance of economic individualism but does not destroy its principal form. Consumer sovereignty, at least in form, remains intact. Such inconspicuous economic power sets the limits of individual choice rather than makes the choice for the individual. So private power is exercised behind the scenes. Private power is inherently irresponsible. The essential characteristic of private economic power in the capitalist world is that it is inconspicuous. Its exercise seldom causes overt resentment.

Private power is there, but unnoticed. It is one of the dirty little secrets of modern capitalism. And the more secret it is, the more powerful it is. Nothing enhances private power so much as the denial of its existence.[1]

At its worst, inconspicuous private power rigs the rules of the game in favor of the powerful and then blames the game or the government for the biased outcome, thereby avoiding responsibility and maintaining power. Inconspicuous private power turns basic economic institutions into tools for its own account. Private power can reap the benefits of the silent fix or the insider tip and avoid its responsibility for the spread of corruption and moral dry rot. It can generate cost push inflation, insist on the government's culpability, goading government officials into draconian measures against inflation, and then it can blame the resulting victims of unemployment for their own plight. Inconspicuous private power can corrupt regulatory agencies. It can even distort the developmental processes of powerful nations.[2]

Conspicuous public power determines and enforces rules. It is exercised by government, but not necessarily on the behalf of government. That is, government often serves special interests when it exercises its conspicuous power. Inconspicuous private power is the special interest served by government. It uses government to change the rules of the game or to enforce the existing rules of the game in its favor. Inconspicuous private power is exercised largely by giant corporations and is the subject of this chapter. Such power is not bound by the market; corporate power transcends the market. That is, it goes "beyond supply and demand."[3] Private economic power is not measured adequately by market concentration ratios because it goes beyond the ability to surpass one's competitors in the market.[4]

Power of real social significance has always involved the ability to surpass the market itself, not just surpass the market competition. This kind of power is possessed to a unique degree by very large corporations. The power of a very large corporation goes beyond competition in the exchange arena, to control of the resources, technologies, and laws on which exchange is based. It goes beyond the hubbub of the exchange arena, to control of the processes of production and reproduction. The degree of this corporate power in the economy is measured by the degree of corporate control over the rules of the game (not directly observable), but also by control over assets, receipts, and incomes. These latter are directly observable in terms of the total assets, receipts, and profits of very large corporations. And in terms of all three, the power of very large corporations has grown considerably in recent years. Corporate control is not only exercised through ownership of assets and through receipts of sales revenues and profits. Corporate control is also exercised through joint ventures, interlocking directorships, credit arrangements, dealership contracts, franchise agreements, mutual forebearance, tacit collusion, industry associations, licenses, patents, and other avenues of mutual cooperation and mutual restraints.[5]

The Corporation Defined

The corporation is not merely a convenient middleman between the shareholder of a company and the actual buyer of a good or a service produced by the company. It is far more than that. The corporation is an instrument of private economic power. It is the predominant instrument of private social control in the modern capitalist economy. As a means of social control in the capitalist economy, the corporation is at least as important as the other means of social control. Corporate administration must be ranked with market competition, government regulation, and union negotiation as a key part of the modern processes for controlling individual and collective action. The corporation is an extraordinarily powerful institution. Through it, a handful of executives can manage the activities of thousands of workers spread all over the globe. Through it, the ownership of assets worth scores of billions of dollars can be concentrated in a few hundred hands. Through it, many billions of dollars in sales revenues can be collected and then reallocated to a myriad of uses. Through it, the transfer prices of many thousands of imported and exported raw materials, parts, and finished products can be administered so as to minimize tax payments or minimize union employment. Through it, whole communities can be abandoned and whole new ones created. Nevertheless, the entire corpus of neoclassical economic theory can be constructed without ever mentioning the corporation. In neoclassical theory, it is as if the corporation does not exist. In reality, on the other hand, the corporation is the most powerful institution to have evolved under capitalism.

In U.S. law, the corporation is a person, with all the rights of a citizen, except the right to vote. The corporation became a legal person almost exactly a century ago due to a series of truly remarkable Supreme Court decisions which interpreted the Fourteenth Amendment in a way that gave the corporation all the immunities from state action granted to a natural person. In cases in 1886 and 1888, the Supreme Court defined the corporation as a legal person, covered by the Fourteenth Amendment. These decisions extended to the corporation all the immunities intended for the freed slave. Apparently, John Brown died to free the Southern Pacific Railroad.[6] The consequences of that erroneous Supreme Court decision have been more profound than the Dred Scott decision, which effectively legalized slavery in nonslave states and made the Civil War almost unavoidable. Did the Supreme Court, in that long-ago decision, create something which only much later would become a Frankenstein monster? We have never as a society thought very seriously about whether we want corporations to be treated in the same way as natural persons. Nevertheless, that is how we now treat them, in law. And, that is the legal foundation of our corporate capitalism. The corporation is treated like a person, even though it has emerged to be the dominant socioeconomic institution of our time.

The corporation concentrates the control of giant sums of capital into a few hands. The corporate board of directors and the corporate management then allocate the benefits and the burdens of that concentrated capital to the creditors, pensioners, shareholders, wage workers, managers, customers, suppliers, and communities who live off, own, work for, buy from, sell to, tax, or subsidize the corporation. The corporation allows for the delegation of power from the principal owners through the board of directors, to the top executives and down to the line managers. The corporation makes very little allowance, however, for the exercise of power by groups other than the principal owners and the top managers. Hindered by their institutionalized powerlessness, pensioners, wage workers, customers, suppliers, and communities often must shoulder most of the so-called "external" costs of production while the principal shareholders and top managers enjoy most of the benefits. The corporation, not the market, is the principal allocation mechanism in late capitalism. Those made powerful through the corporation share the benefits; those made powerless bear the costs. The corporation attracts to itself the society's best and brightest, to serve it in its line and staff positions, research and development positions, and to produce for its profit everything from rocket boosters to road salt. But who actually controls the corporation?—And for what purposes?—are perennial questions.[7] Do the managers control the corporation? If so, for what purpose—to pursue their own pet technological projects, to pay themselves huge incomes, or to play the role of economic statesmen? Do the shareholders, or some subset of them, control the corporation? If so, what are they trying to do—raid the corporate treasury for themselves at the expense of the other shareholders, maximize the profits of all shareholders, or build a commercial empire for their children to inherit? The question of corporate control, like nearly every other question regarding the corporation, boils down to a question of power: Who holds it and why? After all, in its purest form, the corporation is an instrument of power. Furthermore, the problems of our corporate age transcend the evil or righteousness of individual corporate moguls. The corporation has become a social problem because of its structure, size, and power, not because individual corporate executives are naughty.

CORPORATE POWER AND ECONOMIC PERFORMANCE 87

The pre-eminence of the giant corporation, not the pre-eminence of some particular form of market, is a universal characteristic of late capitalism. That is, while all late capitalisms contain giant corporations as dominant forms of economic organization, they do not contain the same forms of markets. So it is *corporate* capitalism, not *monopoly* capitalism, that is found universally in developed capitalist systems. (This is not to say that Baran and Sweezy's classic was in error, just misnamed.[8]) An organizational form, the giant corporation, rather than a market form, the monopoly, is a universal trait of late capitalism. The reason is simple: as a means of social control, the corporation is more important to developed capitalism than the monopolized market. Even so, this obvious, universal characteristic of late capitalism is seldom recognized as such.

Mainstream economists still pay more attention to counting the number of market participants than they do to monitoring the growing powers of the giant corporation. This ignorance about the true nature of modern capitalism is most unfortunate. Unknown to orthodox economists, ours is corporate capitalism, not monopoly capitalism. The corporation yields immense power in corporate capitalism. But the fact that formal monopoly is quite rare leads most economists to conclude that private economic power is equally rare. Their fact is correct. Their conclusion is not. They miss the emergence of the dominant economic institution of our age.

The New Face of Corporate Power

Assets, Receipts, and Profits of Very Large Corporations

The power of the giant corporation is hard to measure directly; perhaps that is why many orthodox economists miss its significance. Nonetheless, corporate power is best measured by its control over assets, receipts, and profits. What has happened to this control over time (time-series data) and what this control looks like across industries (cross-section data) are of major significance. In the United States, corporate power has grown over the postwar period. It now reaches deeply, though unevenly, into every sector of the U.S. economy. That reach is measured in the following two tables. Table 4-1 gives a time-series look at growing corporate power, while table 4-2 gives a cross-section view of spreading corporate power. Both tables are based on information provided by the U.S. Internal Revenue Service. The data are for corporations that filed tax returns with the IRS. The tables reflect direct control through ownership only. They do not reflect other indirect forms of control such as franchising, lending, or interlocking

Table 4-1. Total Assets, Total Receipts, and Net Income (Less Deficit) of All Reporting Corporations and of Corporations with $250 Million or More in Assets for Selected Years, 1965–1982 (in Billions of Dollars)

	Assets		Receipts		Net Income	
Year	All Units	Large Only	All Units	Large Only	All Units	Large Only
1965	1,724	862	1,195	374	74	37
	100%	50%	100%	31%	100%	50%
1975	4,287	2,790	3,199	1,451	143	90
	100%	65%	100%	45%	100%	63%
1980	7,617	5,358	6,361	3,229	239	158
	100%	70%	100%	51%	100%	66%
1981	8,547	6,165	7,026	3,675	213	147
	100%	72%	100%	52%	100%	69%
1982	9,358	6,881	7,025	3,647	154	113
	100%	74%	100%	52%	100%	73%

Source: Internal Revenue Service, *Statistics of Income, Corporate Income Tax Returns* (Washington, D.C.: Government Printing Office, various years). 1982 returns are the latest available as of April, 1987.

boards of directors. Even so, the tables show that the power of corporate giants has grown over time (table 4-1) and has spread widely (table 4-2).

In table 4-1, the columns labeled "All Units" contain data for all filing corporations, while the columns labeled "Large Only" contain data for filing corporations with $250 million or more in assets. The table begins with 1965 because it was in 1965 that large corporations' ownership of all corporate assets reached the 50 percent mark. By 1982 the large corporations' ownership proportion had increased to 74 percent. In 1965 the large corporations accounted for 31 percent of all corporate receipts. Their share of receipts had risen to 52 percent by 1982. Large corporations accounted for half of all corporate net income in 1965. Their share of net income had risen to 73 percent in 1982. So, whether measured by assets, receipts, or net income, the power of large corporations has steadily grown over the last few years. The trend extends back in time much further, as well.[9]

Table 4-2 shows the spread of the large corporation into all of the industrial classifications in the U.S. economy for one year, 1982. The table shows the number of tax returns filed by corporations and the number of tax returns filed by corporations with $250 million or more in assets in each of

Table 4-2. Corporate Tax Returns and Returns with $250 Million or More In Assets, By Industry, in 1982

Industry	Number of Returns	Number of Large Returns	Industry Assets	Assets of Large Returns
Transport. & Pub. Util.	115,470 100%	284 0.2%	919.9 100%	837.4 91.0%
Mfg.	259,106 100%	657 0.3%	2,060.7 100%	1,637.7 79.5%
Fin., Insur. & Real Est.	461,630 100%	1,875 0.4%	4,987.5 100%	3,908.8 78.4%
Mining	36,676 100%	79 0.2%	192.4 100%	129.5 67.3%
Trade	839,547 100%	198 0.02%	753.4 100%	274.6 36.4%
Services	819,706 100%	64 0.008%	237.9 100%	64.8 27.2%
Constr.	282,345 100%	26 0.009%	153.1 100%	25.2 16.5%
Agr., Forest. & Fishing	91,320 100%	6 0.007%	50.4 100%	2.8 5.6%

Note: Assets are in billions of dollars.

Source: Internal Revenue Service, *Statistics of Income, 1982 Corporate Income Tax Returns* (Washington, D.C.: Government Printing Office, 1985).

eight major industrial classifications. It also shows the total corporate assets in each industrial classification and the assets of corporations with $250 million or more in assets in each industrial classification. The different industrial classifications are listed by degree of large corporate control in that class. The large corporation was most dominant in the transportation and public utility class. In 1982 large corporations controlled 91.0 percent of all assets in the transportation and public utility class. Those large corporations filed only 0.2 percent of all tax returns in that industrial class. This means that a tiny fraction of large corporations (only .2 of 1 percent) owned over 90 percent of all assets in transportation and public utilities. A somewhat lower degree of control is encountered in the next three industrial classifications of table 4-2: (1) manufacturing: (2) finance, insurance, and real estate; and (3) mining. In these three classifications, the tiny fraction of large corporations operating in each class owned from about three-fourths to two-thirds of all assets in their industrial class. The control of large corporations drops off sharply after these three classes. In trade and services the large corporations own only about one-third and one-fourth of total assets. Then in construction, large corporations own only about one-sixth of total assets. The large corporation has barely penetrated the agriculture, forestry, and fishing classification. But even there, the signs may be ominous, because the large corporations already own about one-twentieth of all assets in that class.

With only a few possible exceptions, ours is corporate capitalism—a capitalism dominated by the large corporation. And the exceptions, as indicated by table 4-2, are in industrial classifications that account for a relatively small amount of assets. Generally speaking, as the degree of large corporation control declines, the total assets in each class also decline.

Diversification and the Rising Conglomerate

In addition to the prevalence of giant corporations, another important characteristic of corporate capitalism is the large and growing degree to which corporations have become diversified.[10] A diversified corporation is a conglomerate—a company engaged in several unrelated economic activities. Diversification yields power. A conglomerate is never dependent on one industry or on one market. A conglomerate has a range of choices available to it that are not available to a single-industry company. In these choices lies power—the power to wait and the power to redeploy. The conglomerate can change customers and suppliers, can change from union to nonunion, and can change from external to internal sources of finance. It can move from country to country, playing one country off against another to obtain the maximum tax, regulatory, and union breaks possible. The conglomerate also has a greatly enlarged power to make reciprocal deals.[11] In sum, the conglomerate is the corporation in its most powerful form, and its power is not really due to its position in any one market, but is due to its diversification into a wide spectrum of markets and industries. The power of the conglomerate resides in the whole of its commercial empire, not in any one of its market parts.

Table 4-3 shows the extent of conglomeration (diversification) by industrial classification for the United States in 1982. Table 4-3 measures the extent of conglomeration in terms of the way in which employees are deployed. If all employees are deployed in the core business of the company, then the company's degree of diversification (the last column in table 4-3)

Table 4-3. Employment Diversification by Industry, 1982

Industry Classification	Employment in Same Category	Employment in Other Categories	Total	Other as a Percent of Total
Manufacturing	12,773	6,835	19,608	34.9
Minerals	627	128	755	17.0
Wholesale trade	3,720	310	4,030	7.7
Retail trade	13,072	1,035	14,107	7.3
Construction	4,017	270	4,287	6.3
Selected services	10,222	431	10,653	4.0
All	44,431	9,009	53,440	16.9

Note: Employment is in thousands.
Source: Bureau of the Census, *1982 Enterprise Statistics: General Report on Industrial Organization* (Washington, D.C.: U.S. Government Printing Office, 1986).

would be zero. Or, if all the company's employees are deployed outside the core business of the company (rather unlikely), then the company's degree of diversification would be 100 percent. The most diversified industry, by far, is manufacturing. In companies whose primary activity is manufacturing, 34.9 percent of their employees (not counting those at auxiliary offices and sales branches) were deployed in an unrelated industrial classification.

So it is no accident that performance in the U.S. manufacturing sector has been poor. Relative to other industrial classifications, too many of its employees have been deployed in activities outside of its core manufacturing business. U.S. manufacturing was too diversified, even in 1982, before the most frenzied merger and acquisition wave ever to sweep across U.S. industry had crested. If the data were available for 1987, the degree of diversification in manufacturing would be very much higher. Running a distant second to manufacturing is minerals, primarily due to the diversification drive of major oil companies. In the typical minerals company, 17.0 percent of its employees outside of its auxiliary facilities and sales branches were deployed in activities outside of its core minerals business. The other industrial classifications, though by no means free from diversification, have been only lightly touched by it up through 1982. Later data on diversification of employees do not exist.[12] But some 1982 data do exist that indicate the direction of movement for a few industrial classes. For manufacturing, minerals, and construction, the Bureau of the Census tabulated new capital expenditures made by companies both inside and outside their core businesses. In manufacturing, 47.3 percent of capital expenditures were made outside the core business; in minerals, 23.2 percent; and in construction, 31.4 percent.[13] So, in manufacturing, almost half of 1982 capital expenditures were made to diversify out of the company's core business. This disinvestment in manufacturing was clearly the drive behind the deindustrialization of the U.S. economy in the 1980s.

The deindustrialization has had serious effects on the U.S. economy, but it has also been to the benefit of those manufacturing corporations who have successfully diversified out of the industrial heartland. A more glaring example of the conflict between private gain and public interest is hard to come by. Diversifying corporations have broadened their power base while the communities they left have lost their economic livelihoods. Diversification into powerful commercial empires—I call them imperial conglomerates—the accompanying deindustrialization, and the rising social costs of corporate capitalism are new phenomena which have remained largely outside the realm of mainstream economics. The imperial conglomerate has risen to power and has begun using its power to strip many communities of their economic bases, and the economics profession has looked the other way.

Diversification out of manufacturing is an extremely important process, warranting a mini-case study: U.S. Steel (USS) and General Motors (GM), both leading enterprises in the U.S. manufacturing sector, have embarked on major diversification programs for the 1980s. To signify its commitment to diversification, USS has even become USX. David M. Roderick is chairman of USX. He is a trained accountant with no operating experience in steelmaking. Roger B. Smith is chairman of GM and is also an accountant with limited operating experience. (It is very instructive to note that the most famous pioneer in conglomerate enterprise was Harold Geneen, who was trained as an accountant and who also had very limited operating experience.) Under Smith's leadership, GM has rapidly diversified out of the auto industry. In 1984 GM bought H. Ross Perot's Electronic Data Systems, Inc. (EDS) for $2.5 billion. EDS was a leading data processing company and a major defense contractor, making it a prime high-tech company. GM paid $5 billion for Hughes Aircraft Company in 1985. Hughes is also a major defense contractor, a leader in advanced electronics, and a maker of communications satelites—another prime high-tech company for diversification through acquisition. After acquiring EDS and Hughes, GM then bought out H. Ross Perot's share in GM for $700 million in 1986. Perot's fate at GM is instructive. Perot had been the entrepreneurial chairman of Electronic Data Systems. When he moved to GM he disagreed with Smith's leadership of GM. Perot was highly critical of the large bonuses GM gave to upper management, while many workers received little or were on extended layoff. Perot was quite comfortable with engineers and with the details of day-to-day operations. Smith was not. Perot has been a highly successful entrepreneur. Smith has not. Perot left. Smith stayed.

Roderick of U.S. Steel has diversified out of steel by buying into oil and natural gas, at just about the worst time—right before a sustained decline in energy prices. Roderick became chairman in 1979 and has shut down about 150 plants and related facilities. But he paid $6.5 billion in 1982 for Marathon Oil Company. USX also paid about $2.4 billion for Texas Oil and Gas Company. Roderick has diversified his holdings but at great expense. The emerging imperial conglomerate has run into serious difficulties in digesting its newly acquired empire. In addition to a decline in energy prices and continued competitive pressure from steel imports, Roderick is also having difficulty transforming the stodgy Midwestern steelmaker into a well-managed, high-tech conglomerate. The 50,000 or more steelworkers who have lost their jobs under his chairmanship may be having an even harder time, though.

In both cases, diversification contributed to the decline of manufacturing in the United States and to the decline of the communities dependent upon manufacturing. In both cases, diversification was the strategy used by powerful corporations to try to expand their power. In both cases, steel and autos, the diversifying manufacturer has used the cash flow generated from liquidating portions of its old core business to buy into new businesses. In both cases, domestic market share and employment shrank in the old manufacturing core, while financial commitment to new ventures expanded. And, in both cases, imports pushed into the vaccuum left by the diversification. As USX moved out of steel, however, it covered its retreat with repeated calls for more protection against imports. This made sense, in spite of the fact that USX wanted out of steel as fast as it could get out. Protection from imports kept margins up in steel, which helped provide the cash flow needed to finance diversification. As GM has been moving out of autos, it has wanted to disinvest at a slower pace. So, its more gradual withdrawal has been covered by forming a joint venture with its major foreign competitor (Toyota, in Fremont, California). In steel and autos, it is impossible to assign realistic weights to the independent causal role of rising imports versus diversifying conglomerates in the decline of the domestic manufacturing sector. That is, it is not possible to say whether USX and GM decided to diversify because of import competition or the import competition expanded because they decided to diversify. Both are partially correct.[14] Nor is it possible, at this early time, to say how successful the diversification of USX and GM will be. USX is presently under severe pressure to divest some of its energy acquisitions and GM is struggling to make its acquisitions fit together into a coherent whole. At one time, GM was considered a model of the ideal corporation, but now it seems that GM cannot even make a decent small car. Although many questions remain unanswered, it is possible to say that the struggle of conglomerates to continue growing defines the major issues of corporate capitalism.

New Features of Corporate Organization

Driven by diversification and by the concomitant deindustrialization, capitalism in the United States continues to evolve into ever larger corporate power structures. The dominant form of evolving corporation clearly is the conglomerate.[15] And out of the evolution of the conglomerate, two new features of corporate organization have become important.[16] First, the corporation has developed a new form. Second, the corporation has developed a new function. The new form is the modular form. The new function is the accumulation and allocation of financial capital. The new corporate form and the new corporate function are adaptations to the accumulating power and size of the diversified conglomerates.

With the modular form adapted by conglomerates, the corporation has managed to divide itself into separable modules that can be unplugged readily from one conglomerate and plugged into another. Each module is a semi-independent profit center which can produce and distribute its own line of commodities. Most modules originated as free-standing corporations, but after acquisition by a larger corporation, they are reorganized into the new modular form. Each module is organized so that it can perform its own daily operations—production and marketing—for itself, independently of other modules. But each module is also designed so that its finance function is performed at a higher organization level—at the level of the corporate head office. These new modular forms are ideal building blocks for constructing diversified conglomerate empires, ideal for the organizational revolution. They are analogous to the interchangeable parts of the old industrial revolution, except they are the interchangeable parts of a newly emerging organizational revolution. The interchangeable part and the profit-center module are both new technologies. The difference is that the technological frontier has moved from physical production to social control. The interchangeable part was a technology of physical production. The profit-center module is a technology of social control.

Each profit-center module is designed to funnel its profits upward to a conglomerate's head office—any conglomerate's head office, since the modules are interchangeable. The head office does not participate in the day-to-day operations of its modules. The head office does not participate in the production of goods or services; the lower-level operatives in its modules do that. What commodities are produced by its profit centers is beside the point to the head office. It can discard the modules and their products and add new modules with their new products as opportunity dictates.

The ability to discard old modules and add new ones is extremely important, just as important as the use of interchangeable parts. It makes the conglomerate greater than the sum of its parts. The conglomerate, as a whole, is not dependent upon the production of any particular product or upon the structure of any particular exchange interface (market). So market structures and competing products no longer constrain it. The conglomerate has broken free of the market, even though its profit-center modules have not. That is, a particular module still produces a specific product line for a specific market. Entering or leaving that market could be very difficult, for the specific profit-center module. But for the conglomerate, entering or leaving that market is very easy. To enter, the conglomerate simply buys the module serving that market. To leave, the conglomerate simply sells the module serving that market. The module in question could be a free-standing, independent corporation, or it could be a dependent subsidiary, owned by another conglomerate. Since it can enter new markets and leave old ones at will simply by buying old or selling new profit-center modules, the market no longer exerts any effective social control over the conglomerate enterprise. Each operating part of the conglomerate enterprise remains dependent upon the market it serves. But the conglomerate enterprise has become larger than the sum of its parts. The power of the conglomerate resides in the whole, not in any one of the parts. Such an enterprise has become more powerful than any of its markets. Such an enterprise has become an *imperial conglomerate*, because the old mechanism of social control—the market—no longer controls it. Free of outside social control, the conglomerate can pursue its own objectives, at the expense of whoever are too weak to defend themselves against it. While the neoclassical theory of the firm does not have a clue to what is really going on in the economy, the rise of the imperial conglomerate is transforming society profoundly.

Each conglomerate head office is the high-tech nerve center of a vast commercial empire composed of modular profit centers that funnel their profits into the head office. The head office is the highest level of the imperial conglomerate. It determines overall policy and it maps out long-term strategy. The head office also sets the financial objectives to be met by all the operating modules and monitors their financial performance. The profits generated by the modules are what count, not the products produced, nor the communities served. The head office is run by a highly skilled cadre of line and staff managers whose new function is to monitor the profit performance of each semi-independent profit center and to accumulate and reallocate the financial capital of the commercial empire as a whole. To do so, all the latest advances in technology are used to collect, transmit, process, and store vast flows of data. Whole armies of computer operators, programmers, and technicians of every stripe are employed to feed the vast data network centered at the head office. The best-trained MBA's and the highest technological achievements are used by this new level of conglomerate organization and control. The highest salaries are paid to managers and technicians at the head office, and new executive talent is recruited from the head office managerial cadres.[17] So it should come as no surprise that an assignment to the head office in highly desired by aspiring managers, by those who aspire to membership in the "MBA priesthood."

The powerful imperial conglomerate uses its resources and its prowess to produce money, not commodities. The commodities are a kind of by-product, or at best, a means to an end. Production of commodities is not the end; production of money is. And neoclassical economics, though it assumes "profit maximization" in its theory of the firm, does not understand the profound implications of making money instead of making goods. Money is the lingua franca of conglomerate management. Driven by the imperial conglomerate's needs for a method and a theory of social control, modern management is developing into a unified discipline, with money as its common denominator. The evolving principles of modern management are universal. They apply to any imperial conglomerate. Whether the conglomerate's operating modules sell rocket boosters or road salt, the objective of the diversified enterprise as a whole is to make money. So the art of making money is universally applicable to all enterprises. Young people studying for their MBA learn a common language and a common subject—money. They do not study engineering. They do not need to learn how to make things. Others will do that for them. Products are made and services rendered at the lower level of the operating division. Highly trained managers waste little of their career time at the operating level. Instead, they move quickly to the conglomerate head office, where they oversee the lower operating divisions, assuring that each division makes its required financial contribution to the overall corporate effort. At the higher corporate level, the engineering and technical details of each operating division become irrelevant. They are not a part of modern management. Everything is translated into the lingua franca of management. Profit rates, or minimum profit "hurdles," can then be used to compare the performance of operating divisions that produce totally different kinds of things and render totally different kinds of services. Money and how to make it are the universal stuff of modern management. The future leaders of the corporate economy need to learn the pecuniary principles of money making, not the physical principles of science and technology.[18] Profitability is what counts. Productivity is left to lower levels. The giant, diversified corporation has evolved to make money, not goods.[19] This simple truth has profound consequences.[20]

Generally stated, the financial and physical flows of the corporate economy have become severely unbalanced. Financial flows do not match the needed physical flows. The financial flows have become so distorted that the economic system fails to provide a regular and sufficient flow of income to large numbers of individuals and families who need it to maintain a reasonably acceptable lifestyle. In the 1980s the distortion has reached a level of unreasonableness that can only be described as madness. Two examples: Falling agricultural prices have threatened the survival of the family farm while millions of people have gone hungry. Steel mills have shut down all over the industrial heartland while bridges, roads, public buildings, and public housing have all deteriorated to dangerously substandard conditions. The physical performance of the economy falls far short of what is needed. And yet, the financial performance of the stock market has soared to new heights, junk bonds have been snapped up in unprecedented amounts by once conservative pension funds, and takeovers have accelerated to a frenzied pace.

Power and Macro Performance

The Misery Index

The objectives of macroeconomic policy are full employment and price level stability, neither of which have been achieved in the United States for any length of time since the Second World War.[21] Table 4-4 illustrates that fact with what economists generally refer to as the misery index. The misery index is simply the sum of the inflation rate and the unemployment rate. The higher the index, the higher the deviation of the macroeconomy from its desired path of full employment without inflation. The deviation can be due to either inflation or unemployment. Although unemployment is more costly than inflation, the index weights them equally. This bias in the index is offset, to some degree, by implicitly setting the full employment rate at a zero rate of unemployment, a rate too low to be practical. Table 4-4 uses the unemployment rate for the civilian labor force and the rate of inflation in the consumer price index to compute the misery index. In spite of the

Table 4-4. The Misery Index, 1960–1986

Year	Unemployment Rate	Inflation Rate	Misery Index
1960	5.5	1.6	7.1
1961	6.7	1.0	7.7
1962	5.5	1.1	6.6
1963	5.7	1.2	6.9
1964	5.2	1.3	6.5
1965	4.5	1.7	6.2
1966	3.8	2.9	6.7
1967	3.8	2.9	6.7
1968	3.6	4.2	7.8
1969	3.5	5.4	8.9
1970	4.9	5.9	10.8
1971	5.9	4.3	10.2
1972	5.6	3.3	8.9
1973	4.9	6.2	11.1
1974	5.6	11.0	16.6
1975	8.5	9.1	17.6
1976	7.7	5.8	13.5
1977	7.1	6.5	13.6
1978	6.1	7.7	13.8
1979	5.8	11.3	17.1
1980	7.1	13.5	20.6
1981	7.6	10.4	18.0
1982	9.7	6.1	15.8
1983	9.6	3.2	12.8
1984	7.5	4.3	11.8
1985	7.2	3.6	10.8
1986	7.0	1.9	8.9

Source: Economic Report of the President, 1987.

misery index's shortcomings, it is still instructive to note that only twice in the 1970s and the 1980s has the index dipped below the double digit level. It went below in 1972, during phase II of the Nixon Administration's wage-price control program, but rose after the tremendous OPEC price hike of 1973. It went back below the double digit level in 1986, but it is certain to rise thereafter, as inflation has already begun to accelerate once again in 1987. (Inflation is running at about 4 percent for the first half of the year.)

The corporate economy performed poorly as measured by the misery index, and as measured by the real wage rate it was able to generate for workers. With 1977 set as the base year, adjusted hourly earnings in the private nonagricultural sector equaled 100 in 1977, according to President Reagan's own Council of Economic Advisers. Then wages peaked at a whopping 100.5 in 1978, plunged down to 92.6 in 1981, and stood at 94.9 in 1986—just below the 95.0 mark reached clear back in 1969.[22] Workers were worse off in 1986 than they were ten years earlier, in 1977. Of course, there were more people working in 1986 than in 1977, 17.6 million more. So the economy had managed to produce many more jobs over the ten-year period, 19.1 percent more. But the previous ten-year period (1967–1976) also saw the economy generate many more jobs—19.3 percent more.[23] So the job pool grew no faster in the later period than the earlier, even though the need for jobs outstripped their availability—which is the same thing as saying that the unemployment rate has remained too high. In sum, the macro performance of the U.S. economy has been truly miserable, particularly since the high water mark of the 1960s. This poor performance is a direct result of the rising power and deteriorating performance of the U.S. corporation.[24] The physical performance of the large U.S. corporation has left a lot to be desired. Walter Adams and James W. Brock state:

> By most objective standards, America's coporate giants have not performed very well over the last fifteen years. They have lost markets to the Japanese and the newly industrializing countries. They have lagged in innovation. The quality of their products has often been inferior and unreliable. And, taken together, America's five hundred largest industrial corporations have failed to generate a single new job since 1970.[25]

Power Is a Substitute for Performance

When the objective is to make money, not produce a good or a service, power is a substitute for performance. The conglomerate, with its modular form of organization, is uniquely well designed for exercising power. Its modules allow it to exercise a hit-and-run strategy—a new and striking phenomenon in the corporate world, made possible by the evolution of the conglomerate and its modules. The conglomerate can readily buy into an industry by acquiring a free-standing corporation and converting it into a module. Then the conglomerate's head office can either cut the module's product quality or raise the module's product price. Either one, price boost or quality cut, enlarges the gross margin on sales available for cash flow transferral to the conglomerate head office. In this way, the head office uses the module as a "cash cow," milking its former reputation with customers and its accumulated assets to the maximum. Then, when the module is sucked dry of tangible and intangible assets, the conglomerate head office can sell it off, relying on the greater fool principle to provide a buyer. (According to the greater fool principle, no matter how much you pay for something, there is always a greater fool somewhere who will pay more.) The conglomerate can then move on to buy into another industry or market, doing the same thing there. The hit-and-run strategy leaves a whole string of milked companies and deindustrialized sectors of the economy, where imports quickly move in to fill up the vacuum left by the departing conglomerate, and where the workers languish in long-term unemployment. The conglomerate benefits financially at the expense of the physical well-being of the workers and communities.

Revenues and profits can be enhanced by exercising power through the hit-and-run strategy or by improving performance. The latter is generally much more difficult because it involves producing better goods or services or producing the same goods and services more efficiently—things for which the leaders of U.S. corporations are simply not trained and things that short-sighted takeover artists find it unprofitable to allow. Numerous economists, none of them neoclassical, have analyzed different aspects of the drive for corporate power and the decline of corporate performance.[26] Prominent among them was the late John M. Blair, Chief Economist of the U.S. Senate Anti-Trust Subcommittee from 1957 to 1970 and the father of administered price theory, Gardiner C. Means. Blair and Means both showed at great length how market power was used to push up administered prices in major sectors of the U.S. economy. They both explained that administered inflation—the pushing up of the general price level by a rise in administered prices—could cause inflation in the face of rising unemployment.[27] Powerful corporations who administered their prices upward could actually make more money by making fewer goods (and employing fewer workers). Alfred S. Eichner developed a pricing model based on the realities of corporate power, and tied the model to the struggle over relative income distribution. Breaking dependence on inadequate neoclassical micro theory, Eichner has provided a valid micro foundation for the further development of post-Keynesian economic theory.[28] Since 1978, those developments have been published in the *Journal of Post Keynesian Economics*. Abba P. Lerner applied developments in administered price theory to Keynesian macroeconomics, explaining a phenomenon he called "flation." Flation is continued inflation with stagnating employment. It is due, primarily, to the exercise of pricing power and is extremely resistant to traditional aggregate demand management policies.[29] Uncurbed by an effective incomes policy of some sort, the drive by imperial conglomerates to appropriate more of the national income has driven up the national price level and has driven down the national pool of jobs. The old tradeoff between employment and inflation has become a draconian one. In fact, it took the Reagan Administration six years of dreadfully high unemployment to bring the inflation rate in the United States down to a crawl in 1986, only to see it begin climbing once again in 1987. (See table 4-4; this was written in May of 1987.) The Reagan Administration, aside from its misguided attacks on trade unions, did nothing to alter the underlying economic power that generates administered-price inflation. The result, described by Wallace C. Peterson, was an overloaded economy—an economy unable to meet the basic needs for jobs and incomes for all members of the society it serves, without fostering an unacceptably high rate of inflation.[30]

The widespread exercise of corporate pricing power causes inflation, even with high unemployment—a major, perhaps fatal, breakdown in the performance of corporate capitalism. Administered price inflation—inflation caused by powerful corporations setting higher and higher prices—generates an intensified conflict over the relative income shares of different economic interests. The conflict frequently deranges the political process, yielding undemocratic groups power far beyond their numbers. The rentier interest has become particularly powerful in the United States in recent years, while the poor have suffered. Alfred S. Eichner states:

> The fact is that the government, harkening to the outcry of rentier groups, has continually intervened in the economy in an effort to bring a halt to rising prices. Yet without an adequate understanding of the basic economic forces at work, this intervention has succeeded only in transforming the wage-price spiral into a political trade cycle. With aggregate demand unnecessarily curtailed, physical output has been irretrievably lost, the secular growth rate has been held far below what it should have been and—most serious of all—many Americans have been deprived of the employment opportunities which they had every right to expect. Indeed, all of the government's efforts to alleviate poverty at home have been of minor import compared to the disastrous consequences of its misguided policies to control domestic inflation.[31]

Table 4-5 shows how the rentier share of personal income in the United States has actually increased in recent years. In their long fight against inflation, the Reagan and Carter Administrations were kind to the rentier, but not to the poor. Reaganomics proved unusually lucrative for the rentier, as it pushed their income share up to a peak of 17 percent of total personal income. While the rentier was doing very well, the official poverty rate rose significantly, pushing an average of about 8 million more people into poverty in the United States in the first half of the 1980s than were there during the last half of the 1970s.[32] Even though the exercise of conglomerate pricing power was to blame for the inflation, it was the poor who suffered in defending the rentier share against the rising prices.

The exercise of corporate power causes deterioration not only in macro

Table 4-5. Personal Rentier Income, 1940–1986 (Billions of Dollars)

Period	Personal Dividend Income	Personal Interest Income	Personal Rentier Income	Total Personal Income	Rentier Share
1929	5.8	6.9	12.7	84.3	15%
1940–44	4.3	5.2	9.5	122.1	8%
1945–49	6.1	7.3	13.4	190.7	7%
1950–54	8.7	11.5	20.2	268.4	8%
1955–59	11.3	18.6	29.9	353.1	8%
1960–64	14.7	29.6	44.3	455.0	10%
1965–69	20.6	49.2	69.8	655.5	11%
1970–74	24.9	86.0	110.9	1,003.8	11%
1975–79	38.4	163.2	201.6	1,643.7	12%
1980–84	64.3	363.4	427.7	2,679.8	16%
1985	76.4	476.2	552.6	3,314.5	17%
1986	81.2	475.4	556.6	3,487.0	16%

Source: *Economic Report of the President* (Washington, D.C.: Government Printing Office, 1987).

performance but in micro performance as well. Although this chapter deals with macro performance, at least a word about micro performance is needed. Probably the worst performance failure at the micro level is the failure of powerful manufacturers to bear the full costs of their activities. Nearly 40 years ago, K. William Kapp concluded his pathbreaking study of social costs with a harsh indictment:

> As soon as one passes beyond the traditional abstractions of cost-price analysis and begins to consider the omitted truth of social costs, it becomes clear once more that the alleged beneficial orderliness of the competitive process is all but a myth. For, if entrepreneurial costs do not measure the total costs of production, the competitive cost-price calculus is not merely meaningless but nothing more than an institutionalized cover under which it is possible for private enterprise to shift part of the costs to the shoulders of others and to practice a form of large-scale spoliation which transcends everything the early socialists had in mind when they spoke of the exploitation of man by man.[33]

A recent example of shifting to others the costs of making a profit is the astounding behavior of a few powerful asbestos producers, who continued exposing workers and consumers to harmful levels of asbestos, long after the producers knew that such exposure could cause disability and death.[34] This extremely insensitive performance may not be that exceptional. Although few powerful corporations have been found to knowingly cause the disability and death of their workers and customers, Marshall B. Clinard and Peter C. Yeager document extensively that corporate business frequently shades off into criminality.[35] Both the micro and the macro performances of corporate capitalism in the United States leave room for improvement. Social monitoring and social control are long overdue.

The financial flows generated by corporate capitalism are out of balance. Disinvestment and speculation run at fever pitch while the funds cannot be found to provide fulfilling work and adequate lifestyles for all. Social monitoring and social control through an incomes policy are required.[36] The physical flows generated by corporate capitalism are also out of balance. Whole industrial communities are allowed to collapse as conglomerates redeploy their assets elsewhere. The numerous physical needs of the homeless and the poor go unmet while new industrial parks spring up like toadstools across the suburban landscape. Corporate capitalism's effluents, or "external costs," also need much tighter monitoring and social control, not only to prevent further decline in the quality of the environment but to prevent widespread disability and death. A reinvigorated Occupational Safety and Health Administration and a vastly expanded Environmental Protection Agency are required to reinstitute the community's social control over the quality of life.[37] Furthermore, legislation establishing social control over plant closing and deindustrialization is also needed, perhaps in the form of mandatory economic impact statements on major corporate restructurings and also in the form of mandatory severance payments to affected workers and communities. New legislation is also required, at the federal level, to mandate the written transmittal of notice 90 days or longer before major plant closings.

Conclusion

Three Trends

Corporate power has been greatly enhanced by a technological revolution in organization. Through modular divisions and computerized head offices, the former organizational size constraints on commercial enterprises have been overcome. Now, organizations of immense size and global scope can be managed quite effectively. The imperial conglomerate has risen to globe-straddling size and imperial power. The imperial conglomerate is not dependent on any one market, not even on any one nation. It has risen above them. We are in the midst of an epoch-making revolution, an organizational revolution of scope and significance equal to the epoch-making revolution which saw the rise of the modern nation-state.

The revolutionary changes accompanying the imperial conglomerate's rise to power seem to have gone further in the United States than in other nation-states. The penalties of taking the lead, as Thorstein Veblen might have called them,[38] are just visible. Three trends are of major significance: (1) deindustrialization, (2) import penetration, and (3) income disintegration.

Deindustrialization is one of the most important economic phenomena of the closing of the twentieth century. The movement of the U.S. economy's center of balance out of industry and into a whole hodge-podge of services has not only devastated the communities of the so-called rustbelt with plant closings but has also fundamentally altered the structure of jobs in the economy.[39] The high-wage, unionized, industrial core is drying up because the imperial conglomerate is disinvesting from it as expeditiously as possible. The expanding service sector has not provided high wage jobs fast enough to raise average real wage rates, so real wages have stagnated. In the past, labor productivity rose rapidly in the industrial core but slowly in the service sector. If this differential productivity growth continues, and there is no reason to believe that it has changed, then the stagnation of real wages may be difficult to remedy. Furthermore, the service sector, with the exception of government and education, has been very hard to organize. So the stagnation of the labor movement is also likely to intensify as the center of balance continues shifting out of union industries and into nonunion services.

Import penetration into the deindustrialized industrial core has filled the vacuum left by the disinvestment of the imperial conglomerate. U.S. manufacturers have either abandoned the field through disinvestment, allowing a flood of imports to replace their production directly, or they have engaged in a strategy of "outsourcing." They have reduced their reliance on domestic, union production by purchasing intermediate parts and products from low-wage foreign producers operating export platforms behind the protective shield of repressive host governments. The foreign producers often form joint ventures with imperial conglomerates so the imperial conglomerate can take advantage of tax breaks given to foreign investors by often corrupt host governments. Such joint ventures are even being used to move the low-wage, nonunion production methods and the tax breaks given to foreign investors back into the U.S. workplace (Toyota and General Motors). The future remains unclear, but some projections of the main drift in the international relations of the imperial conglomerate are in order. If the United States continues a policy of aggressive devaluation of the dollar in a vain attempt to stop the trade deficit, foreign producers will be forced to move into the shielded domestic market. (The domestic market would be shielded by what amounts to a dirty float rather than by a wall of tariffs. A dirty float occurs when a nation states publicly that its exchange rate is free to float, but then artificially depresses its value privately.) The U.S. trade deficit would then decline as formerly imported products become produced internally. The dirty float would preserve the principle of free trade in form, if not in substance. At the same time, it would facilitate the importation of repressive workplace practices developed by foreign producers in export platforms and brought into the U.S. workplace when joint ventures are formed with imperial conglomerates. Even if the United States does not keep the dollar low, these trends are likely to continue. For if the low exchange rate strategy is abandoned, more overt protectionist measures are certain to be adopted, bringing about more or less the same kinds of adaptations on the part of imperial conglomerates and their foreign allies and affiliates.

Import penetration and continued international changes are sure to intensify the disintegration of the U.S. income distribution. The U.S. income distribution is disintegrating in that insufficient income is distributed to the lower strata. The poor and near-poor are receiving insufficient income in two senses. First, they are receiving insufficient income to maintain a growth in effective demand sufficient to generate full employment. Second, they are receiving insufficient income to maintain a reasonable level of living of their own. The income distribution is also disintegrating in the sense that consensus is being eroded away. That is, the conflict over real income is getting harsher as inequality is increasing. Because the poor and near-poor lack political clout, they will continue to bear the brunt of the burden of adjusting to the ever higher income share going to the supporters and managerial cadres of the imperial conglomerate. Under the current dispensation, the rentier class is highly unlikely to share in the adjustment burden. So any inflation resulting from the depreciated dollar or from the administered prices of imperial conglomerates will be resisted in the traditional manner—by draconian cuts in welfare programs and in other government programs that benefit the poor, and by high interest rates, tight money, and increased unemployment. In short, the distribution of income will continue disintegrating into entrenched inequality and structurally generated insufficiency of effective demand.

The Implications for Social Control

The visible hand of management, exercised by the imperial conglomerate, is replacing more and more of the invisible hand of the market.[40] Our economy is still a dual economy, but the market half is shrinking, and the administered half is expanding.[41] The imperial conglomerate exercises increasing power, but it does so in the shadows. The private power of the conglomerate does not serve the public purpose. It serves the conglomerate's private purpose. If the public purpose is to be served, the nation state must do so, for it is the only institution of broad scope and sufficient countervailing power to have evolved as a specific instrument of the general will. Even if the nation state shoulders its responsibility, the growing global dimension of corporate power will make social control increasingly difficult. At the global level, a strengthening of the economic powers of the United Nations and its agencies is needed. In the United States, the need for democratic economic planning must finally be taken seriously by the federal government. The imperial conglomerate already takes its planning very seriously. It aggressively plans the short-run accumulation and reallocation of profits at the expense of whoever is too weak to resist. In spite of the need to do so, no methods or channels have been constructed that can curb the social irresponsibility of the imperial conglomerate and that can turn the private planning of the imperial conglomerate to the public purpose. This, assuming we do not blow up the planet, is the single most important challenge facing the Western democracies at the close of the twentieth century.

Notes

1. See John Kenneth Galbraith, "Power and the Useful Economist," *American Economic Review*, Vol. 63, March, 1973, pp. 1–11. Also of interest is John Kenneth Galbraith, *The Anatomy of Power* (Boston: Houghton Mifflin, 1983).

2. Further discussion, in the appropriate historical context, is in Douglas F. Dowd, *The Twisted Dream*, 2nd ed. (Cambridge: Winthrop, 1977).

3. See John S. Gambs, *Beyond Supply and Demand* (1946; Westport, CT: Greenwood Press, 1976).

4. Further discussion is in William M. Dugger, "The Shortcomings of Concentration Ratios in the Conglomerate Age," *Journal of Economic Issues*, Vol. 19, June, 1985, pp. 343–53.

5. John R. Munkirs, *The Transformation of American Capitalism* (Armonk, New York: M.E. Sharpe, 1985).

6. The best discussion of the Supreme Court's remarkable interpretation of the Fourteenth Amendment is Walter Prescott Webb, *Divided We Stand: The Crisis of a Frontierless Democracy* (New York: Farrar and Rinehart, 1937), pp. 66–85.

7. The most recent addition to the corporate control literature from the radical perspective is Christos N. Pitelis, "Corporate Control, Social Choice and Capital Accumulation: An Asymmetrical Choice Approach," *Review of Radical Political Economics*, Vol. 18, Fall, 1986, pp. 85–100. The classic is Adolf A. Berle and Gardiner C. Means, *The Modern Corporation and Private Property*, rev. ed. (New York: Harcourt, Brace and World, 1968).

8. Paul A. Baran and Paul M. Sweezy, *Monopoly Capital* (New York: Monthly Review Press, 1966).

9. Berle and Means describe the trend of concetrating power during earlier periods in their classic *The Modern Corporation and Private Property*, rev. ed.

10. The growth of diversification is examined further in William M. Dugger, "Centralization, Diversification, and Administrative Burden in U.S. Enterprises," *Journal of Economic Issues*, Vol. 19 September, 1985, pp. 687–701.

11. A reciprocal deal is simple: If you will buy my product, I will buy yours. The more diversified a company is, the more different products it buys and sells, giving it more opportunities to engage in reciprocal dealing. An excellent example of the strength of reciprocal dealing is the "offset" program offered to the British government in 1987 by the Boeing Corporation. Boeing, a U.S. company, used reciprocal dealing to beat out a powerful British company—British General Electric—in bidding for a lucrative British defense contract. What apparently tipped the scales was the fact that Boeing offered to "offset" each dollar spent by the British Government on the contract with $1.30 spent by Boeing on farm out work to British industry. See Steve Lohr, "Boeing's Coup in Britain," *The New York Times*, January 8, 1987.

12. Earlier data are tabulated and analyzed in Dugger, "Centralization, Diversification, and Adminsitrative Burden in U.S. Enterprises."

13. Bureau of the Census, *1982 Enterprise Statistics: General Report*.

14. The preceding mini-case drew on my personal conversations with former U.S. steel workers and with former GM managers, and on Walter Adams and James W. Brock, *The Bigness Complex* (New York: Pantheon, 1986); Ralph Nader and William Taylor, *The Big Boys: Power and Position in American Business* (New York: Pantheon, 1986); Jonathan P. Hicks, "U.S. Steel: New Name, New Era," *The New York Times*, July 9, 1986; and John Holusha, "Acquisition is Expected to Acid GM Plans for Diversification," *The New York Times*, June 6, 1985. Further discussion is in Barry Bluestone and Bennett Harrison, *The Deindustrialization of America* (New York: Basic Books, 1982).

15. A pioneer in the conglomerate movement is Harold Geneen. See Harold Geneen with Alvin Moscow, *Managing* (Garden City, NY: Doubleday, 1984). But also see Anthony Sampson, *The Sovereign State of ITT* (New York: Stein and Day, 1973).

16. Two orthodox economists have written widely on these new features, but neither has understood the real importance of the new form and new function taken on by the conglomerate. See Alfred D. Chandler, Jr., *The Visible Hand: The Managerial Revolution in American Business* (Cambridge: The Belknap Press of Harvard University Press, 1977) and Oliver E. Williamson, *Markets and Hierarchies: Analysis and Antitrust Implications* (New York: Free Press, 1975); Oliver E. Williamson, "The Modern Corporation: Origins, Evolution, Attributes," *Journal of Economic Literature*, Vol. 19, December, 1981, pp. 1537–68.

17. For an insightful but unjustifiably optimistic insider account, see Thomas J. Peters and Robert H. Waterman, Jr., *In Search of Excellence* (New York: Harper and Row, 1982).

18. Further discussion is in Peter Cohen, *The Gospel According to the Harvard Business School* (New York: Penguin, 1973).

19. Thorstein Veblen originally made the distinction between industrial and pecuniary. See his *The Theory of Business Enterprise* (1904; Clifton, NJ: Augustus M. Kelley, 1975).

20. Some of those consequences are discussed in Adams and Brock, *The Bigness Complex*. For a more personal view see Nader and Taylor, *The Big Boys: Power and Position in American Business*.

21. Further discussion of recent developments in macro performance and in macro theory is in Wallace C. Peterson, "Macroeconomics: Where Are We?" *Review of Social Economy*,

Vol. 45, April, 1987, pp. 64-76.

22. *Economic Report of the President* (Washington, D.C.: Government Printing Office, 1987), p. 292.

23. *Ibid.*, p. 282.

24. Adams and Brock agree, particularly for the steel and auto industries. See their *Bigness Complex*.

25. *Ibid.*, p. xi.

26. My small contribution is William M. Dugger, *An Alternative to Economic Retrenchment* (Princeton: Petrocelli, 1984).

27. A convenient place to read both of them is Gardiner C. Means et al., *The Roots of Inflation* (New York: Burt Franklin, 1975). See Means, "Simultaneous Inflation and Unemployment: A Challenge to Theory and Policy," pp. 1-31, and John M. Blair, "Inflation in the United States: A Short-Run Target Return Model," pp. 33-67.

28. Alfred S. Eichner, *The Megacorp and Oligopoly* (1976; White Plains, NY: M.E. Sharpe, 1980).

29. Abba P. Lerner, *Flation* (Baltimore: Pelican, 1973).

30. Wallace C. Peterson, *Our Overloaded Economy* (Armonk, NY: M.E. Sharpe, 1982).

31. Eichner, *Megacorp*, p. 271.

32. U.S. Bureau of the Census.

33. K. William Kapp, *The Social Costs of Private Enterprise* (1950; New York: Schocken Books, 1971), p. 233.

34. Paul Brodeur, *Outrageous Misconduct: The Asbestos Industry on Trial* (New York: Pantheon, 1985).

35. Marshall B. Clinard and Peter C. Yeager, *Corporate Crime* (New York: The Free Press, 1980).

36. Further discussion of incomes policy (wage-price controls) is in Jerry E. Pohlman, *Inflation Under Control?* (Reston, VA: Reston Publishing, 1976).

37. Further discussion of environmental and workplace regulation is in Lester B. Lave, *The Strategy of Social Regulation* (Washington, D.C.: Brookings Institution, 1981) and Daniel M. Berman, *Death on the Job* (New York: Monthly Review Press, 1978).

38. He first used the concept in Thorstein Veblen, *Imperial Germany and the Industrial Revolution* (1915; New York: Augustus M. Kelley, 1964).

39. For recent discussions see Warner Woodworth, Christopher Meek, and William Foote Whyte, Eds., *Industrial Democracy: Strategies for Community Revitalization* (Berverly Hills: Sage, 1985).

40. See Chandler, *The Visible Hand: The Managerial Revolution in American Business*.

41. The classic is Robert T. Averitt, *The Dual Economy* (New York: W.W. Norton, 1968). But see also Robert T. Averitt, "The Dual Economy Twenty Years Later," *Journal of Economic Issues*, Vol. 21, June, 1987, pp. 795-802; and John R. Munkirs and Janet T. Knoedler, "The Dual Economy: An Empirical Analysis," *Journal of Economic Issues*, Vol. 21, June, 1987, pp. 803-11. Averitt and Munkirs are both pathbreaking researchers into economic dualism and the accompanying corporate power. But neither investigates, at much length, the crucial role played by the rise of the imperial conglomerate.

5 NATIONAL ECONOMIC MANAGEMENT AND THE SUPRANATIONAL ECONOMY
John Willoughby

Introduction

Economic disruptions of the past 20 years have periodically focused the American public's attention on international economic problems. The determinants of energy and food prices, plant location, the value of the dollar, and domestic financial stability all have global dimensions; and if newspaper articles and television reports are any indication at all of popular consciousness, many Americans recognize this new reality. Unfortunately, an expansion of our regional vision does not guarantee a more cosmopolitan populace. External economic disturbances are just as likely to generate an inward-looking hostility. There certainly is evidence that many U.S. citizens would support a more nationalistic economic program, but specific protectionist proposals have received surprisingly little coherent support in Congress. There are two plausible explanations for this anomaly. Corporations and government agencies with strong interests in overseas trade and investment can effectively lobby representatives to prevent measures that would restrict international economic intercourse. Or the public itself may believe that no measure—however useful for particular sectors of the populace—could really improve the general welfare of U.S. citizens.[1]

If these propositions are correct, the growing interconnectedness of the U.S. national economy with the rest of the world has become linked to a sense of national civic powerlessness. After all, informed journalistic analysis tells us that factories close as a result of import competition; farms fail because of global overcapacity; and the relative prices of currencies gyrate in response to global cries and whispers about interest rate movements. Given this proclaimed reality, who would not quail helplessly before the world economic behemoth?

Any economics essay that explores the relationships between power and the supranational economy must first confront this sense of disenfranchisement, for this view is not just a popular one. It is also related to a basic theme in recent academic work on macroeconomics and economic regulation. As world integration proceeds, the story goes, there is less and less that an individual state can or should do to regulate a citizen's or corporation's economic contact with those residing beyond the nation's borders.

There is much that is impressive and insightful in this theoretical work, but there is also a curious lacunae. According to standard theory, national powerlessness results from the mechanical working out of stock and flow adjustments to changing economic variables. In these models, the logic of pecuniary maximization takes place in an institutional vacuum. The evolving structures of financial and manufacturing corporations are less important than the technological changes and competitive processes that drive any individual firm's production and marketing decisions. This is a familiar proposition in neoclassical theory. Developing organizational capabilities are epiphenomena of more "basic" economic forces.

International economists have always placed great emphasis on the operation of blind economic processes. Seventeenth and early eighteenth century theorists such as Thomas Mun were able to analyze international trade in this manner because fewer restrictions constrained the global world of commerce. It was possible to observe patterns of commodity exchange freed from parochial limitations, and this more amoral, international environment helped give birth to economics as a distinct discipline. Of course, the mercantilists believed that the state did have the organizational ability to manipulate economic flows. National political power was crucial to these theorists' understanding of how the world ought to work.[2] Today most Western economists hold the reverse proposition: economic processes should and can rule over national economic management.

These dualisms of international economy versus national politics or economic process versus institutional power have important theoretical uses. They are, however, ultimately sterile if we are concerned with designing, advocating, or just thinking about appropriate responses to contemporary economic "laws." A neglect of power within economic institutions leads to a paradoxical overvaluation of structural rigidity. Corporate managers certainly do attempt to maximize economic return and much of the external world they face is given, but the effort to increase net revenue always involves attempts to change the external environment as well. The power capability of a corporation—that is, the ability of this economic institution to transform the circumstances it faces—should be a key part of any analysis of our economic world. Moreover, the power capabilities of the state are also important to consider. It may be possible for a national government to introduce policies that enlarge or restrict a corporation's transformative capacity. If we neglect this potential, we illegitimately exaggerate the structural rigidity of the economy. Popular folk wisdom and sophisticated economic theory can both reach misleading conclusions.

The general proposition that institutional forms and power capabilities matter is not controversial. Nor does it contradict the traditional insight that rapid advances in transportation and communication technologies are a major reason for the internationalization of production, trade, and finance. In this chapter, however, I abstract from these commercial innovations and instead explore the equally important implications that flow from the integration of commodity and money capital circuits within the networks of supranational corporate power.[3]

World Economic Interdependence and the Withering of National Economic Control

Imagine an economic world in which all economic agents are solely concerned with the maximization of some monetary asset. Imagine also that there are no significant international restrictions on the competitive process that this profit seeking impulse generates. These two assumptions place us squarely in the field of most economic paradigms. If we further accept the Keynesian proposition that aggregate employment is demand constrained, then we have entered the arena of open economy macroeconomics. We are ready to ask the central policy question: How can a nation-state act to ensure the prosperity of its citizens?

Twenty years ago—as the postwar fixed exchange rate, relatively free currency convertibility system that we call Bretton Woods began to unravel —many economists had sanguine responses to this question. Flexible exchange rates could permit the relatively quick and painless adjustment of a nation to changing competitive relations. If the United States began to lose its competitive edge, the dollar could devalue, exports and import-competing industries (the tradeable sector) would expand, and employment would stabilize at high levels. Any alternative effort to resolve international disequilibria without changing the exchange rate would either lead to prolonged unemployment or efficiency-sapping trade and capital controls.[4]

This finding for the market determination of relative currency values appealed to most monetarists. Robert Mundell argued that an easy or tight money policy would be more powerful in this more flexible environment than expansive or austere fiscal policy. A falling or rising interest rate would stimulate international capital outflows or inflows, and depreciate or appreciate the national currency. In this way, attempts to expand or contract production rates through changing the money supply would powerfully affect the tradeable sectors of the economy. This finding contradicts Keynes' own closed-economy intuition that aggregate demand would respond only inelastically to interest movements, and an antifiscal corollary to Mundell's analysis was that an internationalized currency regime would make national fiscal policy weaker. The state's attempts to stimulate demand would raise interest rates, appreciate the currency, and thereby crowd out the national economy's tradeable sector.

There is a political as well as technical message in this 1960s argument for flexible exchange rates. If monetary policy could be more effective than fiscal interventions in stabilizing the economy, then one could not use employment creation as a strong rationale for directed government spending programs. Rather, the monetary authorities should be encouraged to lower interest rates and let markets distribute any excess labor supply to the most efficient productive sectors. This conclusion obviously weakens one argument for state expenditures. The internationalization of the economy became associated with increasing calls for fiscal passivity.[5]

As we entered into the brave new 1970s world of flexible exchange rates and relatively general currency convertibility, it soon became apparent that the precise arguments of this new conservative macroeconomics were inadequate. The abandonment of the pure Bretton Woods model coincided with rising unemployment and increased price instability. The complacent promises of the late 1960s were not fulfilled, and theory had to adjust.

The major innovation of this period was that of the rational expectations school, but this reaction to theoretical disarray was particularly unilluminating. The basic premise, that economic agents can effectively anticipate the future, is implausible because it is not even obvious that anyone currently understands which variables regulate or predict our economic present and future. Moreover, even if we had a well-specified model, policy makers might not be able to regulate the key economic variables.

The most pointed example concerns the domestic money supply. An attempt to expand the money supply can, for example, lower short-term interest rates, increase inflationary expectations, and then lead residents to enlarge their relative holdings of assets denominated in foreign currency units.[6] This devaluation of domestic monetary imbalances—if carried far enough—will generate pressures for a repressive monetary policy. This vicious policy cycle, however, can actually produce a vicious downward spiral. Government authorities concerned about weakened national creditworthiness allow long-term real interest rates to ratchet upward and tolerate higher levels of domestic unemployment.

This is one plausible explanation of the upward creep in the "full employment" target rate through the seventies and early eighties. The internationalization of the money circuit of capital has undercut the validity of those early monetarist theories that suggest a relatively simple and benign way to manipulate trading relations and domestic employment. Neither fiscal nor monetary policy appears to work very well. Theory now tells us what much of the public may already understand: the nation-state is not really able or willing to undertake policies that would improve the economic lives of its national citizens.

The Integration of Industry, Trade, and Financial Asset Management in Supranational Institutions

What accounts for the theoretical failures of the past 20 years? Why did economists not anticipate the potential for prolonged fiscal and monetary austerity as the economy internationalized?[8] There is no single answer to this general problem, but there is one obvious failing in the early open economy macroeconomic literature that provides important clues. Many 1960s theorists assumed that trading and direct foreign investment relationships would regulate the behavior of the financial sector.[9] This perspective is not hard to understand. In our efforts to combat money fetishism in the lay public, we tend to give the world of finance a ranking below production and trade. Moreover, most empirical data seem to verify this premise. American financial and insurance institutions, for example, were responsible for only about 5 percent of the total gross domestic product generated by all U.S. industry during the late 1970s and early 1980s. During this same period, the manufacturing sector's contribution has been about 25 percent.[10]

The problem with this approach is that it abstracts from the historically important interconnections between international capitalist finance and production. The growth of over-the-border productive and trading facilities has always been intimately associated with the expansion of banking. The firm's pecuniary maximization efforts involve itself with more than engineering, productive location, and marketing decisions; portfolio management is a significantly important activity for most large enterprises.[11]

This need to manage financial balances does not in and of itself prove that money management activities create a different economic world than that imagined by theorists. Most multinational corporations would probably argue that their major decisions still center on the production and distribution of commodities. The relatively small size of asset management departments, however, obscures the influence of speculation on the economic system as a whole. The manipulation of financial assets by large corporations radically compresses economic time; the rapid generation of winnings and losses forces every firm to speculate. Short-term efforts to anticipate interest rate and exchange rate movements can have enormous and cumulative impacts on competitive conditions within the "real" world.

Underlying trading and direct foreign investment realities are certainly important factors determining exchange rate movements. The massive U.S. trade deficits of recent years combined with the piling up of short-term debt obligations are probably behind the current rise in the value of the yen and Deutsch Mark. On the other hand, the trade deficit itself flowed largely from the dollar's appreciation during the first half of the 1980s. The United States' competitive position had not strengthened significantly during the late 1970s and was not a powerful cause of this earlier exchange rate movement.[12] It is no longer appropriate to assume that finance is the tail whose wagging helps balance the body of the "real" economic dog. (Today, our dog has perhaps two heads: one real and the other financial.) This integration of financial productive and commercial maximization efforts within the supranational enterprise poses tremendous challenges for the theorist and policy maker. It is not possible to focus on trade competitiveness without also worrying about destabilizing money market reactions. As *The Economist* puts it during an earlier period of disruptions in the relative value of national currencies,

> The men at Bretton Woods lived in an age when it seemed conceivable that movements of capital could be controlled so as to compensate for swings in trading balances. No one then envisaged that the world's financial centers could be as closely linked as an everyday bread-and-butter business. Nor that there would be such huge sums looking for the best return on them as there are today in the hands of multinational and American corporations.[13]

The Nature of Transnational Corporate Power and the Roots of the New Economic Liberalism: Historical Examples

This new institutional environment has not gone unnoticed by more astute political commentators. Social Democratic politicians, for example, have proposed a "Gnomes of Zurich" thesis to explain why progressive macroeconomic management has had such a dismal record over the past 20 years.[14] Here, it is argued that the power of finance has effectively undermined any sustained efforts toward progressive economic reform. More pessimistic versions of this thesis would suggest that any measures to redistribute income and wealth by reflating the economy and imposing moderate controls on capital are destined to fail. The British Labor government's sustained inability to stabilize the pound between 1964–1970 and 1974–1979 without fiscal and monetary repression seems to provide some support for this thesis.

More recently (in early 1983) François Mitterand reversed his Keynesian and redistributive policies in the face of severe inflationary and foreign exchange difficulties. *The Economist*'s grateful response to this retreat from social democracy certainly seems to represent the voice of the banking gnomes.

> President Mitterand deserves more cheers than jeers for the choices he has made since Sunday, because in the process he has saved France and Europe from much worse ones that were on offer.
>
> The alternative being pressed on the Socialist president this week was Bennite protectionism; to go on television and announce that the franc was not going to be devalued by the 'speculation of anti-socialist bankers': but that the government would introduce a raft of controls on imports and capital movements.... It would have had dire economic and political consequences across the world.[15]

Despite its intuitive plausibility, there are some difficulties with this interpretation of British and French social democratic economic failures. The crudest gnome version suggests that transnational interests are able to act coherently and even conspiratorially against a moderately progressive state. It is not implausible to assume that most bankers and industrialists were worried about the possible policies of Harold Wilson and François Mitterand. On the other hand, there is less evidence that exchange rate speculation is a very effective way for capital to buy the implementation of policies they support. There are two reasons for this: corporate leaders often have difficulty in agreeing on an appropriate general economic policy, and, in any event, speculation can undermine policies that most of the business world might favor.[16]

One of the better examples of this last point occurred in Japan after the unilateral devaluation of the dollar in 1971. On August 15th of that year, President Nixon abolished any stable price relation between dollar and gold and temporarily imposed a 10 percent tariff surcharge on nearly all imports of manufactures. Washington introduced this policy to force the permanent devaluation of the dollar, so the success of this program obviously depended on the grudging acquiescence of the United States' major economic competitors. Resistance to Nixon's policy was especially strong in Japan. Both the government and the corporate world complained about this unfriendly act, although no significant liberal Democratic politician wished to endanger military or economic ties by raising threatening punitive action against the United States.

Given this self-imposed limitation, the success of any Japanese effort to resist the dollar's devaluation depended on the central authority's ability both to buy dollars and to limit institutional efforts to sell dollars for yen. This last goal required direct intervention into the foreign exchange operations of Japanese corporations and banks. Thus, the state placed a quota on the amount of dollars which each foreign exchange bank could convert into yen. This system forced banks to hold dollars which were likely to be devalued. As *The Economist* put it: "The commercial banks...feel that they are being treated in a most uncomradely and unJapanese way."

This conflict was not limited to the world of banking finance. Soon all corporations began to pressure the Japanese government.

> What worked well when Japan's total trade was worth a few billion dollars a year is distinctly leaky now that a single month's turnover on Japan's foreign trade exceeds $3 billion [in 1971 dollars]. A small change in the timing of conversions from dollars into yen could easily account, therefore, for the inflow of $4 billion in the two weeks from August 13th. By restricting conversion by the commercial banks, the central bank was threatening them with a massive loss on their dollar position. The banks said they would soon have to restrict their purchase of dollar bills as well as refuse dollar remittances from overseeas. The guns that the commercial banks put at the head of the central bank, therefore, was that Japan's official policy would soon lead to an actual disruption of trade.[17]

This minor postscript to the August 1971 Nixon shock is revealing on two accounts. In the first place the regulation of capital flows almost immediately requires the regulation of trade. This has always been true in some ultimate sense, but now, a partial, ad-hoc state policy will collapse quite quickly if the government neglects to extend controls. Secondly, this defeat of state intentions can occur even if most business interests agree with the government's goals. Presumably most Japanese exporters applauded the state's efforts to resist the revaluation of the yen. And yet their immediate fears of the devaluation of their dollar assets frustrated any actions which might have effectively promoted more long-term interests. In this case, the interpenetration of industrial and financial accumulation processes gave the corporate world the power to frustrate certain policies but not to create an alternative framework of economic management.

These two conclusions help explain the paradoxical results of contemporary state-corporate interaction. Government policy is not impotent. Indeed, the decisions of monetary and fiscal authorities have profound effects on the world economy. On the other hand, the new speed of business response to government interventions seems to have channeled policy toward fewer attempts to control corporate behavior directly. President Mitterand and Prime Minister Wilson before him, for example, failed to implement trade and capital control measures—even though one might have expected a more sympathetic consideration of these measures from leaders of their political predilections. This creeping trend toward economic liberalism is in striking contrast to the immediate postwar period. Then most European state leaders deployed extensive trade and exchange controls in order to preserve employment.[18] We can assume that business interests of that time did not always appreciate these efforts, but it is doubtful that liberal economic policy would have succeeded in establishing capitalist growth in the late 1940s more effectively.

The institutionalized integration of all arenas of pecuniary maximization has undermined the simpler versions of open economy macroeconomic theory, but the related failures of liberal employment and growth policies have not stimulated effective governmental efforts to control this institutional environment. If the Gnomes thesis is inadequate, what other theory can help account for this paradox?

The answer to this question requires an approach that also focusses on the behavior of state agents as well as on the power of finance capital. A significant "school" within the postwar political science literature, for example, has stressed the creation of multilateral "regimes": orderly and predictable frameworks for dispute management which may or may not have institutional locales (such as General Agreement on Tariffs and Trade or the International Monetary Fund), but which do depend on certain cultural and political understandings and/or stable power relations.[19] This approach provides a useful counterweight to the gnome view of the world because it alerts us to the possible existence of a generalized postwar social democratic, liberal, and conservative political commitment to a relatively unregulated international economic order. Rather than assuming state-corporate hostility, a better synthesis is one that examines the interaction of supranational business (the gnomes) and national government in an environment that is already economically liberal.[20]

More specifically, I would hypothesize a three-step process driving governments toward economic liberalism:

1. In response to international economic imbalances, nation-states occasionally take ad-hoc steps to control the trading and financial activities of supranational enterprise.

2. These measures generate new corporate efforts to circumvent or minimize the impact of the state action—even if the corporate managers agree with the general thrust of the government's policy.

3. Given the speed of this response, the state regulators are unable to control these new developments and, faced with the choice between stricter controls and deregulation, government officials abandon the now discredited program. This sequence of actions tends to make similar regulatory efforts even more difficult to implement in the future.

The rise of Eurodollars in the mid-1960s is the most spectacular example of this process. The Johnson Administration's efforts to control U.S.-based lending to overseas multinational institutions resulted in a nearly four-fold explosion in dollar balances held in "foreign" banks between 1964 and 1969. Wachtel notes:

> Like a Tom and Jerry cartoon-chase sequence, a new strategy is devised once the lumbering cat [the government] discovers it has been outwitted by the resourceful mouse [the supranational banks].[21]

This and other unsuccessful administrative efforts to limit inflationary pressures and the dollar drain culminated in monetarist credit restrictions in 1966–1967 that produced a mini-recession. In retrospect, these measures were indicative of the political economic future. Three examples will suffice. First, the 1971 Nixon Administration's unilateral devaluation of the dollar eventually resulted in a less regulated international monetary system—despite initial early 1970s efforts to tighten capital controls (or at least to separate a trade-based currency exchange rate from a capital account based rate).[22] Second, the 1973 OPEC price rise eventually increased the power and influence of private international banks rather than promoting a coordinated state response to North-South financial problems. Most of the more industrially sophisticated, less developed countries lost complete access to public finance, and the present debate over the Third World debt crisis largely excludes any approach that would regulate the major banks' activities. This contemporary policy discourse is in striking contrast to the statist, New International Economic Order debates of the mid-1970s. Finally, the second oil price rise of 1979 combined with intensifying balance of payments and domestic inflationary difficulties in the United States to produce a much more severe credit shock than that of 1966 and 1967. The result was high real interest rates and an intensification of deregulatory presures—as financial institutions and other corporations agitated for the right to adjust to the new economic environment without government intervention or approval. The conservative nature of contemporary American economic policy has clear international roots.

The Need for Institutional Reform: A Return to Antitrust Traditions?

Most citizens should be alarmed by the progressive deregulation of the world economy. This internationalizing dialectic has created a much more erratic macroeconomic environment which is especially characterized by higher unemployment. The negative consequences of the supranational order, however, go beyond these employment (and price stability) problems. Richard Cooper has noted that the more open world economy has tended to redistribute income away from immobile factors of production toward mobile ones,[23] and this implies that the dynamics of the open world economy shift resources from labor to capital. Intensified competition forces firms to consider relocating their production facilities, and this threat weakens the bargaining power of trade unions who represent workers much less able to move.[24]

The redistribution of resources to business also works its way through the government's fiscal system. More and more nation-states have attempted to attract industrial and banking capital by providing tax and regulatory relief as well as a subsidized infrastructure.[25] Even though there is not strong evidence that tax giveaways are an efficient way to attract industrial capital, few governments can afford to alienate local and international businesses clamoring for putative relief. Moreover, corporations can often circumvent differential corporate profit rates through transfer pricing procedures that shift surpluses from high tax to low tax areas.[26]

The negative distributional and macroeconomic implications of the new world economy have prompted several proposals to strengthen the power of state policy. The most moderate advocates support the closer coordination of fiscal and monetary policy. Coordinated policy might be able to attenuate monetary disturbances and thereby permit the efficacious return of the naive Keynesian policies of the past. The 1978 Bonn economic summit represents a modest experiment of this sort; Germany agreed to a minor reflation of its economy in return for a Carter Administration pledge to deregulate domestic energy prices. The Reagan Administration is now attempting to coordinate interest rate adjustments with Japan and Germany to stabilize exchange rates, and more ambitious officials have also expressed the desire for fiscal policy coordination. None of these proposals would mitigate the regressive distributional effects of intensified capital mobility to which we have already referred.

Despite these efforts, the general prospects for effective policy cooperation are not very auspicious. The Carter-Schmidt measures collapsed in the face of the political economic disruptions of 1979, and economic stagnation in the late 1980s will also make it difficult for Secretary of the Treasury Baker's plans to succeed. Unstable macroeconomic conditions have combined with supranational institutional power to make even this limited form of coordination problematic.

A left-wing social democratic response to global economic difficulties would, at first glance, not attempt to create an internationally integrated policy world. Instead, its "alternative economic strategy" aims to reconstruct the national economy by reintroducing the trade and foreign exchange controls so essential a part of the postwar world. One clear thrust of these proposals is to subordinate the banking system to the needs of national accumulation. This could require the nationalization of the major banks and, in the case of England, the partial dismantling of the City of London.[27]

The proposals to deconstruct globally and reconstruct nationally are appealing. The social democratic programs directly address the institutional issues raised in this chapter. Nevertheless, most national governments could not implement such a program without international acquiescence. Perhaps only the United States could break its traditional trading and investment links unilaterally without suffering extensive short-term damage, and it is precisely the U.S. government which would be organizing opposition to any leftist, nationalist effort of the sort once contemplated by the Bennites in England and the CERES group in France. For these reasons, some European theorists have written about the need to develop a planned trading system, but this, of course, is a much more ambitious proposal than macroeconomic policy coordination. This radical alternative is much more likely to founder on the shoals of international conflict than the liberal Keynesian one.

Are there any less ambitious alternatives available to policy makers? In contrast to the foregoing proposals, Wachtel has argued for a four-pronged banking and trade reform policy that involves: (1) the creation of a public authority which could buy up funds from the Eurodollar market; (2) the use of these funds as reserves for bonds which would be issued in exchange for Third World debt held by supranational banks; (3) The establishment of a reserve ratio for international accounts as well as increased reporting requirements for global banks; (4) The imposition of trading restrictions on countries that systematically violate labor rights.[28]

This proposal is appealing because it would not require an unrealistic amount of international cooperation for its implementation. It might temporarily succeed in both reducing some of the destabilizing Eurodollar transfers endemic to world economy and restricting the mobility of some industrial capital. On the other hand, the proposal does not really address the fundamental institutional matrix that supports the new supranational economy: transnational corporations will still be institutions that integrate their use of financial, commodity, and productive resourses. Regulatory measures of the sort that Wachtel proposes will be ultimately ineffective if corporations maintain the ability to shift large financial balances merely by altering their monthly trading patterns.

Nevertheless, these proposals are intriguing in their use of the U.S. regulatory and antitrust traditions. It might be possible to use this inspiration to design programs that would limit the ownership of industrial and financial enterprises to one national economy. The most radical extension of this idea would force the selling of most foreign subsidiaries in the United States as well as overseas. This redistribution of ownership need not be especially disruptive; national firms could still trade goods and services as well as buy and sell rights to technology. Banks could still manage financial assets, but there would have to be strict limits on the amount of such balances that could be held outside the country by corporations and individuals. This policy would be much easier to implement if most ownership rights were already restricted nationally.

There are obviously great barriers to the implementation of a global antitrust politics. Indeed, the growth of the supranational economy has provided a key theoretical rationale for the dismantling of some judicial restrictions on the behavior of large corporations within the United States. Now, some industrial organization theorists use contestable market theory to suggest that the lower barriers to entry brought about by intensified global competition can produce the beneficent results of perfect competition—whether the industry remains oligopolistic.[29] Even if we grant some logical validity to this thesis, one could certainly make a cogent argument for more severe limitations on the internationally oriented accumulation decisions of the giant firm. Purported efficiency gains through trade and foreign investment must be balanced against the loss of economic welfare associated with the decline of effective national economic management.

There are, of course, other political and cultural objections to antitrust measures. Many hold to a "cult of bigness" and assume that giant corporations are large because they are more efficient and advanced. It is difficult for any theoretical argument to sway such an opinion; this unclear thinking may especially apply to that large number of professional and managerial U.S. citizens whose future seems dependent on the continued prosperity of the large corporation. I am sure that nearly every economics professor has at times consulted with a pragmatic but secretly starry-eyed student who dreams of becoming an international business representative. There are some rather humble, if economically secure, beneficiaries of supranational corporate power, and a political strategy to reassert national economic control must address those who may worry about the security of their positions within a particular firm.

Although proposals to dismantle supranational networks of corporate power are unlikely to garner immediate political support, there are theoretical advantages to the articulation of such a position. Social scientific knowledge is meant to empower by indicating how social processes either advance or frustrate our ability to construct a more humane environment. Unfortunately, recent advances in international macroeconomics have blocked this practical imperative behind knowledge creation.[30] Most political and economic theorists take for granted the contemporary ownership structures of international capitalism and then develop models that often indicate how powerless or counterproductive national fiscal and monetary interventions will be. This conclusion has its convenient uses for politicians who wish to maintain their popular support. Policy makers can claim that their failures are really the result of uncontrollable economic events. Some of the most popular leaders of the West have embraced this short-term fatalism with a vengeance. Margaret Thatcher, in particular, vigorously celebrates the need for the British people to adjust to the harsh realities of international competition.

Standard neoclassical theory seems incapable of constructing a theoretical framework that questions the premises of this conservative theory and practice. A more adequate understanding of global corporate power and our ability to control it requires both a multifaceted institutional approach and a critical political vision.

Notes

1. This may explain the striking ability of some pro-business politicians to argue that specific trade control measures pander to "special interests."
2. Heckscher points out that this new emphasis on organizing state policy according to consistent economic principles was also—and, perhaps, primarily—against the disintegrative, particularistic tendencies of Medieval society. Eli F. Heckscher, *Mercantilism*, rev. ed. (London: George Allen and Unwin, 1955), pp. 33–44.
3. This exploration is ultimately inspired by Veblen's attempt to analyze the rule of finance within the modern firm. Thorstein Veblen, *The Theory of Business Enterprise* (New York: Mentor Books, 1958).
4. Another, more "Keynesian" proposal of the late 1960s called for the creation of an international reserve unit in relation to which all national currencies would be fixed. This more ambitious version of the SDR initative would permit periodic devaluations or revaluations, but this framework would interpose an administrative procedure between the gains and losses of reserves and the determination of appropriate exchange rates. Fritz Machlup, *Remaking the International Monetary System: The Rio Agreement and Beyond* (Baltimore: The Johns Hopkins Press, 1968).
5. For the most compelling early articulation of this open-economy emphasis on monetary policy, see Robert A. Mundell, *International Economics* (New York: The Macmillan Company, 1968).
6. Richard N. Cooper, "Economic Mobility and National Economic Policy," in *Economic Policy in an Interdependent World: Essays in World Economics* (Cambridge, MA: The MIT Press, 1986), pp. 85–86.
7. The pressure will be especially strong for those countries whose national money is also an international reserve currency. The twentieth century British experience is particularly instructive.
8. The economic history of the 1920s indicates a possible connection between an unstable and stagnant world economy and attempts to preserve a liberal system of international exchange. This experience lay behind Keynes's own protectionist arguments during the 1930s and early 1940s. For a detailed economic history of this period, see Derek H. Aldcroft, *From Versailles to Wall Street, 1919–1929* (Berkeley: University of California Press, 1981). For a brief commentary on Keynes' perspective, see John Willoughby, "A Reconsideration of the Protectionism Debate: Keynes and Impport Controls," *Journal of Economic Issues*, vol. 16, June, 1982, pp. 555–61.
9. Thus, Fritz Machlup wrote in the mid-1960s:

> Counterflows of private capital induced by "financial corrective" may in rare circumstances remove the need for real adjustment. But in more usual circumstances the correction of the imbalance will be only temporary and the need for real adjustment merely postponed.

"The Capital Account and the Balance of Payments," in *Maintaining and Restoring Balance in International Payments* (Princeton: Princeton University Press, 1966). p. 170.

10. OECD, *National Accounts, 1972–84*, Vol. II (Paris: OECD, 1986), p. 49.
11. Mira Wilkins points out, in fact, that the first U.S.-based international banking operations evolved from trading companies who "found trading in money to be more lucrative than trading in goods." Mira Wilkins, *The Emergence of Multinational Enterprise: American Business Abroad from the Colonial Era to 1914* (Cambridge: Harvard University

Press, 1970), p. 13. Stephen Hymer makes a similar argument when analyzing the rise of the modern supranational corporation. See "The Multinational Corporation and the Law of Uneven Development," in J. Bhagwati, Ed., *Economics and World Order from the 1970s to the 1990s* (Basingstoke, Eng: Macmillan, 1972).

12. The merchandise trade deficit of the United States hovered between 25 and 34 billion between 1977 and 1981. Given the inflationary conditions of this period, there was some real improvement in trade competitiveness during most of the Carter years. *Economic Report of the President, 1987* (Washington, D.C.: Government Printing Office, 1987), p. 361.

13. "When the Dollar Was Devalued," *The Economist*, Vol. 240, No. 6678, August 21, 1971, p. 53.

14. Harold Wilson first attacked the Gnomes of Zurich during the mid-1960s. Anthony Sampson, *The Money Lenders: Bankers and a World in Turmoil* (New York: Viking Press, 1981), p. 207.

15. "Le Bon Choix," *The Economist*, Vol. 286, No. 7282, March 26, 1983, p. 11.

16. Bob Jessop makes the argument that businesses will often not be able to articulate a common stance that reflects the interests of "capital in general." Bob Jessop, *The Capitalist State* (New York: New York University Press, 1982).

17. "The Rising Yen," *The Economist*, Vol. 240, No. 6680, September 4, 1971, pp. 57–58.

18. As Milward puts it:

> The response of the European economies to their increasing international payments difficulties was not, however, as it had been in 1920, to deflate, but, with the exception of Italy, to maintain inflationary boom conditions while increasing the level of control over foreign trade.

Alan S. Milward, *The Reconstruction of Western Europe, 1945–51* (Berkeley: University of California Press, 1984), p. 465.

19. The regime literature can be widely divergent. Steven Krasner, for instance, has argued that trading and finance regimes are mainly dependent on continued U.S. hegemony, while John Ruggie has stressed the shared commitments of most state managers to some form of liberal Keynesianism. For a further exploration of these perspectives, see Stephen Krasner (Ed.), *International Regimes* (Ithaca: Cornell Press, 1983).

20. this approach does not explain the formation of a liberal Keynesian regime, but rather concentrates on explaining its historical reproduction.

21. Howard W. Wachtel, *The Money Mandarins*, (Pantheon Books, New York, 1986) p. 100.

22. This attempt to separate trade from capital accounts was France's first reaction to the Nixon shock. "Waiting on the Six," *The Economist*, Vol. 240, No. 6678, pp. 55–9.

23. Richard N. Cooper, "Economic Mobility and National Economic Policy," in *Economic Policy in an Interdependent World: Essays in World Economics* (Cambridge, MA: the MIT Press, 1986), pp. 71–122.

24. This conclusion tends to contradict the argument that intensified international competition will suppress profits more than wages. It is possible that a strong labor movement might be able to resist wage-cutting strategies and force corporations to accept a lower profit share. This is the scenario outlined by Andrew Glyn and Bob Sutcliffe in *British Capitalism, Workers and the Profit Squeeze* (Harmondsworth, Eng: Penguin, 1982). On the other hand, it is plausible to expect that capital would eventually relocate and eventually capture a larger global share of income. I am grateful to Sam Bowles for first suggesting these ideas.

25. Even the United States has played this game. In order to attract U.S. banks away

from their havens in the Cayman Islands and elsewhere, the Federal Reserve created deregulated and tax free enterprise zones for International Banking Facilities. Wachtel, *The Money Mandarins*, Pantheon Books, New York, 1986, pp. 110–118.

26. E.J. Kolde writes:

> No tax system, however involved, can be expected to fully incapacitate the transfer-pricing mechanism. Indeed, it appears that as a multinational firm matures and develops greater operational integration among its affiliates, the opportunities for employing the transfer price tend to increase sharply irrespective of national tax laws.

E.J. Kolde, *The Multinational Company* (Lexington, MA: DC Heath and Company, 1974), p. 193.

27. A British example of this leftist nationalism is: CSE London Working Group, *The Alternative Economic Strategy: A Labour Movement Response to the Economic Crisis* (London: CSE Books, 1981).

28. Howard Wachtel, *The Money Mardarins*, pp. 204–214. Wachtel's other reforms focus on policy coordination issues that are similar to already outlined liberal planks.

29. Elizabeth Bailey, "Foreword," in W.J. Baumol, J.C. Panzer and R.D. Willig (Eds.), *Contestable Markets and the Theory of Industrial Structure* (New York: Harcourt, Brace and Jovanovich, 1982), p. xx.

30. Jurgen Habermas is one of the most recent theorists to discuss the liberatory potential of knowledge. See the discussion of Perry Anderson, *In the Tracks of Historical Materialism* (London: Verso, 1983), pp. 55–67.

6 ECONOMIC POWER AND THE POLITICAL PROCESS

Jerry L. Petr

Economics as a separate science is unrealistic, and misleading if taken as a guide in practice. It is one element—a very important element, it is true—in a wider study, the science of power.

—Bertrand Russell

The Golden Rule of Politics—he who has the gold, rules.

—Mark Green

Introduction

This chapter is an essay in political economy—specifically, the political economy of power. It is an examination of how the "Golden Rule of Politics" (cited above) really works. It is, therefore, an exploration of the impact of economic power on political processes.

In the political economy of the United States, this is an era of bicentennialism. Our political charter was drafted in 1787 and is being heralded, celebrated, and critiqued. Our economic ideology is traced back to Adam Smith's *An Inquiry into the Nature and the Causes of the Wealth of Nations*, published in the year of our Declaration of Independence, 1776. Not coincidentally, both Smith's *Wealth of Nations* and the U.S. Constitution are documents in which "power" is an important consideration. The Constitution organizes and distributes political power; Smith analyzes institutional structures for the prevention or mitigation of abusive economic power. Thus eighteenth century informed minds were clearly attuned to issues of power and its disposition.

In the subsequent two centuries, the forms that power takes and the mechanisms by which it is employed have evolved and developed; unfortunately, its analysis by economists has atrophied. Smith and the Constitution dealt with the world as they found it; academic economists have increasingly analyzed a theoretical world as they would like it to be. And in that complex but arid world of assumed abstractions, analysis of the political exercise of economic power is as rare as a Marxist on the Council of Economic Advisers.

That is, perhaps, a slightly hyperbolic statement. Unlike dodo birds, some political economists still live, scattered in small and nonobtrusive clusters on the fringes of academic respectability. And it is from the heterodox precincts of academe, as well as from the halls and cloakrooms of Congress and the courts, that much of the substance of this chapter is drawn.

We will not trace here the regression of political economy from its eighteenth and early nineteenth century analytical interest in the reality of economic power to its late twentieth century antiseptic ideology of impersonal powerlessness. We may observe that such analytic atrophy was convenient for those who acquired and used the unremarked power. We will note, with J. K. Galbraith, that "...the [intellectual] conditioning that served the industrial power was not necessarily either contrived or visibly sychophantic. But its service to economic interest was, nonetheless, the test of its acceptability."[1] And we assert that the steady erosion of the analysis of the political economy of power was additionally useful because, in an ostensibly democratic and participatory society, the less visible power is, the more effectively it can work its will.

Despite its musty smell, if not downright un-Americanism, an old-fashioned political economic analysis of the economic muscle behind the turns of public policy is the subject of this chapter. It will argue that power is the ability to influence or direct the activity of others, that much power is exercised through political processes, and that such processes are influenced by economic factors. And as plausible as that sequence appears to be when boldly stated in black and white, it remains murkily obscure when viewed through the opaque lens of much of contemporary economic theorizing.

The Exercise of Power

C. Wright Mills noted three decades ago that "The very rich in America are not dominantly an idle rich and never have been."[2] In his context, Mills had reference to the economic role of the rich in the production of goods and services. In our context, his observation can be brought to bear on the political role of the rich in the production of rules and expectations. As government, in the United States and throughout the developed world, has, of necessity, come to play an increasingly significant economic role, holders and representatives of wealth have likewise become increasingly active in influencing, shaping, and channeling such government participation. The very rich in America, either individually or collectively (in corporate form), are also not dominantly an idle rich in the arena of political power and social control.

Power, as we discuss it in this chapter, refers to the ability to influence our social environment, our community, to act as we wish it to. Power is the ability to influence the course of events, to cause things to happen in the social environment, or, of equal importance, to prevent them from happening.

Obviously, within a market economy, money is an important source of such power or influence. Given sufficient money (economic power) one can cause a new automobile to appear in one's garage, or one can prevent the destruction of one's lawn by soil insects. But such examples, consistent with elements of our fundamental ideology, reinforce the idea that "economic power," in our society, is a non-coercive means to self-fulfillment. It represents the freely chosen allocation of one's financial resources among alternative uses via mutually beneficial transactions. But it is also separate from the exercise of one's political power via the ballot box and the ethic of "one person, one vote."

Our ideological pillars of consumers' sovereignty and political democracy support a social myth of economic and political self-determination beyond the reach of the powerful arms of external forces. Ideologically, consumers' sovereignty and political democracy are instruments by which each of us, as individuals, exercises power over our own circumstances and well-being, and protects ourselves from subjugation to the power of others. They are elements of a self-directed, individualistic ideology in which each person is master of his fate, captain of her soul.

In this chapter, however, we part the curtains of mythology to view a social system in which unequal influence over "rules of the game" is a reality, in which some persons write the script by which others must act, in which, in fact, there are both puppets and puppeteers. And we explore ways in which economic power is instrumental in the attainment of those political results.

Americans are fond of asserting that we are a society governed by laws, not by men (persons). The significance of that assertion is that power, or coercion, or control, is exercised via a process of participation and consent, not by personal whim or conceit. We laud such an evolutionary step in social institutions as a mark of civilization or progress.

Consequently, we see the law, or the government that formulates, implements, and interprets policies via law, as the repository and the embodiment of legitimate power. So, in this chapter, we focus our investigation on government, both as direct agent of publicly wielded power and as indirect permissive or prohibitive influence on privately wielded power. We specifically examine how economic power is brought to bear on those governmental processes.

In a more subtle version of Mark Green's "Golden Rule," Randall Bartlett has written:

> To the degree that inequality exists in the distribution of wealth, it implies inequality in both market and political power distributions.... It is a basic conclusion of economic theory that the allocation of resources arising from the operation of a market system will reflect the initial distribution of wealth and the structure of the market.... It is also the inevitable result of rational, self-interested action on the part of all agents in an uncertain world that the outcome of decisions in the political realm, even when organized democratically will also reflect this same distribution.... In either the political or the market operations of a society such as the one we have been describing, the wishes of the agents with the greatest wealth will carry the greatest weight. It is not a new "conspiracy" that makes it so. It is merely the action of self-interested rational men.[3]

It is our task in the remainder of this chapter to understand more specifically why this broad and intuitively persuasive generalization should be so, and, more specifically, how it is so.

The structure of the discussion in this chapter follows the structure of our government itself. School children learn, we hope, something of the principle of "separation of powers" by which we divide the legislative, executive, and judicial functions of government. This trifurcation of the exercise of public power into writing the rules ("Policy Formulation"), administering the rules ("Policy Implementation"), and adjudicating disputes ("Policy Interpretation") presumably has the advantage of further diminishing the possibility of capriciousness or exploitative abuse of power. As we shall see, however, each of these separate aspects of the political process is itself subject to the influence of concentrated economic power.

Our objective here is to consider the most significant interactions between economic power and the political process in each of these three major components of the American exercise of public authority: policy formulation, policy implementation, policy interpretation. In each case the influence of economic power over the political process is formidable, and in each case to attempt to understand political processes without consideration of the role of economic power is both inadequate and misleading. Each of these three avenues for the exercise of economic power is summarized briefly at this point and then more fully developed throughout the remainder of this chapter.

In a contemporary polity, power is exercised via rules (laws); obviously one of the most effective ways of wielding power in any society is to be the maker of those rules (or at least to influence their making). We here call this rule-making activity "policy formulation" and focus on Congress as the principal locus of such activity. Those who influence Congress influence the rules, and those who are influential in campaign funding certainly influence Congress. Particular attention in this "formulation" segment of the chapter is consequently placed on the role of money and "the moneyed" in campaign financing, particularly via Political Action Committees (PAC's). (In fact, PAC may better indicate "Preferred Access to Congress.")

But is also important to move beyond the obvious and direct exchange of contributions for consideration in understanding the role of economic power in policy formulation. Formulation of the formal guidelines by which we live is also shaped by the availability of influential information and argument which can be placed before the policy makers. To that end, the founding, financing, and functioning of "think tanks" (nongovernmental privately supported research and policy analysis organizations) are relevant to establishing the terms of the debate, the perception of options, and the quality and quantity of information that is available to policy formulators. Think tanks depend upon money, and money comes from centers of economic power. Therefore we will examine the dual impact of PAC's (financed by wealth) in providing a source of political muscle to influence policy formulation, and think tanks (financed by wealth) in providing the concomitant intellectual support to allow policy makers to acquiesce to political pressure with the clear conscience provided by confirmatory argument.

Finally, of course, at one further remove from the legislative process, policy formulation takes place within a cultural environment which provides standards of acceptability. Galbraith, in his 1983 *Anatomy of Power*, described "conditioned" power as power which "is exercised by changing belief."[4] This "conditioning" of a whole society to accept a proferred set of attitudes "is central...to the functioning of the modern economy and policy...."[5] In our society such conditioned power is exercised via major institutions of education, religion, and popular media. They, too, are dependent on economic power and wealth for their well-being, viability, and social standing and acceptability.

Once policy has been formulated (rules have been developed) by rule makers influenced by economic power, using information provided by economic power, in a cultural environment conditioned by economic power, the rules must be enforced. The enforcement function, herein identified as "policy implementation," is assigned to the executive or administrative branch of government. Implementation is the responsibility of the various regulatory commissions and agencies that "police" the participants in our modern economy.

Again, we examine the opportunities for the exercise of economic power over political process and highlight two of them. One might be called an "identity factor" as we observe the staffing of significant public regulatory positions by people drawn from the ranks of the economically powerful regulatees. The second power path is the "absorption factor" as the regulatory or supervisory body becomes absorbed by the attitudes, perspectives, preferences, and mind set of the "target" population. We will find examples of both processes as we look at defense oversight, regulation of auto safety and efficiency, environmental protection, antitrust action, and traditional areas of rate and service regulation. The footprints of economic power are easily found on the turf of policy implementation.

Finally, the judicial branch is responsible for interpretation of the rules which, in turn, influences the impact of those rules on community life. Therefore judicial theory, judicial processes, and the personnel who develop and implement those theories and processes provide still more avenues for the exercise of power. Given the analyses of the "Warren Court" or the "Rehnquist Court," and the importance and contention attached to court appointments, it would be very difficult to argue that a court is but a "neutral," "objective," or "dispassionate" explicator of reality. Courts are, rather, framers of reality through the various and diverse sensibilities, preferences, and even prejudices which they bring to the interpretive function.

Thus it is that trends or fashions in legal scholarship and practice, such as the current popularity of "law and economics," are significant conduits for social policy messages and influences. In its dominant "Chicago" variation, the law and economics perspective suggests "that economic theory can provide the underpinnings for a normative theory of law with the use of economic efficiency as the decisional criterion to guide the development of the law."[6] As the economic theory cited here is neoclassical microeconomic theory, in which Pareto optimality and/or utility or wealth maximization are the touchstones of validation, the normative criterion is one based on unfettered market practice, reflecting the power emanating from a status quo distribution of income and wealth.

> It would appear also that the Pareto-criterion rests upon, and may be considered as an extension of, a certain ethical system. This is the ethical system in which justice is what justice can get in the market, in which ethics is the ethics of bargaining, and in which values are the values of a middle class, bourgeois society; in short, in which everything is (at least potentially) up for sale, in which there is a (potential) market price on considerations of equity, all this albeit within, yet structured by, some vague limits imposed by assuming the status quo system of social control and working rules (as well as income, wealth, and power distributions). The Pareto-criterion represents the ethics of a business society and the economic theology of that society, an ethics of the market. The "simple" assumption is not only specific to a civilization but represents its ethical quintessence.[7]

Thus interpreted, economic analysis of law implies using law and interpretation of law to cause the society to conform more closely to the theoretical norm of the "free market." Those who have market strength are thereby advantaged, and economic power again embraces political power.

The burden of this chapter then is that economic power in the form of personal and collective wealth and income is an important influence on public policy formulation, implementation, and interpretation. There is an important, perhaps dominant, connection between economic and political power which is underestimated and underanalyzed by economics as conventionally practiced in the United States. We now look at each of these areas of influence (policy formulation, policy implementation, and policy interpretation) more closely.

Public Policy Formulation

This country's most "successful" business executive in 1986, Lee Iacocca, defended his $20 million income from Chrysler Corporation by wrapping himself in the folds of a version of the "American Dream." "That's the American way. If little kids don't aspire to make money like I did, what the hell good is this country?"[8]

Iacocca's assertion arguably is a cogent statement of the dominant American ethos. It is, unarguably, a statement of values; and values lie behind and presumably influence public understandings, public approbation, and, ultimately, public policy. According to opinion polls, the American public has an unrequited political love affair with Lee Iacocca— precisely because he represents what "we" idealize.

B. F. Skinner, in one of his more controversial books, argued that the "pre scientific" self-determining "autonomous man" (the fictitious individual of free will) must be replaced in our "scientific" understanding by the knowledge of human behavior determined by environmental forces (the acceptance of human beings as conditioned actors). As he concluded *Beyond Freedom and Dignity*, he asserted that:

> It is the autonomous inner man who is abolished, and that is a step forward. But does man not then become merely a victim or passive observer of what is happening to him? He is indeed controlled by his environment, but we must remember that it is an environment largely of his own making. The evolution of a culture is a gigantic exercise in self-control.[9]

Skinner's reference to human control by an environment of man's "own making" and the ultimate reliance on "self-control" are both plural references. To Skinner, we, collectively, control ourselves as individuals. The significant point for this chapter and this discussion of the formulation of public policy is that, whether we totally accept Skinner's view of behavioral manipulation, or only partially acknowledge the influence of cultural norms and influences on human actions, we recognize ourselves as creatures responsive to and reflective of societal values. When those values are articulated by Lee Iacocca (and similar spokespersons), those oracles become arbiters of acceptability and respectability in matters of taste, preference, emulation, and expectations. They establish parameters within which public policy must find its legitimacy.

In his classic sociological study published a generation ago, C. Wright Mills captured the essence of this argument.

> Whenever the standards of the moneyed life prevail, the man with money, no matter how he got it, will eventually be respected.... It is not only that men want money; it is that their very standards are pecuniary. In a society in which the money-maker has had no serious rival for repute and honor, the word "practical" comes to mean useful for private gain, and "common sense," the sense to get ahead financially....

> A society that narrows the meaning of "success" to the big money and in its terms condemns failure as the chief vice, raising money to the place of absolute value, will produce the sharp operator and the shady deal. Blessed are the cynical, for only they have what it takes to succeed.[10]

The point then is that economic power, in a society that venerates such power, establishes a climate of opinion and a set of values within which public policy is formulated. Further, it shapes and guides the mass institutions through which a mass consciousness is formed and articulated. So it is not sufficient to note that, in general, social values conform to the attitudes and preferences of the powerful. Institutions including religious, educational, and journalistic also are dependent upon, and responsive to, concentrated wealth. It is surely not remarkable to note that private wealth owns the journalistic media, supports the charitable and religious institutions, and endows the universities. Is it more remarkable to suggest that the degree of such economic support is correlated with the degree of comfort the wealth holders find in the product of those institutions?

Transferring these ideas more specifically to the political realm, analyst Elizabeth Drew quotes Richard Wirthlin, pollster, as follows:

> People make decisions based upon the way they see the world, and the way they see the world is conditioned by the information they have; and money can influence not only the information they have but also the perceptions they have, and therefore influence who wins and who loses.[11]

Wirthlin here suggests a more direct influence that may be exerted by power and wealth to affect policy outcomes. Finding nebulous environmental influences on social thought and values rather too indirect an expression of interests, and control over the formative institutions of social attitudes too long-term for highly visible results, the holders of economic power have taken steps to concentrate and formalize the channels of influence and control. One set of these channels takes the institutional form of "independent" research institutions or think tanks. Within the context of this chapter, the role of think tanks can be understood as the transformation of generally predominant cultural values into specific sets of policy recommendations by means of a scientifically reputable research and validation process. Thus the think tank industry has grown apace with government and government's need for policy studies and informed guidance.

Think tanks, or public policy research organizations, have existed for decades. Of the present major players in the brainproduct league, the Hoover Institution, founded in 1919, and the Brookings Institution, incorporated in 1927, are two of the longest-lived. These "independent" organizations have never been (can never be?) free of ideological or partisan bias. (The Hoover Institution was early an avowedly anti-Marxist organization.) But this institutional form has been viewed in recent years as a vehicle for increasingly more direct and active policy influence. Although the American Enterprise Association (later the American Enterprise

Institute for Public Policy Research, or AEI) was founded in 1943 by Johns-Manville chairman Lewis H. Brown as concrete embodiment of a wish "to restore free-market economics in the aftermath of the New Deal,"[12] and as a counterweight to the perceived "liberalism" of the Brookings Institution, the rise of the most actively ideological agenda has been advanced by the rapidly growing "new kid on the block," the Heritage Foundation. As Brookings and AEI (both of whom receive significant portions of their $10–15 million annual budgets from corporate America, its executives and foundations) have apparently settled into moderately differentiated occupancy of the establishment political center, from which they function as alternating "governments in exile," the Heritage Foundation has aggressively pursued a more strident role in shaping national policy.

And whereas the "centrist" positioning of Brookings and AEI has been attributed, in part, to "their concern for maintaining a flow of funds from middle-of-the-road" individuals and institutions,[13] it is clear that a good deal of not-so-centrist funding is available to advance a more conservative agenda via Heritage. Founded in 1973 by Paul M. Weyrich and Edwin J. Feulner with the support of a $250,000 contribution from Joseph Coors (who reportedly continued gifts on the order of $350,000 per year into the 1980s),[14] Heritage had grown to a size similar to Brookings and American Enterprise Institute by 1986 (with a dollar income in 1986 of over $14 million).[15] Although Paul Weyrich left Heritage to establish the Committee for the Survival of a Free Congress (now the Free Congress Political Action Committee,[16] Edwin Feulner remained as Heritage president. The influential activist role of Heritage is indicated by journalist Dom Bonafede who reported:

> ...Feulner reported during an interview that the Reagan Administration had adopted 61 percent of the 1,270 recommendations included in Heritage's massive study, *Mandate for Leadership*, a 20-volume, 3,000-page work setting out the policy options available to a conservative Administration. The study was presented to Reagan 10 days after his election.[17]

Additionally, according to Bonafede, in 1982 Fuelner "estimates that he goes to the White House about once a week."[18]

The tenor of the policy advice that contributors buy for their $14 million may be reflected in the Bonafede list of the Heritage cast of characters: it has included Russell Kirk, George Gilder, William Simon, Louis Lehrman, Midge Decter, Norman Podhoretz, Thomas Sowell, and Herman Kahn.[19] William Casey has been listed as a major contributor.[20] Edwin Meese was a active 1970s participant in Heritage activities,[21] and the impetus for the Strategic Defense Initiative ("Star Wars") can be traced to a

Heritage Foundation 1982 report titled "High Frontier."[22] "Urban Enterprise Zones," a domestic policy proposal in President Reagan's 1982 State of the Union Address, also was a Heritage initiative.[23]

It is not difficult to see that money, supporting think tanks with their analysis and publication arms, can be a significant factor in policy formulation. And one should keep in mind that it is not just the more avowedly political think tanks that illustrate the impact of economic power on political policy. One would have to be extremely naive to assume that the more "moderate" think tanks are totally unaware or unconcerned about the impact of their policy studies on their potential for fund raising from the American "establishment." "He who pays the piper, calls the tune"; those who can offer more pay, call more tunes.[24]

Furthermore, a recent think tank innovation, initiated by the imaginative energies of the Heritage Foundation, is extending influence beyond policy suggestions into personnel matters. Establishment of an "Academic Bank," a computer registry of hundreds of conservative scholars, allows Heritage to suggest appropriate applicants for government positions, testifiers before Congressional committees, authors of policy studies, participants at workshops and on task forces, and more.[25] Such efforts at creating an intellectual network, supported by the economic power base of the Heritage contributors, provide yet another cutting edge to this tool of policy influence.

This emphasis on the Heritage Foundation as one of the currently more vigorous and effective idea lobbies should not imply that all connections between economic resources and political power are made by the political right. There are think tanks of a "liberal" persuasion (such as the Institute for Policy Studies, the Urban Institute, the Center for Tax Justice) which also have exerted political influence. Two inferences may be drawn from the Heritage example, however. One is that a type of dialectic may well operate in this realm of policy influence, whereby the success of more overtly ideological groups from one portion of the political spectrum may well spur efforts to create counterforces from other political positions. The second is that those who can gather the most economic support for "their" think tank, all other things being equal, are likely to have the most political influence via this tactic. Historically, and consistently, moneyed interests have tended to be conservative interests.

But conception is only part of the life story of a national policy. The think tanks provide the intellectually fertile environment, and the necessary opportunity for policy conception to occur; but after appropriate gestation the eagerly nurtured policy must be ushered into the world via formal legislative action. Rule-making is the culmination of the policy formulation process and takes the form of an official resolution or appropriation or regulation or prohibition. The Strategic Defense Initiative, or Urban Enterprise Zones, conceptually benefitting from the fertile environment of the Heritage Foundation, need formal legislative approbation before they become real factors in American life. For this birthing process, the midwife is often money (economic power).

It is neither polite nor accurate to argue that money buys specific policies in the way that cash in one's pocket buys vegetables at the supermarket. But policies are enacted by people (legislators) who are convinced of their importance; legislators are elected to their positions via political contests; and money is a significant factor in determining which candidate (and therefore what policy preferences) will be successful. That common sense conclusion is research-supported, as reported by political scientist Gary Jacobson who, after an extended study of the 1980 and 1982 Congressional elections, concluded, "Campaign spending has a significant impact on the outcomes of congressional elections"[26] and, more specifically, "...money played a central role in the Republican victories of 1980 and avoidance of disaster in 1982...."[27]

The weight of the dollar in the ballot box has been a long-standing concern in the American political system, but without notable success in curbing its influence. A thumbnail sketch by Michael Malbin reports some of the relevant regulatory history, beginning with the Corrupt Practices Act of 1925, continuing through the Hatch Act of 1940, and the Federal Election Campaign Act (FECA) of 1971. Malbin notes that FECA Amendments of 1974, largely adopted in response to the Watergate demonstration of connections between economic and political power, supplemented by additional 1976 amendments, provide much of the current campaign finance legislation.[28]

But each adjustment to campaign financing restrictions seems to generate a yet-more-creative circumvention. The current marvel of political financing, the Political Action Committee, is the contemporary embodiment of such creative influence-buying and the most rapidly expanding conduit through which economic power can be transformed into policy formulation.

Along with the rapid, impressive, and perhaps somewhat frightening growth of PACs since the 1974 Congressional attempts to "curb the role of money and the influence of its contributors in campaigns"[29] the descriptive and analytic literature attempting to cope with the PAC phenomenon has grown correspondingly.[30] This chapter can only present a few highlights concerning trends in the development and activities of these proliferating organizations.

In the period from 1974 through 1984 the number of PAC's registered with the Federal Election Commission grew from 608 to 4,157.[31] PAC contributions to Congressional candidates over that same time span grew from $8.5 million in 1974[32] to $130.3 million in 1986.[33] This growth in numbers and spending also made the PAC's more significant in relative terms as sources of funds. In House races, for example, in 1974 PACs provided 17 percent of total campaign expenditures [34]; by 1986, the PAC contribution was 37 percent of the total.[35] More impressive, in 1986, "194 of the 434 current Members received 50 percent or more of their campaign funds from...PACs...."[36]

But important beyond the growth of PAC numbers and financial significance are other interesting evolutionary patterns. For example, although in 1974 the dominant PAC category was "labor" PACs, that category has been relatively slow to expand (an average of 12 percent increase in their numbers each year during the late seventies and early eighties) compared to "corporate" PACs (21 percent per year growth rate) and "nonconnected" or "ideological" PACs (with a 47 percent annual growth rate).[37] When we further note that the most rapidly growing PAC category, the ideological PAC (of which examples are the National Conservative Political Action Committee (NCPAC) and the Committee for the Survival of a Free Congress (CSFC)), is predominantly (by about a 2:1 ratio) composed of PACs which are "conservative" in outlook,[38] we may infer a definite rightward tilt in the direction of PAC political influence. Of course, it should not be surprising that the moneyed segments of a society would be conservative about policy directions in that society. After all, they have the positions and perquisities that are worth conserving.

We therefore have in the United States: (1) the rapidly increasing importance of PACs as a source of campaign funding; and (2) the steady relative expansion of the more conservative political position among active PACs. Add to those developments a significant third. PACs are increasingly directing their funding activity to incumbents. For example, in 1986, "PACs made record investments in House incumbents, giving a total of $65,514,435 to incumbents, compared with only $8,657,485 for their challengers.... The 6 to 1 ratio in PAC support for House incumbents over challengers represents by far the highest disparity in PAC giving for an election cycle since comprehensive data on federal campaign finance activity first became available in 1972."[39] The incumbents won 98 percent of those contested seats.[40]

Coincident with the expansion of PACs as a campaign finance force has been the related decline of political party structures and discipline. In the Democratic Party, this is, in part, was due to the "democratizing" reform of the 1970s. The net result of these financial, ideological, and institutional shifts has been the growing receptivity of elected officials of both parties to a more conservative political outlook. As analyst Jacobson noted,

> The shift to the right in national politics after the 1980 election was not simply a consequence of more Republicans in Congress (or the Republican in the White House).... Democrats did not, for the most part, vigorously resist the conservative tide; the electoral costs of doing so appeared to be high, the costs of not doing so, negligible. And one reason was clearly the current system of Congressional campaign finance.[41]

Or, confirmingly,

> Some Democratic office-holders have gone out of their way recently to support the new politics of capital formation and deregulation. Thus, another possible strategy might be to use campaign contributions as one way of winning and keeping friends of business in both parties. On the case of one member of the House whose conversion from a "labor Democrat" to a "business Democrat" was allegedly helped along by generous contributions from corporate PACs see Dennis Farney, "A Liberal Congressman Turns Conservative: Did PACs Do It?" *Wall Street Journal*, July 29, 1982, p. 1.[42]

Playing the same theme, Fred Siegel, writing in *Dissent*, calls this phenomenon "'Republicanizing' the Democrats" as he bemoans the "disaster" of the "growing dependence on business for campaign financing."[43]

And all of these political changes and policy influences have consequences in the real world of everyday life. Policy reflects and reinforces power. Journalist Thomas Edsall, remarking on the same trends we have been here examining, noted that:

> ...The cumulative impact of these changes in the political system... has been to contribute to an extraordinary alteration in economic policy, which produced, as a result of tax and budget legislation passed in 1981 and 1982, increased taxes and lost government benefits for every income group except for those making in excess of $75,000 a year. For a family earning over $200,000, the net gain over four years from this legislation has been about $17,000, largely in reduced taxes, while the marginal family making $8,000 to $13,500 a year—the working poor—had a net loss of just under $1,000 in lowered benefits and increased taxes over the same period.[44]

But perhaps even more important than any particular ideological tilt to any immediate distributional shift is the impact that such concentrated, motivated, and directed money has on the general operation of the political process. Political observer Elizabeth Drew has written:

The point is what RAISING money, not simply spending it does to the political process. It is not just that well-armed interests have a head start over the rest of the citizenry.... It is not just that citizens without organized economic power pay the bill for the successes of those with organized economic power. It is not even relevant which interests happen to be winning. What is relevant is what the whole thing is doing to the democratic process. What is at stake is the ideal of representative government, the soul of this country.[45]

The foregoing discussion of think tanks and PACs, idea development and electoral influence, explains in part some of the connections between economic power and the political process in the area of policy formulation—the development of the rules by which we each must live. But that is only one element of the power process. We now turn to the subsequent enforcement of those rules.

Public Policy Implementation

The preceding pages present the argument that there is ample reason to believe that economic power (read: "money") exerts significant influence on the formulation of public policy. That is not to say, with the Marxists, that public policy is solely a reflection of the interests of the bourgeoisie. The argument here is more complex and more subtle, and does allow for the probability of policy enactment which is noncongenial to the interests of economic power. But the political game does not stop at the point of policy formulation; it continues into the realm of policy implementation.

Our consideration now turns to precisely that process of carrying out, administering, executing the policies (rules) that flow from our legislative bodies. In a sense, all laws (enacted policy statements) are "regulations" because they regulate one or another entity's behavior; but we will here focus primarily on regulatory policies more narrowly considered. We discuss policies designed to "regulate" business behavior in a capitalist society, and we do that on the presumption that if economic power is to be effectively employed in any area, it could be expected to be most visibly utilized in those areas that directly involve the actions of the economically powerful (or the wealth possessors).

The central point to be made here is that the development of a policy to control, influence, guide, and direct business behavior "in the public interest" doesn't necessarily lead to the intended execution of that policy. In addition to the obvious human failings of ignorance, short-sightedness, misapprehension, and error, which may well flaw any private or public decision, we must also consider policy "subversion" by those effected, interested, and powerful enough to attempt such action. Again, "money talks" and we here consider its voices in those public offices where regulatory policies are to be implemented. Once again we emphasize the "political" aspect of such analysis, and bemoan the ritualistic economic assumption of the corporation as a massless point on an economic plane, responding to exogenous forces but exercising no power in its own right.[46]

Major regulatory efforts in the U.S. economy, whereby the general public via its elected representatives has seemed to gain some element of control over socially damaging economic activity, have occurred in two primary waves and have had two different focal points. The first regulatory push was nurtured by populist reactions to perceived abusive behavior by concentrated economic power, took place during the late nineteenth and early twentieth century, and is exemplified by creation of the Interstate Commerce Commission (1887), Federal Power Commission (1930), Federal Communications Commission (1934), and the Civil Aeronautics Board (1938).[47] These actions, and these regulatory bodies, were generally industry-specific and were directed toward "economic" regulation primarily focused on price, service, and rates-of-return.

The second regulatory wave was the era of "social regulation" of the 1970s. Cutting across industry lines, this regulatory effort, exemplified by the creation of the Environmental Protection Agency (1970), the Occupational Safety and Health Administration (1970), the Consumer Product Safety Commission (1972), and the National Traffic Safety Commission (1970),[48] was responding more to the deleterious consequences of an increasingly powerful and sophisticated technology on the quality of life of a population growing in numbers but not in command of the information base necessary to make enlightened citizen or consumer judgments. As it turns out, an impressive case can be made that even in cases where policies were formulated which appeared originally to work to the disadvantage of centers of wealth and power, the combination of economic, political, and social muscle possessed by the "regulatees" eventually bent policy implementation substantially in accord with their wishes.

The "economic" regulation referred to above has existed for a sufficient length of time to allow rather careful analysis of its consequences. Any simplistic conclusions must be misleading, and the overall pattern of regulatory performance is mixed.[49] But even a casual survey of the literature of regulation offers a preponderance of opinion that in the area of economic regulation, the regulated have sufficiently often "captured" the regulator so that what was intended in formulation has been subverted in implementation. Therefore, we find, from Grant McConnell:

The outstanding political fact about the independent regulatory commissions is that they have in general become promoters and protectors of the industries they have been established to regulate.[50]

And, further, from George Stigler,

...regulation is acquired by the industry and is designed and operated primarily for its benefit.[51]

Or finally, from Walter Adams and James Brock,

...the symbiotic identification of the board with the carrier tainted the regulatory process, and eventually led to the capture of the process by those who were to be subject to it. In the end, the trunk-line carriers were allowed to operate a cartel created, sanctioned, and protected by the government.[52]

The reasons for such "capture" or eventual conformity of viewpoints are complex and not necessarily based on venality. Economic power (wealth) is a resource; resources have functional utility (instrumental value); and one of the functions of resources in the hands of those subject to regulation is to provide "their side of the story" to the regulator. The multiple avenues of opportunities for the impact of economic power on the administration of regulatory policies are well captured by Henry L. Bretton:

Because it can open doors closed to the general public, penetrate walls of secrecy, remove obstacles to action endemic to administration and expedite otherwise protracted proceedings, alter official set priorities, even cause "iron laws" of administration to be suspended or at least bent, monetary pressure can do wonders; and it need not be corrupt. At work here are essentially the same stimuli as when money works on Congress or other legislative bodies.... Not inconsequential in this connection is money's capacity to overpower administrative resistance with the aid of superior background information, secured through liberal dispensation of funds accumulated for such purposes. Money can also out-perform any other manifestation of "the public interest" in the number of contacts it can make with key administrators, the number of witnesses it can mobilize, transport, and deploy in strategic places at critical moments. It can also, with the aid of private investigative agencies if necessary, accomplish its objectives by ferreting out any weaknesses and vulnerabilities in any office or in any bureaucrat. It is for these or similar reasons, that outside interests increasingly perform as partners of public administration in the drafting of policy proposals, or recommendations for legislative action, and of government regulations or interpretation of regulations.[53]

Therefore, as in the cases of think tanks and PACs discussed earlier, economic power allows actions to be taken, channels to be used, ideas to be marshalled, pressure to be exerted on behalf of the economically powerful, which are not available to the economically powerless. It must therefore be expected, and is surely not remarkable, that the ways in which the administrative branch of government executes its responsibilities will necessarily reflect those unequal influences. "One person, one vote" becomes an unconvincing guarantee of democratic processes. To return to the work of political scientist Grant McConnell, in a discussion of the "independence" of independent regulatory commissions,

> The judicial model was influential, but freedom from "politics" was also an important motivation. Unfortunately, what was achieved was not freedom from all politics, but freedom only from party and popular politics. The politics of industry and administration remained....
>
> Thus it is incorrect to charge that the commissions have been irresponsible. They quite obviously have been responsible—indeed, particularly responsive—to the industries with which they have been associated.[54]

And to sharpen the point a bit, Justin Dart, member of President Reagan's "kitchen cabinet," noted that "talking to politicians is 'a fine thing, but with a little money they hear you better.'"[55]

The matter under discussion is, however, not merely an issue of the judicious application of economic resources in the pursuit of a desired policy objective. Policies are implemented (or not) by people, and influence over personnel decisions is one more arena of activism for the economically powerful. Possessors of economic power have the ability to influence the selection of those who will be responsible for policy implementation. And, again, the notion of a government of laws, not of "men," is less than a full description of political-economic reality. Of course it makes a difference whether a Department of the Interior is headed by a Stewart Udall or a James Watt; whether the Federal Trade Commission is directed by a Michael Pertschuk or a James Miller; and whether the Environmental Protection Agency is headed by a William Ruckelshaus or an Anne Gorsuch. As a former CAB chairman noted, "...the philosophy of the Civil Aeronautics Board changes from day to day. It depends who is on the Board as to what the philosophy is."[56]

Given the speculation, fear, hope, and apprehension that publicly surrounds the appointment of new members to the Federal Reserve Board, or the Securities and Exchange Commission, or the Federal Trade Commission, we can hardly quarrel with the notion that the issue of "who" affects the determination of "what." The important point is that the question of "who" is not divorced from matters of economic power and influence.[57]

To the current generation of social scientists and informed citizens, the fate of the "independent regulatory commissions" may be only a dim historical memory; but we have seen a contemporary replication of the interplay between economic power and regulatory activity during the first 15 years of "social" regulation. It is a repetitious history. In their 1986 work, *The Bigness Complex*, Walter Adams and James Brock capture the point with cogent brevity. "In short, just as bigness can mobilize its power to obtain protection against competition, so too can it wield power to subvert social regulation."[58] The possessors of economic resources are able to threaten, cajole, lobby, mislead, marshall public opinion, and simply "persuade" in ways not available to the not-so-powerful. And often the interests opposed to effective implementation of the regulatory mandate are of sufficient economic size or political importance that persistence or resistance on the part of the regulator is reckless or futile. Claims of "national interest" or "competitive disadvantage" are effective in dealing with an economically insecure society. Strategies that Adams and Brock describe as useful in fighting air bags as a component of auto safety are also useful in matters of gasoline mileage requirements, or bumper crash resistance, or toxic waste, or water quality, or acid rain, or stack emissions, or workplace safety.[59]

As this chapter was being drafted, front page newspaper stories were dealing with mine-owner influence over regulatory processes in the area of coal mine safety. In a piece of investigative reporting concerning the demotion of an overly effective investigative squad employed by the Mine Safety and Health Administration (MSHA), *Wall Street Journal* reporter Bryan Burrough referred to the alleged "Burger King approach toward regulation: allowing coal companies to 'have it their way'."[60] In this mine-safety episode, the central role of a MSHA head who had previously been a Kentucky coal operator was symbolic of the relationships and influences possible in the symbiotic atmosphere of overlapping realms of economic and political power.[61]

Discussion of social regulation and economic power provides an opportunity to illustrate the linkages and interconnections between various influential tools available to the economically powerful. Consider first a specific regulatory venture, the Superfund program, and then the broader issue of regulation in general. The Superfund was created by Congress in 1980 to facilitate the cleanup of particularly nasty hazardous waste dumps. It was financed primarily by levies on the chemical industry, and was both economically and politically unpopular with some of the more economically powerful chemical and mining interests.

In this chapter we have discussed the use of economic power to influence both policy formulation and implementation. In the case of the Superfund, for example, Elizabeth Drew has noted,

The champion PAC-money raiser in 1980 was Charles Grassley, Republican of Iowa, who raised more than seven hundred thousand dollars from PACs in his successful effort to defeat the incumbent senator, John Culver.... A great deal of Grassley's money came from oil interests and chemical interests, after Culver had guided through Congress a bill requiring these companies to contribute to a "superfund" to clean up toxic-waste sites.[62]

Thus we have an example of political financing as a disciplinary device in the area of policy formulation.

But, unfortunately for the industry, the Superfund was in place. Therefore, attention turned to implementation. Influence over appointment of a long-time Colorado opponent of the EPA, Anne Gorsuch, to head that agency, and the subsequent appointment of former Cordova Chemical "public relations flash"[63] Rita Lavelle to administer the Superfund seemed effectively to subvert an uncongenial policy. Although both Ms. Gorsuch and Ms. Lavelle came to unhappy ends in their administrative roles, the ability of economic power to move in multiple arenas is illustrated in this depressing example.

On a broader scale, Thomas Edsall provides a similar look at a double-barreled exercise of economic power on public policy. In discussion of activities that fall into our category of policy "formulation," Edsall notes the origin and activity of the Center for the Study of the American Business System headed by Murray Weidenbaum at Washington University of St. Louis. This relatively modest think tank, founded in 1975 with major support from the John M. Olin Foundation and James B. McDonnell (of McDonnell-Douglas Corporation),[64] contributed to the intellectual climate of opinion in which policy is formulated with a "sustained critique of government regulation."[64]

Weidenbaum's staggering estimates of the economic cost of accumulated government regulations over business, although treated skeptically by many, were congruent with the Reagan Administration's ideological posture and were brought to the top of the government's economic agenda when Professor Weidenbaum was named chairman of the Council of Economic Advisers.

Thus, in the establishment of the Weidenbaum think tank, economic power initially bought ideas. But through the power of political appointment it also reached well into the realm of policy implementation. Edsall credits Weidenbaum with providing

...justification for one of the major policy initiatives of the Reagan administration—that is, the across-the-board drive to reduce the scope and content of the

Federal regulation of industry, the environment, the workplace, health care, and the relationship between buyer and seller. The Reagan administration's drive toward deregulation was accomplished through sharp budget cuts reducing enforcement capabilities; through the appointment of anti-regulation, industry-oriented agency personnel; and, finally, through the empowering of the Office of Management and Budget with unprecedented authority to delay major regulations, to force major revisions in regulatory proposals, and, through prolonged cost-benefit analyses, to effectively kill a wide range of regulatory initiatives.[66]

Although our attention has been focused on the influence of economic power on the implementation of social and economic regulatory policies, we should not totally limit our discussion of policy implementation to the regulatory area. Government implements, administers, executes many other policy directives, and those also are subject to the influence of economic power.

Will a few rhetorical questions suffice? Do defense contractors play a role in decisions concerning the implementation of defense appropriation measures? Adams and Brock remind us that

> ...In the Reagan administration, for example, Boeing has provided the assistant secretary of the navy for research systems and analysis, the deputy undersecretary for strategic theater nuclear forces, the deputy director of the Defense Department's Office of Intelligence and Space Policy, the assistant secretary of defense for international security policy, the associate director of presidential personnel in the national security field, and the deputy head of the president's transition team for the Department of Defense.[67]

Do representatives of the nuclear energy industry influence decisions on licensing, supervising, and regulating construction of nuclear power facilities? Adams and Brock cite a case of a two-unit nuclear power plant, approved in 1967 for construction by Consumer Power Company at an estimated total cost of $256 million. After numerous delays, investigations, overruns, 2nd revisions, finally, in 1984, the project was scrapped, without completion, after the expenditure of $4.1 billion.[68]

Does the steel industry influence the implementation of "Voluntary Restraint Agreements" or "Trigger Price Mechanisms" in the import of steel? Does the automobile industry have an input into the implementation of "voluntary" export quotas for foreign automobiles?

Or is it more surprising to realize that an educated professional segment of the Academy, economists, in their predominant pronouncements and pedagogical tracts, exhibit either disinterest or ignorance that "money makes the world go 'round'"?

Policy Interpretation

As promised earlier in this chapter, discussion of the impact of economic power will be extended beyond its role in policy formulation (legislation) and policy implementation (administration) to complete the triumvirate by considering policy interpretation (adjudication). The focus of this consideration will be the contemporary "law and economics" movement among legal scholars and practitioners.

Current surveys of the realm of law and economics correctly emphasize the considerable range of scholarship and practice that is placed under that rhetorical umbrella.[69] For example, Mercuro and Ryan assert that the rubric covers conventional antitrust and regulatory analyses (discussed in the previous section), "property rights" economics, public choice theorizing, neoinstitutionalism, and critical legal studies, in addition to our main concern in the remaining paragraphs of this chapter, the "new" law and economics.[70] In fact, as John R. Commons realized decades ago, all economics, properly understood, is "law and economics."[71] Or, in Warren Samuels's terms, "the economy is a system of power, of mutual coercion, of reciprocal capacity to receive income and/or to shift injury—whose pattern or structure and consequences are at least partially a function of law."[72] All allocation and distribution activities take place within a social context, whose parameters are determined by law. As thoughtful writers in this area are careful to note, even the absence of a specific legal statement confers, or permits, rights just as surely as the presence of a specific legal statement may transfer them.

In our economy, understood as a web of rights, tacit and formal, which govern and determine the final distribution of goods and income, the ideas by which those rights are legitimated are all-important. Therefore we turn now to consideration of the ascendant new law and economics movement of the Coase/Posner variety. (Ronald Coase, economist, provided the specific economic grounding for the dominant contemporary law and economics perspective with a 1960 article, "The Problem of Social Cost"[73]; Richard Posner, jurist, contributed the fundamental legal analysis in his 1972 work, *Economic Analysis of Law*.[74]

Before we specifically consider the Coase/Posner positions (which, together with other contributions from that school shall henceforth be our reference for the term *law and economics*), let us further reflect upon the role of law in our society. We can perhaps imagine a rather primitive, "lawless" society in which we may assume "might makes right." Presumably we there refer to physical might. Or, imagine a more sophisticated "free market" society, which is surely not "lawless" for it is law that protects and preserves the system of property and contract necessary for a market to function. In this free market, "money makes right." That is, decisions follow the dictates of effective demand. Where law, or the state, actively intervenes to modify free market decisions (to re-shuffle rights), presumably it does so in respect of some valuative norm other than money or effective demand. Such norms might be rooted in equity, nationalism, religion, or in the recognition of market failures due to externalities, etc. In other words, legal intervention to change unalloyed market outcomes is the result of a considered social judgment concerning value preferences.

As conventionally understood and interpreted, the Coase/Posner school would reduce the domain of countermarket intervention and expand the domain of market, or market-like outcomes. Coase's agrument (Coase's "theorem") is that "in a competitive economy with zero transaction costs and perfect information, the allocation of resources will be efficient however the law distributes original entitlements."[75] This outcome occurs as a result of motivations for compensation payments to guide resources "to productive uses that maximizes the aggregate market value of the two parties' joint product."[76]

In lay terms, the idea is that, under appropriate assumptions, regardless of legal determination of rights, if free exchange is possible individuals will arrange trades and compensation among themselves which ultimately mimic the allocative decisions of a free market.

Posner's contribution is to take the next step and to affirm the Coase "efficiency principle" as a standard for judicial action. Obviously Coase's assumptions of zero transaction costs and perfect information seldom hold, and automatic allocative efficiency is not assured. Judge Posner

> ...has advanced the following rule to guide the law in promoting efficient resource use in the absence of efficient market exchanges: "Assign the relevant entitlement to that party who would have pruchased it in an exchange market in which the conditions of the Coase Theorem were satisfied."
>
> The idea is simple enough. Economic analysis relies on competitive market models of efficiency. When efficient outcomes cannot be obtained and the law must intervene, entitlements are to be conferred to produce the result an efficient market would have. In an efficient market, the relevant right would eventually have worked its way to the party who would have paid the most for it. The general principle, then, is to assign entitlements by simulating or mimicking the market....
>
> Posner's intention is to translate into law so far as possible the implications of the Coase Theorem.[77]

Such analysis provides the basis for the legal institutions which permit the sale of pollution rights and marketing of airport landing privileges, but are additionally extended to matters of child custody, organ transplantation, and other realms of human activity often thought to be beyond the reach of utilitarian economics.

Although an abundant, complex, and contentious literature has grown up around this law and economics movement, we confine our discussion here to two aspects of the phenomenon.

The first observation is, as must be apparent from the previous few paragraphs, the thrust of the Coase/Posner doctrine is to use the law to reinforce market power, rather than to counterbalance or counteract it. Quite baldly stated, as in the following comment by Judge Robert Bork, a Posner disciple, on the issue of government regulation of corporate size:

> The difficulty with stopping a trend toward a more concentrated condition at a very early stage is that the existence of the trend is prima facie evidence that greater concentration is socially desirable. The trend indicates that there are emerging efficiencies or economies of scale—whether due to engineering and production developments or to new control and management techniques—which make larger size more efficient. This increased efficiency is valuable to the society at large, for it means that fewer of our available resources are being used to accomplish the same amount of production and distribution. By striking at such trends in their very earliest stages the concept of incipiency prevents the realization of those very efficiencies that competition is supposed to encourage.[78]

At this writing, Judge Bork is a nominee to the Supreme Court who, if confirmed, will explicitly take this market power bias to the nation's highest tribunal.

The presumption that what is, is right (efficient, optimal) strips a patina of civilization from community life, narrows the moral vision of a society to the criterion of "efficiency" or "wealth maximization," and too often accompanies that ethical judgment with a disclaimer that any normative judgment at all is being made. But, of course, "An efficiency appraisal of the law must presuppose an initial assignment of entitlements that reflects some conception of distributive justice."[79] The market is an arena for the exercise of power, and success in the market is highly correlated with one's initial power position. "Pareto-optimum as a decision rule thus becomes an instrument of power play, of mutual coercion, allowing the perpetuation of privilege."[80]

An elegant and succinct summation of this concern is offered as follows:

> No one who has read Professor Posner's elaborate and refined work and the large literature which has grown out of it, designed to establish these utilitarian

underpinnings of the law, could fail to profit. This is not, I think, because it succeeds in its ostensible purpose, but because its detailed ingenuity admirably forces one to think what else is needed besides a theory of utility for a satisfactory, explanatory, and critical theory of legal decisions. It becomes clear that in general what is needed is a theory of individual moral rights and their relationship to other values pursued through law, a theory of far greater comprehensiveness and detailed articulation than any so far provided.[81]

On the other hand, if one assumes that markets are efficient allocators and distributors of resources and income, one need not be concerned that the attendant power is unequally distributed. Such inequality is reward for productive contribution by the more-favored and is motivation to further effort and productivity on the part of the less-favored. The market itself, in this view, is an appropriate arbiter of moral rights.

Whatever the "objective" merit of the law and economics movement, it is clearly a direction of judicial thought which must appeal to the self-interest of the possessors of economic power. The use of law to reinforce their position rather than to counterbalance it in pursuit of other societal values must be an appealing attraction. And as we have argued earlier in this chapter that those with economic power have disproportionate political power (to influence judicial appointments, for example) one can understand the purportedly bright futures of judges such as Posner and Bork. To put a softer point on it, "The actions of government influence the distributions of wealth and income, and the distribution of wealth and income influence the actions of government."[82]

Finally, to make a second significant point about the contemporary law and economics movement, this legal theory confirmatory of market power is having a major impact in American legal thought and in legal education. One legal scholar describes law and economics as "...the most important thing that has happened in legal thought since the New Deal" and "the most important thing in legal education since the birth of Harvard Law School."[83] Its influence is growing in cases with economic context (such as antitrust, trade restrictions, corporate liability, securities fraud) consistently opposing government intervention in what are argued to be various manifestations of efficient marketing. Economic analysis is being extended even to traditionally noneconomic judgments such as the right to free counsel in civil rights suits or legalized baby sales. Judge Posner argues that failure to obtain counsel on a contingency basis leads to a "natural inference...that he doesn't have a good case," and that parents who value a child the most will pay the top price and "are likely to give it the best care."[84] Therefore we see the widening and increased utilization of yet one more avenue for the exercise of economic power on public policy.

Conclusion

This chapter provides a lengthy and somewhat fragmented assemblage of argument and evidence bearing on the issue of the relationship between economic power and the political process. It asserts that such influence is significant and is embedded in areas of policy formulation (through cultural influence, purposeful social research, and political campaign financing), policy implementation (via staffing, pressuring, persuading, or undermining regulatory processes), and policy interpretation (with the assistance of creative market-enhancing legal theories). As we draw this analysis to a conclusion, perhaps the major surprise is that the subject matter or the direction of argument of this chapter should be much in doubt. One can hardly deny the utility of money (certainly economists never have); why should that utility be overlooked, unrecognized, or unused in the political arena?

C. Wright Mills insightfully and presciently analyzed American society a generation ago.

> Within American society, major national power now resides in the economic, the political, and the military domains. Other institutions seem off to the side of modern history, and, on occasion, duly subordinated to these. No family is as directly powerful in national affairs as any major corporation; no church is as directly powerful in the external biographies of young men in America today as the military establishment; no college is as powerful as the National Security Council. Religious, educational, and family institutions are not autonomous centers of national power; on the contrary, these decentralized areas are increasingly shaped by the big three, in which developments of decisive and immediate consequence now occur.
>
> Families and churches and schools adapt to modern life; governments and armies and corporations shape it; and, as they do so, they turn these lesser institutions into means for their ends.[84]

And Warren Samuels gives us our final admonition. "The structure of social power is what counts, and not individual choice in a power vacuum."[86] Would that more economists could learn that truth.

Notes

1. John Kenneth Galbraith, *The Anatomy of Power* (Boston: Houghton Mifflin Company, 1983), pp. 113–114.
2. C. Wright Mills, *The Power Elite* (New York: Oxford University Press, 1956), p. 108.

3. Randall Bartlett, *Economic Foundations of Political Power* (New York: The Free Press, 1973), p. 156.
4. Galbraith, *Anatomy...*, p. 5.
5. *Ibid.*, p. 6.
6. Nicholas Mercuro, "Contributions to Law and Economics: A Survey of Recent Books," *The Journal of Economic Education*, Vol. 17, No. 4, Fall, 1986, p. 297.
7. Warren J. Samuels, "Welfare Economics, Power, and Property," in Warren J. Samuels and A. Allan Schmid (Eds.), *Law and Economics: An Institutional Perspective* (Boston: Martinus Nijhoff Publishing, 1981), p. 44.
8. *The Wall Street Journal*, April 28, 1987, p. 4.
9. B. F. Skinner, *Beyond Freedom and Dignity* (New York: Alfred A. Knopf, 1971), p. 215.
10. Mills, *The Power Elite*, pp. 346–347.
11. Elizabeth Drew, *Politics and Money* (New York: Macmillan, 1983), p. 146.
12. Sidney Blumenthal, *The Rise of the Counter-Establishment* (New York: Times Books, 1986), p. 32.
13. William J. Lanouette, "The 'Shadow Cabinets'—Changing Themselves as They Try to Change Policy," *National Journal*, Vol. 10, Feb. 25, 1978, p. 296.
14. Dom Bonafede, "Issue-Oriented Heritage Foundation Hitches Its Wagon To Reagan's Star," *National Journal*, Vol. 14, March 20, 1982, p. 507.
15. The Heritage Foundation, *1986 Annual Report*, p. 2.
16. Robert K. Landers, "Think Tanks: The New Partisans?" *Editorial Research Reports*, Vol. 1, No. 23, June 20, 1986, p. 467.
17. Bonafede, "Issue-Oriented...," p. 502.
18. *Ibid.*, p. 504.
19. *Ibid.*
20. Micheal R. Gordon, "Right-of-Center Defense Groups—The Pendulum has Swung Their Way," *National Journal*, Vol. 13, No. 4, January 24, 1981, p. 129.
21. Blumenthal, *...Counter-Establishment*, p. 48.
22. *Ibid.*, pp. 306–308.
23. *Ibid.*, pp. 49–50.
24. A useful discussion of the growth and influence of conservative think tanks is contained in Thomas Byrne Edsall, *The New Politics of Inequality* (New York: W. W. Norton & Co., 1984), pp. 117–120.
25. Blumenthal, *...Counter-Establishment*, pp. 48–50.
26. Gary C. Jacobson, "Money in the 1980 and 1982 Congressional Elections," in Michael J. Malbin (Ed.), *Money and Politics in the United States* (Chatham, NJ: Chatham House Publishers, Inc., 1984), p. 65.
27. *Ibid.*
28. Michael Malbin, "Introduction," in Malbin (Ed.), *Money...*, pp. 7–9.
29. Marc Leepson, "Campaign Finance Debate," *Editorial Research Reports*, Vol. 1, No. 12, March 29, 1985, p. 235.
30. The Federal Election Commission, Common Cause, and The Congressional Quarterly Press are prolific sources of information on the role of PAC's in campaign finance. Other campaign "watchdogs" such as the Public Affairs Council, Citizens' Research Foundation, and the League of Women Voters have also sponsored and published helpful PAC information.
31. Leepson, "Campaign Finance Debate," p. 239, and Federal Election Commission, *Record*, February, 1987, p. 10.
32. Michael J. Malbin and Thomas W. Skladony, "Appendix: Selected Campaign Finance

Data," in Malbin, *Money...*, p. 296.

33. Data for 1986 PAC expenditures on Congressional races come from Common Cause. The PAC expenditure on House races in 1986 was $84.6 million (April 7, 1987, press release), and on Senate races was $45.7 million (February 13, 1987, press release).

34. Jacobson, "Money...," p. 39.

35. Common Cause, April 7, 1987, press release.

36. *Ibid.*

37. Margaret Ann Latus, "Assessing Ideological PACs: From Outrage to Understanding," in Malbin, *Money...*, p. 143.

38. *Ibid.*

39. Common Cause, April 7, 1987, press release.

40. *Ibid.*

41. Jacobon, "Money...," p. 45.

42. Theodore J. Eismeier and Philip H. Pollock III, "Politics and Markets: Corporate Money in American National Elections," *British Journal of Political Science*, Vol. 16, June, 1986, p. 292 (footnote 18).

43. Fred Seigel, "'Republicanizing' the Democrats," *Dissent*, Summer, 1985, p. 301.

44. Thomas Byrne Edsall, *The New Politics of Inequality* (New York: W.W. Norton & Co., 1984), pp. 21–22.

45. Drew, *Politics...*, p. 5.

46. This point is made cogently in Grant McConnell, *Private Power and American Democracy* (New York: Alfred A. Knopf, 1967), pp. 129–130.

47. Campbell R. McConnell, *Economics*, 10th ed. (New York: McGraw-Hill, 1986), p. 710.

48. Edsall, *The New Politics...*, p. 113.

49. James Q. Wilson (Ed.), *The Politics of Regulation* (New York: Basic Books, Inc., 1980) offers a set of analytical papers on a variety of regulatory activities. Wilson's summary chapter offers a "balanced" appraisal of the regulatory effort.

50. G. McConnell, *Private Power...*, p. 287.

51. George Stigler, "The Theory of Economic Regulation," *Bell Journal of Economics and Management Science*, Vol. 2, Spring, 1971, p. 3, as quoted in Wilson, *Politics...*, p. 358.

52. Walter Adams and James W. Brock, *The Bigness Complex* (New York: Pantheon Books, 1986), p. 228.

53. Henry L. Bretton, *The Power of Money* (Albany: State University of New York Press, 1980), p. 323.

54. G. McConnell, *Private Power...*, p. 289.

55. Quoted in Michael Pertschuk, *Revolt Against Regulation: The Rise and Pause of the Consumer Movement* (Berkeley: University of California Press, 1982), p. 60. (Pertschuk cites Thomas Edsall, "Business Learns to Play New Politics," *Baltimore Sun*, February 25, 1980, p. A7, as his source.)

56. Henry J. Friendly, *The Federal Administrative Agencies* (Cambridge, MA: Harvard University Press, 1962), p. 97, as quoted in G. McConnell, *Private Power...*, p. 286.

57. See, for example, discussion of political influence in the selection of Anne Gorsuch as administrator of the Environmental Protection Agency, in Jonathan Lash, et al., *A Season of Spoils; The Reagan Administration's Attack on the Environment* (New York: Pantheon Books, 1984), pp. 9–14.

58. Adams and Brock, *The Bigness Complex*, p. 260.

59. Discussion of subversion of environmental regulations, for example, can be found in Lash, et al., *Season of Spoils...*, and in Friends of the Earth, *Ronald Reagan and the Ameri-*

can Environment (San Francisco: Friends of the Earth, 1982).

60. Bryan Burrough, "Mine-Safety Agency Disbands Sleuth Squad Despite Its Big Success," *The Wall Street Journal*, June 1, 1987, pp. 1 and 10.
61. *Ibid.*, p. 1.
62. Drew, *Politics and Money*, p. 21.
63. Lash, *Season of Spoils*, p. 42.
64. Edsall, *The New Politics...*, p. 119.
65. *Ibid.*, p. 216.
66. *Ibid.*, p. 217.
67. Adams and Brock, *The Bigness Complex*, p. 339.
68. *Ibid.*, pp. 274–275.
69. One such helpful survey is Nicholas Mercuro and Timothy P. Ryan, *Law, Economics and Public Policy* (Greenwich, CT: JAI Press, Inc., 1984).
70. *Ibid.*, p. IX.
71. Certainly that is one inference one may draw from John R. Commons, *The Legal Foundations of Capitalism* (New York: Macmillan, 1924).
72. Warren J. Samuels, "Interrelations Between Legal and Economic Processes" in Samuels and Schmid (Eds.), *Law and Economics...*, p. 100.
73. R. H. Coase, "The Problem of Social Cost," *The Journal of Law and Economics*, Vol. 3, October, 1960, pp. 1–44.
74. Richard A. Posner, *Economic Analysis of Law* (Boston: Little, Brown and Co., 1972).
75. Mark Kuperberg and Charles Beitz (Eds.), *Law, Economics, and Philosophy: A Critical Introduction, with Applications to the Law of Torts* (Totowa, NJ: Rowman & Allanheld, 1983), p. 5.
76. *Ibid.*, p. 6.
77. Jules L. Coleman, "The Economic Analysis of Law," in J. Roland Pennock and John W. Chapman (Eds.), *Ethics, Economics, and the Law* (New York: New York University Press, 1982), pp. 96–97.
78. Robert H. Bork, *The Antitrust Paradox* (New York: Basic Books, 1978), pp. 206–206, as quoted in Adams and Brock, *The Bigness Complex*, pp. 158–159.
79. Paul Burrows and Cento G. Veljanovski (Eds.), *The Economic Approach to Law* (London: Butterworth, 1981), p. 134, as quoted in Nicholas Mercuro, "Contributions...," p. 304.
80. Warren J. Samuels, "Welfare Economics...," p. 30.
81. H. L. A. Hart, "American Jurisprudence Through English Eyes: The Nightmare and the Noble Dream," *Georgia Law Review*, Vol. 11, 1977, pp. 988–989, as quoted in E. J. P. Mackaay, *Economics of Information and Law* (Montreal: Groupe de Recherche en Consommation, 1980), pp. 94–95.
82. Bartlett, *Economic Foundations...*, p. 196.
83. Professor Bruce A. Ackerman, as quoted in Paul M. Barrett, "A Movement Called Law and Economics Sways Legal Circles," *The Wall Street Journal*, August 4, 1986, p. 1.
84. *Ibid.*, pp. 1 and 14.
85. Mills, *The Power Elite*, p. 6.
86. Samuels, "Welfare Economics...," p. 34.

7 CONCLUDING OBSERVATIONS
Wallace C. Peterson

This final chapter has three objectives. First, it will summarize the major findings and conclusions about power and the economy that emerge from the other essays in the book. Second, it will examine some of the key ways in which market power affects the economy's macroeconomic performance. In general, the ideas and themes contained in the other chapters point toward the firm and the industry, not the economy overall. Thus, it is appropriate to include some comments directed toward the macroeconomic aspects of power. Finally, thoughts are in order with respect to economic theory and market power. As noted in the preface, the neglect of power by mainstream economic theory at both the micro and macro level is a major deficiency of contemporary economics. What can be done about this? To conclude this book, some modest suggestions are offered as to what must be done.

Some General Conclusions

The other chapters in this book are rich with insights and observations about power and its role in contemporary market capitalism. From this richness and from, too, the diversity of approaches to the topic, it is possible to winnow out a number of broad generalizations that inform us about important aspects of economic power, its nature, and where it fits into the economic scheme of things. These get to the heart of the matter and are essential not only to an understanding of power and what it does but also for development of an adequate theoretical frame of reference into which the fact of power can be fitted.

One cannot come away from reading these chapters without an appreciation and understanding of the fact that in our economic, social, and political life, power is a multidimensional phenomenon. Professor Peterson brings this point forcefully home in his opening essay. This, of course, makes both its analysis and incorporation into the theoretical structures of economics an exceedingly difficult task. But in the final analysis, the aspect of power that counts most from the perspective of economics is the ability of people and organizations to have a direct impact upon prices and incomes. If Galbraith is right—and I believe that he is—a dominant characteristic of our age is the thrust of people toward getting control over their lives. In economics, this involves control over one's income, escaping, Galbraith aptly phrases it, from "the tyranny of the market." Economists in the pristine purity of the classroom may extoll the wonders and discipline of the market, but in the rough and tumble of real life no person nor economic organization submits willingly or happily to such discipline. In a variety of ways, the chapters in this book describe and document the major means by which escape from the "tyranny of the market" is accomplished in the modern world. Ultimately, however, these come down to organization and resort to the power of the state!

As respects organization, the discussion and evidence marshalled in John Munkir's essay leaves no doubt that in the private sector, the large, multiproduct, multidimensional corporation has become the dominant—overwhelmingly dominant—economic institution of our time. No other private organization of any nature can match the raw economic power now concentrated in the contemporary corporation. Some years back, one might have argued that the trade union offered significant countervailing force to corporate power. No longer. Across the globe trade unions are on the defensive, their power in decline. In the United States, the Reagan Administration from its beginning moved aggressively to curb the power of the trade unions and to enhance the power of the corporations.

Not only has the private corporation become the dominant economic organization in society but the extent to which economic power is lodged in this institution is steadily increasing. This is the clear message that emerges from Douglas Greer's painstaking research and careful analysis of corporate

CONCLUDING OBSERVATIONS   159

concentration. No matter how concentration is measured—he demonstrates a variety of ways to measure this phenomenon—the evidence is that concentration is on the rise in the American economy. A little understood development that has helped to intensify this trend is an organizational-technological "revolution" within the modern corporation. This is a central point in Professor Dugger's chapter. The essence of this "revolution" is the emergence of the "modular" organizational structure, a development which permits practically unlimited growth in corporate size. As Dugger says, this development means that the "technological frontier has moved from physical production to social control." The economic and social impact of this change is enormous. Out of this has come the "imperial conglomerate," the multifaceted global corporation, largely free from any effective social control by the market, more powerful, perhaps, than all but a handful of modern nation-states. This is a development that Veblen would readily understand, for the real function of this entity is to produce money, not commodities. Production of commodities has become essentially a sideshow, necessary no doubt, but subordinate nevertheless to the larger goal of the accumulation and allocation of financial capital. A skilled cadre of supranational managers and technicians, a new breed, the "MBA priesthood," staff the imperial conglomerate.

From the perspective of the contemporary supranational economy, what these developments mean is an erosion of the power of the individual national state to manage its own economy. There is a sense of "disenfranchisement," of "national powerlessness" before the behemoth that is the integrated world economy. This is a part of John Willoughby's thesis. The other part is that it is not, as standard economics maintains, the normal and impersonal between interplay stocks and flows involving the domestic and the international economy that gives rise to the feeling of "powerlessness." This interplay does not take place in a vacuum, the perspective of mainstream theory; rather, the stock-flow interplay is centered in and filtered through new institutional arrangements of enormous power. These are the supranational corporation and the vast, stateless pool of international liquidity we call "Eurodollars." What was once the "tail" of international money and capital flows now wags the "dog" of trade and goods movements. The ultimate issue is whether the major Western powers, acting in concert, can do what is now beyond the capability of any one acting alone, namely tame the free-wheeling power at loose in the supranational economy so that it is harnessed to the well-being of the world's citizens. It is a formidable challenge.

Stretching above and around all these developments like a great arch or dome is the "marriage" of politics and economics. Mobilizing the power of the state to bend market forces in one's favor is the other major means for escape from the "tyranny of the market." How this is done and how pervasively the economic power centered on the megacorporation has spread through and dominated our political system is explained in depth in Professor Petr's chapter. Unlike the unreal models of conventional theory in which power does not exist, Petr understands that one cannot, in reality, separate economic power and the political process. His essay is an important contribution to restoring life and vitality to economics as "political economy." Rather than allowing it to continue as a discipline that is increasingly empty of empirical content—one characterized by an excessive but all too often sterile preoccupation with mathematics—economists must not lose sight of the fact that most, if not all, of our major propositions can be clearly and simply stated in English. They also can be clothed with numbers readily understood by most citizens. Then with wisdom and imagination economics skills can be brought to bear on the real problems of the real economy.

Power and Macroeconomic Performance

Let us now turn to the matter of how power as defined and analyzed in the prior chapters affects economic performance in the aggregate. Most of the thrust to this point has centered on the microeconomic aspects of market power, but the phenomenon has significant implications for macroeconomics as well. It is to these that we turn.

It is an interesting—although not necessarily a highly important—fact that Keynes had little awareness nor any serious interest in the matter of market power. He was, as is well known, extremely knowledgeable and sophisticated with respect to how a system of mature market capitalism worked with respect to such critical matters as production, jobs, and the price level, but his insights did not extend to the role played by power at the aggregate level of performance. As for as the microeconomic issues of resource allocation and income distribution, Keynes did not question seriously a classical analysis which had no place for the phenomenon of power.

But this won't do. The structure of macroeconomic analysis remains incomplete, unless the fact of economic power is incorporated into that structure. The question is how is this to be done? Macroeconomics, we must not forget, focuses on jobs, output, the price level, and growth. Thus, what counts is the impact that power and its exercise have on these key variables. What is needed is an analysis of how power enters into the process by which output and employment are determined. In working toward this goal we should keep in the forefront of our thinking that, as Galbraith has said, the primary means for escaping from the market and gaining control of price and income is organization and action through the state. With this as backdrop, let us turn to the matter at hand.

There are, in my judgment, two major points of entry for power into macroeconomic performance. They are, first, the price level and, second, the distribution of income and wealth. Let us consider each of these in turn.

In his much neglected chapter 21 ("The Theory of Prices"), Keynes in *The General Theory* pointed up a basic dichotomy in the classical analysis. This centered on their explanation of individual prices by the forces of market demand and supply, but when it came to explaining the general level of prices in "Chapter two" they ignored these "homely" but useful concepts, turning in an altogether different direction. They turned to the money supply and the quantity theory of money to explain the price level. This, however, is a false dichotomy, Keynes said. The proper division is between individual industry and the economy as a whole, and, as he argued in chapter 21, prices can be explained at both levels (micro and macro) by the same forces—namely, demand, supply, and cost. Unfortunately, Keynes did not go beyond this point, being content with the usual classical or neoclassical interpretation of how market forces work at the firm and industry level to determine both price and output. The viewpoint that Keynes implicitly accepts at this point is that the economy is highly competitive—there is no hint that the outcome might be affected by power.

Thus, Keynes set theory with respect to the determination of the price level on the right tract, but his analysis remains incomplete. Power must be brought into the picture if we are to have the complete story of how prices in general are determined. To put this somewhat differently, Keynes saw inflation (or deflation) as resulting from the interplay of demand (both individual and aggregate) and neoclassical supply considerations, the latter being influenced primarily by diminishing returns (increasing costs), bottlenecks and shortages, and the usual upward pressure on wages and other variable costs as output moves closer to capacity. But all this happens within a competitive environment, one basically untouched by power. Nonetheless, Keynes, by rejecting the quantity theory of money as the explanation for the price level, opened the door for the entry of power into the economy's aggregate performance. There are three ways in which this happens. The first two center on corporate power and its impact on pricing, whereas the third focuses on the role of trade unions in wage and price inflation.

The power that bigness and concentration confers upon the corporation is the power to "administer" its prices, to set prices more or less independently of conditions in the market in the which the company operates. Such power is *never* absolute, and its exercise by the corporation is a discretionary act, tempered always by political as well as economic considerations. A review of experience back to the 1930s suggests that two basic patterns of administered pricing have emerged in the American economy. The pioneer studies of Gardner Means in the 1930s discovered that prices in the industries where the firms had substantial power did not decline in the face of collapsing demand during the depression. These firms were able to maintain their prices, thereby shifting the impact of a falling demand into output and jobs by cutting back on both of the latter. Profit margins were maintained, in other words, by holding prices up as much as possible and laying off workers as production was cut back.

The other pattern emerged during the post-World War II period, especially during the inflationary decade of the 1970s. Rather than continuously trying to "maximize" profits as the textbooks suggest, firms in highly concentrated industries pursue a "target return" strategy with respect to pricing. This involves setting prices so as to secure a particular—or "target"—rate of return on the firm's assets. The vehicle is the price "mark-up," the addition of a specific percentage figure to raw material, labor, and other costs to arrive at a profit figure which will achieve the target rate of return. In a recession costs may rise because of declining productivity and high fixed overhead expenses, which puts a squeeze on profits and requires an increase in the price mark-up to maintain the target rate of return. Thus, prices for firms with the power to administer their prices may actually rise in the face of falling demand, as happened in the 1970s. When prosperity returns, prices may stabilize for a while, but sooner or later boom or expansion conditions will begin to push labor and material costs higher. So again the mark-up will be adjusted upward to maintain profits at a level adequate for the target rate of return.

The consequence of this is a "ratchet" effect, which pushes the price level upward from one business cycle to the next. Prices may rise in a recession, stabilize briefly during the recovery, and then rise again in the late stages of the expansion. The process may repeat itself during the next cycle. This was the pattern during the 1970s and earlier. Whether it will be the pattern for the future remains to be seen. One way to curb the inflationary potential inherent in mark-up pricing is through recession and rising unemployment. If a recession is severe enough, the adverse feedback effect upon demand in the concentrated industries associated with rising unemployment curbs the corporation's power to increase price mark-ups. This is what has happened in the 1980s. The 1981–1982 recession was the most severe since the 1930s, with unemployment hovering in the 7 percent range

CONCLUDING OBSERVATIONS   163

well after the recovery. Organized labor showed little inclination after the 1981–1982 slump to be aggressive in wage demands, trying for the most part to hold onto past gains and resist further "give-backs." What the future holds in the way of administered price behavior remains uncertain, but the evidence is strong that when the current merger movement has run its course, the economy will be more concentrated than ever. Consequently, corporate control over pricing will be even stronger.

The third way power enters macroeconomics involves trade unions, money wage rates, and the price level. When these factors are combined with the power of the modern corporation to administer its prices using mark-up pricing as the means, we have a much more complete and realistic picture of price behavior at the macroeconomic level. Although Keynes in *The General Theory* did not recognize the impact of corporate power on prices, individual and in general, he did argue that in the long run the most important single factor influencing the price level was the rate of change in money wages in relation to the rate of change in labor productivity. In chapter 21 in *The General Theory*, he made this point forcefully. All that is needed to complete the picture is to add in mark-up pricing.

Data from the 1960s onward provide strong empirical evidence for the foregoing proposition. Table 7-1 (from the 1987 *Economic Report of the President*) shows the links between productivity, money wage increases, including fringe benefits ("Compensation per Hour" in the table), unit labor costs, and the inflation rate. The latter is measured by the GNP deflator and the CPI. These data trace out the "wage-price spiral" of the 1970s, a spiral which got its start in the Vietnam War with a build-up of military spending unmatched by tax increases. The "demand-pull" inflation of the late 1960s turned into a "cost-push" inflation as workers struggled to keep up with rising prices, and finally was brought to an end by the severity of the 1981–1982 slump. External shocks from worldwide food shortages and the four-fold increases in oil prices exacerbated a cost-push process that was well underway by the opening of the decade.

What lessons are to be drawn from the experience reflected in the data in table 7-1. Three observations are in order. First, it should be clear that the real causes of inflation in the 1970s are to be found in the market power exercised variously by the trade unions, the corporations, and, finally, by OPEC. Second, fiscal and monetary policy are not appropriate instruments for controlling inflationary pressures that originate as these did. Society had in place an appropriate policy instrument in the form of the wage-price "guideposts" developed by the Kennedy-Johnson Administrations, but unfortunately they had no teeth. Yet the principle they embodied is correct. If money (and other variable) costs do not increase any faster than pro-

Table 7-1. Productivity, Money Compensation, Unit Labor Costs, and Inflation: 1960–1986 (in Percent, Annual Average Rates of Change)

Period	Productivity	Compensation Per Hour	Unit Labor Costs	Inflation Rates	
				GNP Deflator	CPI
1960–64	3.0%	4.0%	1.0%	1.2%	1.2%
1965–69	1.8	5.8	3.9	3.5	3.5
1970–74	1.2	7.5	6.3	5.7	6.1
1975–79	1.0	8.8	7.7	7.9	8.1
1980–86	1.2	6.3	5.1	5.4	5.4

* Wage and salaries, plus all fringe benefits, including employer contributions. All data pertain to the nonfarm business sector.

Source: *Economic Report of the President*, 1987, p. 295, *Current Economic Indicators*, October 1987, pp. 16, 24.

ductivity, a power-based, cost-push inflation can be avoided. Finally, and in the absence of a workable incomes policy as represented by the guideposts, it took a severe recession—the most severe since the Great Depression—to end the inflation. The social cost of this was lost output and idle workers. What this shows, of course, is that market power, whether exercised by corporations or by trade unions, is not absolute. It is strongly tempered by the state of the economy, expansions and booms bringing it into play, while downturns and recessions curb its deployment. Since it is likely that a serious inflationary problem will arise again out of the combination of a period of sustained full employment and concentrated economic power in strategically important areas of the economy, a workable incomes policy is a must. Unfortunately, no such policy is in sight.

Economic Theory and Market Power

Let us now turn to the last objective of this chapter, namely, some comments on how the phenomenon of market power can be linked to economic theory. This, perhaps, is the most difficult problem of all, given the structure and nature of mainstream economic theory, and given, too, the complex and diverse forms power takes in contemporary market capitalism.

The first matter to clarify, however, is to state more precisely what is envisioned and what is possible in speaking of a relationship between economic analysis and economic power. Are we looking here for a complete theory of power? The answer is no. That objective is much too broad. To attain that goal all the wisdom of the social sciences would have to be brought to bear on the matter. It is doubtful that such an ambitious project can be undertaken, now or in the foreseeable future. The end sought is much more modest—and more attainable. This is to determine if it is either practical or likely that power can be brought into the existing corpus of economic theory, micro and macro.

Before proceeding, it is worth reminding ourselves what economic theory is supposed to accomplish. It should do three things. First, it should explain how the economy works; second, it should enable us to predict what will happen when change is introduced into the economic system; and, third, it should be prescriptive, which is to say it ought to lead to policies that will correct any malfunctioning of the economic system.

As is well known, economic theory, like economics generally, has two main divisions, microeconomics and macroeconomics. There does not exist a unified body of theory applicable to the whole of economics. This statement will be disputed, especially by adherents of the Rational Expectations Hypothesis (REH), the latest fashion in economic theorizing. REH believers maintain that both micro- and macroeconomic phenomena can be explained on the basis of a common point of departure. This is the "rationality postulate," the belief that all human behavior in the economic sphere is "maximizing" behavior. People as "economic agents" maximize gains, no matter what their form, and minimize cost, also no matter what their form. This, it is argued, provides the necessary and long-sought link between micro- and macroeconomic theory. Why is such a link necessary? One fundamental reason, it is argued, is that aggregate (macro) behavior is nothing more than the summation—that is, the aggregation—of individual behavior. Therefore, for the sake of theoretical completeness, the fundamental force that governs individual behavior must also govern at the aggregate level. This might be termed the "argument of theoretical completeness."

More, however, is involved than theoretical tidiness. The argument also contains an ideological element, one especially crucial to the REH perspective. If we accept the assumption–and it is an assumption–that human behavior is rational in the sense just described, then an extremely important theoretical conclusions folows: there is nothing inherent in a system of market capitalism that either generates instability, or prevents the full utilization of all resources—including the full employment of labor—from being the norm. Under REH, this argument is pushed to its logical extreme, namely, no government policy actions are needed, and, furthermore, no government policy actions can make any difference to the economy's behavior. REH, in effect, abolishes macroeconomics.

There is, however, an alternative perspective and argument, one particularly germane to the matter of market power and its impact upon economic performance.

The argument that macroeconomic theory must necessarily be grounded on the same theoretical foundation as microeconomics rests upon an assumption, not an empirical observation. This is that the macroeconomic whole is nothing more than the sum of its microeconomic parts. It is just as plausible, and philosophically more realistic, to argue that the whole is greater than the sum of its parts. From a theoretical perspective, this has two consequences. First, it undercuts the essentially neoclassical argument that macroeconomics necessarily must have a micreoeconomic foundation. Second—and this follows from the foregoing—macroeconomic theoretical relationships can stand on their own. There may exist, in other words, macroeconomic behavior relationships that are observable, ones that may be—and have been—empirically verified, and which contribute significantly to our understanding of the economy's behavior. Further, they offer a guide to useful policy actions. This is in accord with earlier comments about what theory should accomplish. Furthermore, such relationships do not depend upon the existence of microeconomic roots.

There is an important practical reason for the foregoing argument. It relates to linking power to economic theory, the objective of this section. Economic or market power exists in this society, being as much a characteristic of contemporary market capitalism as is competition, if not more so. That is empirical fact. Yet there is little hope of bringing this empirical reality into contemporary theory if the neoclassical approach dominates both micro and macro theory.

Let us consider, first, the state of mainstream microeconomic theorizing. The entrenched and dominant paradigm is Walrasian general equilibrium theory, a view of how the microeconomic world actually works that has been gaining, not losing strength and prestige in the economic profession. It is the idealized world of rational (i.e., maximizing) human behavior, competitive (i.e., auction) markets, perfect knowledge and resource mobility, and timelessness carried to the complete, logical end. It is a world in which markets always clear (prices are equilibrium prices), no resources go unused (there is no unemployment), and resource allocation is at an optimum (society gets the maximum output of the goods and services it wants). As a theoretical and deductive structure the neoclassical model is a thing of elegance and beauty, made all the more formidable by the deployment of sophisticated mathematics in its support. After all, it was for bringing mathematical perfection to market-clearing, general equilibrium theory that Gerard Debreu received the Nobel prize in economics in 1983.

Do mainstream economic theorists really believe that this idealized model represents reality? Not literally. But what they appear to believe is that is depicts the power of and direction of market forces in the real economic world. They argue that forces found in the neoclassical paradigm come close to real-world economic behavior often enough—especially in the realm of the "long run"—that it may be viewed as essentially correct. No alternative paradigm has yet appeared to challenge the commanding heights it occupies in the realm of microeconomic theory.

As far as market power is concerned, it simply does not—and cannot—exist in the pure Walrasian general equilibrium model. If characteristics of the real economics world are at odds with the neoclassical theory, the fault lies with reality, not the model. Even if a glimpse of power is allowed, as in oligopoly theory, it is treated as essentially a minor aberration, not anything of major importance. Ultimately, markets in the real economic world work essentially as depicted in the Walrasian paradigm. That this is more a matter of faith than empirical reality does not seem to matter. It is the entrenched paradigm, given sanction, prestige, and the trappings of a "hard" science by mathematics, taught to new Ph.D.'s in the nation's "best" graduate schools. The citadel of microeconomic theory will remain essentially untouched by the fact of economic power until it is displaced by a new paradigm. Thomas Kuhn's analysis of the process by which science advances seems especially appropriate with respect to the micro branch of economic theory. To admit the existence of the anomaly of power to the degree that power actually exists in the real economic world threatens the entire neat and elegant structure. So all eyes are simply diverted away from the anomalies. Until a new and more powerful paradigm appears, this will be the situation. Unfortunately, in the domain of microeconomics no such paradigm is in sight.

Turning to macroeconomics the picture is less grim. There are good reasons to believe that macroeconomics will provide the avenue through which the reality of economic power can enter into the realm of theory. In these final paragraphs I will attempt to show why this is likely to be the case.

Until the late 1960s, as is well known, Keynesianism was the dominant macroeconomic paradigm. The upheavals of the 1970s, including unprecedented inflation rates combined with excessive unemployment, bred the monetarist, the supply-side, and the rational expectations challenges to the Keynesian dominance in macroeconomic theory. Although full judgment is not yet in, it is becoming increasingly clear that the basic Keynesian income-expenditure model in spite of its limitations offers the best theoretical model for explaining both the "stagflation" of the 1970s and the debt-driven expansion of the Reagan era. Neither supply-side economics nor monetarism fits the reality of what actually happened during these turbulent years. Rational expectations, in spite of its strong intellectual appeal and hold on an influential segment of the economics profession, is so removed from reality that it cannot offer any practical help in understanding the events of this period.

Thus, we are for all practical purposes left with the Keynesian model as the dominant theoretical frame of reference for understanding the economy's aggregate behavior. This is hardly to be deplored. Not only has Keynesianism survived better the "laboratory" tests of experience over the prior 20 years than the alternatives but its door, unlike that of mainstream microeconomic theory, is not closed to the entry of power into the analysis. How can this be done? The answer was suggested earlier in this chapter. Keynes, as we saw, offered a macroeconomic theory of the price level with supply-and-demand-oriented microeconomic roots. As noted, this aspect of Keynes was largely neglected in the enthusiastic rush after World War II to build and perfect the income expenditure version of Keynes. The experience of the 1970s and the 1980s, however, demonstrates two major things. First, a theory of the price level such as Keynes developed in the neglected chapter 21 of *The General Theory* is absolutely essential for completing the Keynesian "revolution," for providing a macroeconomic theory that explains not only output and employment but prices as well. Second, not only is the Keynesian theory of the price level open to bringing power into the analysis but actually it requires that this be done. As was shown earlier in this essay, pricing behavior in both the 1970s (nearly unchecked inflation) and the 1980s (collapsed inflation rates) must be explained in terms of administered prices and real-world practices of mark-up and target-return pricing. These latter are, pure and simple, manifestations of economic or market power!

One final comment is in order. Although in one sense, as most of the chapters in this book suggest, the drama of economic power is played out at this microeconomic level, its entry into economic theory must come, so to speak, from the highground of macroeconomics. On a practical policy level, the logic of power-based pricing behavior in an expanded macroeconomic paradigm leads to development of an incomes policy. This should be the third element in a triad of macroeconomic policy instruments—fiscal, monetary, and incomes. A workable incomes policy does not now exist, but it must come. If we are ever to reach the desired goal of full employment without inflation, such a policy is the only practical means under

CONCLUDING OBSERVATIONS

current circumstances to blunt the pressure on prices brought into play by market power as the economy moves toward full employment. This will result in a "back-door" entry of power into the house of micreoeconomics. Rather than pursue the theoretical dead-end of trying to force macroeconomics into a microeconomic foundation based on the rationality postulate, economists should turn their talents to constructing a new microeconomics appropriate to a macroeconomics fully aware of the role and importance of power in economic affairs. This would be a worthy goal!

Index

Act to Regulate Commerce (1887), 31
Adams, Walter, 99, 143, 154, 147
Administered prices, 36, 161
Agriculture, Department of, 60
American Enterprise Institute, (AIE), 135
American Tobacco Co., 29, 30
Anational Corporation, 46

Bain Index, 9
Bain, Joe, 11
Ball, George W., 46
Benefit-cost, 6
Bennites, 120
Berle, Adolf, 34, 39
Blair, John M., 100
Bluhdorn, Charles, 53
Bork, Robert, 150
Bretton, Harry L., 143
Bretton Woods, 111, 112, 114
Brock, James W., 99, 143, 145, 147
Bronson, Charles, 2
Brookings Institution, 135, 136
Brown, John, 85
Burlington Railroad, 68
Burrough, Bryan, 145

Capitalism
  American, 1, 8
  Industrial, 27
  Corporate, 87
  Monopoly, 87
Carnation, 69
Carter Administration, 103, 120
Casey, William, 136
Caves, Richard, 59
Census Bureau, 65, 91
Census of Manufacturers, 63
Center for Tax Justice, 137
Center for the Study of the American Business System, 146
Ceres, 120
Chamberlin, Edward H., 4, 34, 35, 37, 44
Chandler, Alfred, Jr., 66
Chase Manhattan Bank, 47
Chemical Bank, 47
Chicago School, 132
Chrysler Corporation, 133
Citicorp Bank, 47
City of London, 120
Civil Aeronautics Board (CAB), 41, 142, 144
Civil War, 29, 85
Clayton Act, 15, 32, 40
Coase, Ronald, 148, 149
Collins, Norman, 11, 12
Comons, John R., 148
Competition
  and the Firm, 4

171

172 INDEX

Imperfect, 4
Monopolistic, 34
Perfect, 15
Pure, 34
Workable, 66
Concentration
   Aggregate, 13, 14, 72, 77
   Four Firm (Four Digit) (FF), 15, 64, 77
   Market or Industry, 13, 14, 77
   Statistical measures, 62–75
Concentration ratio, 13, 16, 63, 77
Conglomerates, 61, 72, 77, 90, 95, 99, 101
Conrail Railroad, 68
Consumer Price Index, 97
Consumer Sovereignty, 83, 129
Continental Airline, 67
Copeland, Morris, 10
Cooper, Richard, 119
Cordova Chemical, 146
Corporation, 29, 85, 88–90
Corrupt Practices Election Act (1925), 138
Council of Economic Advisers, 146
Cost-push inflation, 163
Cournot, August, 62
Coward, Denise, 2
CSX Railroad, 68
Cultural lag, 17

Dahl, Robert, 6
Debreu, Gerard
Decter, Midge, 136
Deindustrialization, 92, 94, 164
Del Monte, 69
Demand-pull inflation, 163
Deregulation, 67
Dissent, 140
Diversification, 91, 93, 94
Dred Scott Decision, 85
Drew, Elizabeth, 135, 145
Dubin, Robert, 5
Dugger, William M., x, 83, 159

Eastern Airline, 67
Economic interdependence, 47
Economic liberalism, 118
Economic man, 35
Economic progress, 33
Edsall, Thomas, 140, 146
Eichner, Alfred S., 100
Elasticities, 11
Electronic Data Systems, Inc., 92
Elitism, 7, 8
Employment Act (1946), 42
Environmental Protection Agency (EPA), 60, 103, 144
Esmark, 69
Etzioni, Amatai, 5
Eurocurrency market, 47
Eurodollars, 118, 159
Exchange rates, 111

Farley Industries, Inc., 62
Farley, William, 62
Federal Communications Commission (FCC), 41, 142
Federal Election Campaign Act (FECA) (1971), 138
Federal Power Commission (FPC), 142
Federal Reserve Act (1915), 32
Federal Reserve Board, 32, 144
Federal Trade Commission Act, 32, 40
Federal Trade Commission (FTC), 41, 144
Feulner, Edward, 136
Fiscal policy, 43, 113, 119, 163
Flexibile exchange rates, 112
Food and Drug Act (1906), 31
Food and Drug Administration (FDA), 31, 60
Forbes, 55
Ford Motor Company, 47, 58
Fourteenth Amendment, 85
Free Congress Political Action Committee (Committee for the

INDEX

Survival of a Free Congress), 136, 139
Full employment, 113

Galbraith, John Kenneth, ix, 44, 128, 131, 158
General Agreement on Tariffs and Trade (GATT), 117
General Electric Corporation, 53, 55
General Foods, 57, 59, 69
General Motors, 92, 93
Gilder, George, 136
Gini coefficient, 18
Global markets, 50
Gnomes of Zurich, 115, 117
GNP deflator, 163
Geotz, Bernard, 2
Gordon, Myron J., 76
Gorsuch, Anne, 144
Government
  Micro-market power, 31
  Micro-marco-market power, 40
Green, Mark, x, 68, 127, 130
Green, Douglas F., x, 53, 158
Guideposts, 163
Gulf & Western, 53

Hall, Robert, 76
Hatch Act (1940), 138
Heritage Foundation, 136
High Frontier, 137
Hirschman-Herfindahl (HH) Index, 14, 63
Holding company, 29
Hook, Sidney, 62
Hoover Institution, 135
Hughes Aircraft Company, 92

Iacocca, Lee, 133, 134
IBM, 57, 59, 72
IBM World Trade Corp., 46

Ideology, 27, 28
Imperial Conglomerate, 95, 100, 103
Import penetration, 104
Income distribution, 105
Incomes policy, 168
Indexes
  Aggregate, 14
  Parital, 14
  Summary, 14
Institutions and institutional, 17, 18
Interdependent sections, 48
Interlocking directorates, 6
International firm, 46
International economy, 111
International Monetary Fund, 117
International Telephone and Telegraph, 62
Interstate Commerce Commission (ICC), 31, 142
Institute for Policy Studies, 137
Institutional drag, 17
Invisible hand, 3

Jacobson, Gary, 138
J.P. Morgan Bank, 47
Japan, steel industry, 45
Jeffersonian democracy, 3
John M. Olin Foundation, 146
Johnson Administration, 118
Johnson, Lyndon B., 46
Joint Economic Committee, 42
Journal of Industrial Economics, 63
Journal of Post Keynesian Economics, 100

Kahn, Herman, 136
Kapp, William K., 102
Kennedy, John F., 46
Kennedy-Johnson Administration, 163
Keynes, John Maynard, 34, 42–44, 112, 160, 161
Kirk, Russell, 136

Kodak, 59
Kuhn, Thomas, 167

Labor's *Magna Carta*, 41
Laissez-faire, 28, 33
Lavelle, Rita, 146
Lehrman, Louis, 136
Lerner, Abba P., 9, 100
Lerner Index, 9, 10, 76
Ling, Jimmy, 53
Locke, Sondra, 2
Macroeconomics, 48, 49
Maisonrouge, Jacques, 6, 46
Malbin, Michael, 138
Marion, Bruce, 67
Marginal productivity, 33
Mark-up pricing, 162
Marshal, Alfred, 17
Marathon Oil, 45
Maximization hypothesis, 12, 35
MBA priesthood, 96
McConnell, Grant, 143, 144
McDonald's, 58
McDonnell-Douglas Corporation, 146
McDonnell, James B., 146
MCI, 68
Means, Gardner C., 34, 36, 39, 44, 100, 162
Meese, Edwin, 136
Mercantilism, 3, 28, 110
Merger guidelines, 15
Merrill Lynch, 70
Metropolitan Life, 70
Miller, James, 144
Miller-Tydings Act (1937), 40
Mills, C. Wright, 129, 134, 152
Mine Safety and Health Administration (MSHA), 145
Misery Index, 97
Mitterand, Francois, 115
Modules, 94
Monetarism, 167
Monetary policy, 43, 113, 119, 163
Mueller, Willard F., 66

Multinational firm, 46
Mun, Thomas, 110
Mundell, Robert, 112
Munkirs, John R., x, 27, 158

Nabisco Brands, 69
National Cash Register Co., 30
National Conservative Political Action Committee (NCPAC), 139
National Labor Relations Act (Wagner Act) (1935), 41, 42
National Labor Relations Board (NLRB), 41
National Resources Committee, 34
Neoclassical economics and theory, 3, 4, 9, 12, 18, 122
New Empirical Industrial Organization (NEIO), 75
New international economic order, 119
Nixon Administration, 98, 118
Nonplanned sector, 48
Norfolk Southern Railroad, 68
Normal profit, 13
Northern Railroad, 68
Northwest Airline, 67
Norton Simon, 69

Occupational Safety and Health Agency (OSHA), 103
Oligopoly, 64
OPEC (Organization of Petroleum Exporting Countries), 118, 163
Oscar Mayer, 69
Ozark Airlines, 67

Pacific Bell, 58
Papandreau, Andreas, 10
Pareto optimality, 133
Perot, Ross, 92

INDEX 175

Pertschuk, Michael, 144
Peterson, Rodney, x, 1, 158
Peterson, Wallace, 157
Petr, Jerry, x, 127
Phillip Morris, 57, 59
Physiocracy, 28
Planned sector, 48
Pluralism, 7, 8
Podhoretz, Norman, 136
Political Action Committee (PAC), 131, 138, 139
Policy, formulation, implementation, and interpretation, 130
Political man, 55
Porter, Michael, 59
Posner, Richard, 148, 149
Poverty rate, 101
Power
  Aggregate, 60–62
  Comprehensiveness, 54
  Corporate, 27, 28, 84, 101, 103, 106
  Corporate coercive, 29
  Corporate, micro-market, 29
  Defined, 12, 129
  Economic, 16, 27, 53–55, 76, 77, 83
  Extensiveness, 54
  Hierarchy of, 18–22
  Industrial, 3, 4, 9, 16
  Intensiveness, 54
  Macro-market, 40, 42
  Market, 16, 34, 53
  Micro-marco-market, 38
  Monopoly, 10–12, 16, 33
  Private, 83, 84
  Public, 84
  Related markets, 59, 60
  Single market, 56
Preston, Lee, 11, 12
Price-cost Margin (Index), 12
Private property, 38
Procter and Gamble, 61
Productivity, 163, 164
Profit maximization, 96
Prudential, 70
Pure monopoly, 13

Ratchet effect, 162
Rational expectations (REH), 112, 165, 166
Reagean Administration, 103, 120
Rehnquist Court, 132
Rentier, 101
Republic Airline, 67
Robinson, Joan, 34, 35, 37, 44
Robinson-Patman Act (1936), 40, 41
Rockefeller, John D., 30
Roderick, David M., 92
Rogers, Richard T., 66
Rothchild, Kurt, 10
Ruckelshaus, William, 144
Russell, Bertrand, 127

Solomon Brothers, 70
Samuels, Warren, 148, 152
Santa Fe-SP Railroad, 68
Security and Exchange Commission (SEC), 41
Self-interest, 3, 28, 33
Sherman Act (1890), 32, 40
Shepherd, W.G., 66
Siegel, Fred, 140
Silberg, Philip, 75
Simon, William, 136
Sinclair, Upton, 31
Skinner, B.F., 134
Smith, Adam, ix, 33, 39, 50, 127, 128
Smith, Robert E., 54
Smith, Roger B., 92
Sowell, Thomas, 136
Sprint, 68
Stallone, Sylvester, 2
Standard Industrial Classification (SIC), 64, 66
Standard Oil, 30, 31
Stevens, Robert, 47
Strategic Defense Initiative (Star Wars), 136
Superfund, 146
Supply-side, 167

Supranational economy, 110
Supranational firm, 46

Target return strategy (pricing), 162
Technology, 17
Texas Air Airline, 67
Texas Oil and Gas, 45, 93
Thatcher, Margaret, 123
The Economist, 114, 115, 116
The Jungle, 31
Third world, 118, 121
Toyota, 93
Trade deficits, 114
Transnational firm, 46
Trigger price mechanisms, 147
Trusts, 29
TWA Airline, 67

Udall, Stewart, 144
Underemployment, 17
Unemployment, 17
Union Pacific Railroad, 68
United Nations, 106
Urban enterprise zones, 137
Urban Institute, 137
U.S. Department of Commerce
   Census of Manufacturers, 12
   Standard Industrial Classification, 12, 15
U.S. Internal Revenue Service (IRS), 87

USX (United States Steel, USS), 92, 93

Vietnam War, 163
Visible hand, 105
Voluntary restraint agreements, 147

Wachtel, Howard, 118
Wage-price Control Program, 98
Walrasian general equilibrium, 167
Warren Court, 132
Watt, James, 144
Wealth of nations, 128
Weber, Max, 5
Weidenbaum, Murray, 146
Western democracies, 106
Wheeler-Lea Act (1938), 40
White, Lawrence, 72
Wiley, Harvey W., 31
Willoughby, John, x, 109, 159
Willox, Clair, 29
Wilson, Harold, 115, 117
Wirthlin, Richard, 135
Wrong, Dennis, 54

X-efficiency, 33, 34
X-inefficiency, 39, 45

Yeager, Peter C., 103